SPIRAL GUIDE

CÔTE D'AZUR

AA
Publishing

Contents

Compiled by Beth Hall
Magazine section and contibutions by Teresa Fisher

Designed by Nucleus Design
Copy edited by Ann F Stonehouse
Verified by David Halford
Indexed by Marie Lorimer

Produced by AA Publishing © Automobile Association Developments
Limited 2007

Published by AA Publishing, a trading name of Automobile
Association Developments Limited, whose registered office is
Fanum House, Basing View, Basingstoke, Hampshire, RG21 4EA.
Registered number 1878835.

ISBN-10: 0-7495-4995-5
ISBN-13: 978-0-7495-4995-4

Cover design and binding style by permission of AA Publishing

Colour separation by Keenes, Andover
Printed and bound in China by Leo Paper Products

Find out more about AA Publishing and the wide range services the
AA provides by visiting our website at www.theAA.com/travel

A02724
Maps in this title produced from mapping © MAIRDUMONT/Falk Verlag 2006
Transport map © Communicarta Ltd, UK

the magazine

A WINTER WONDERLAND

In 1834 two Englishmen –Tobias Smollett and Henry Lord Brougham, a former Lord Chancellor – were forced by a cholera epidemic in Marseille to remain in the tiny fishing village of Cannes. So beguiled were they by the mildness of the winter climate, the beauty of the

Palais Princier, Monaco

coast and the local bouill-abaisse (Provençal fish soup), that they bought a plot of land and built a villa. Other Britons followed, and the French Riviera was born as a fashionable winter destina-tion for the well-heeled of the world, including sovereigns, statesmen, aristocrats, wealthy bourgeois and cour-tesans. Queen Victoria, the Aga Khan, Empress Eugénie (Napoléon III's wife) and King Leopold of Belgium all held court here, and artists and writers flocked to the region, inspired by the magi-cal light scenery. It marked the start of the *belle époque*.

By 1860, when Nice voted to join France, it was already Europe's most sophisticated

Above: The Old Terraces of Nice; Côte d'Azur ticket

winter retreat, ideally located between the fashionable resorts of Monaco and Cannes. The taste for luxury of this opulent high society gave rise to the most exuberant and daring architectural projects, as each statesman vied with his neighbour to create the grandest, most flamboyant villa. Railways, palatial hotels, luxuriant semi-tropical gardens and the fabled promenade des Anglais in Nice were built to meet their needs. In 1865 Monaco – until 1850 the poorest

> **"I like France, where everyone thinks he's Napoleon."**
> Dick Diver in F Scott Fitzgerald's *Tender is the Night*

Boulevard de la Croisette, Cannes

A RUSSIAN ROMANCE

Since the Russian Revolution of 1917 the Côte d'Azur has been a popular destination for Russian aristocrats and émigrés, including such luminaries as Ivan Bunin (the first Russian to win the Nobel Prize for literature, in 1933) and artist Marc Chagall (► 41). It was in the Russian Orthodox Church in Nice that, by an Imperial Manifesto, Alexander III was officially proclaimed heir to the Russian throne, and Russian architects left their mark on the coast with such masterpieces as the Fernand Léger museum in Biot (► 123) and Nice's dazzling Cathédrale Orthodoxe Russe St-Nicolas (► 49). The beautiful Château des Ollières (39 avenue des Baumettes, Nice) was built by Prince Lobanov Rostowsky; on being recalled to Moscow to assume a position in the Russian government, he then gave it to his mistress as a gift of love.

state in Europe – boomed with the opening of the glamorous Monte-Carlo Casino, as fortunes were won and lost by the famous and the fashionable.

It wasn't until 1887 that poet and Dijonais vineyard owner Stephen Liegeard gave the region the glamorous, evocative name it needed to confirm its success – La Côte d'Azur.

Throughout the *belle époque* the area flourished, but it was not until the "Roaring Twenties" that the region became a summer resort, made fashionable by trendsetting American socialites including comic actor Harpo Marx, composer Cole Porter, dancer Isadora Duncan and writer F Scott Fitzgerald (► 16). Under their racy influence swimming came into vogue, and glamorous French fashion designer Coco Chanel started a new fashion craze after holidaying here – the suntan. Up until then, being as pale as possible had been desirable. Soon the Côte d'Azur was the haunt not only of millionaires and royalty, but also of fashion divas, film stars and the greatest artists, writers and thinkers of

> **"Thirst for the sun! Thirst for the sand! Thirst for the clocks that run slow!"**
> Jacques-Henri Lartigue, photographer

The *belle-époque* façade of the Carlton Hotel

LA BELLE ÉPOQUE

Many villas and hotels built in the frothy *belle-époque* style survive on the Côte d'Azur, including the Négresco (► 44–45) and Cathédrale Orthodoxe Russe St-Nicolas (► 49) in Nice; Villa Grecque Kérylos and its elegant rotunda (► 65) in Beaulieu; Villa Ephrussi de Rothschild on Cap Ferrat (► 70–71); and the Monte-Carlo Opéra and Casino (► 93–95). The *belle-époque* style reflects the *dolce vita* of the era, a fusion of the most ornamental and daring features of bygone years – turrets, domes and cupolas; *faïence* and fresco; marble, chandeliers and gilt – the more extravagant the better. Queen Victoria stayed at Nice's Hotel Excelsior Regina for three winter seasons from 1897 to 1899, and the wing she occupied is topped with the Imperial British crown. The Carlton Hotel in Cannes was built in 1912, and its twin cupolas were modelled after the breasts of the famous dancer and courtesan La Belle Otero (► 111) after she appeared in her most famous costume – which revealed her best assets barely covered with precious gems!

the time, including Renoir, Matisse, Picasso, Hemingway, Camus, Sartre and Huxley.

Today the Côte d'Azur continues to draw celebrities to its shores, including Brigitte Bardot, Joan Collins, Elton John and Claudia Schiffer. Despite the advent of mass tourism and low-fare airlines, its resorts remain chic and exclusive with their "see-and-be-seen"

"It is a land of milk and honey, the best milk and the most perfumed honey, where all the good things of the earth overflow."
William Bolitho,
Camera Obscura

promenades, their beautiful sun-soaked beaches and bustling harbours full of millionaires' yachts. After nearly two centuries the aptly named Côte d'Azur, with its enticing, electric blue sea, remains the home of the rich and famous and the most glamorous playground in the world.

Walking among the cacti and succulents of Èze's Jardin Exotique

An A–Z
of Local Cuisine

Dining on the Côte d'Azur is a magical experience. With all the brilliant, sun-drenched colours, alluring fragrances and strong, earthy flavours of the Mediterranean, it is a veritable feast for the senses.

*A*ioli is a delicious garlic mayonnaise, often served with shellfish.

Expect to pay at least €40 per person for a bowl of the region's world-famous *b*ouillabaisse (a rust-coloured fish stew with 12 different kinds of fish), or try *b*ourride – poor man's fish soup.

The *C*heese course is always a treat – try the delicious local *C*hèvre (goat's cheese) called banon, served wrapped in oak leaves.

Hearty *d*aube de boeuf (a beef stew with red wine, cinnamon and lemon peel) is especially warming in winter months.

*E*stocaficada (stockfish stew) is one of the most ubiquitous dishes in coastal restaurants.

Petit *f*arcis (savoury stuffed courgettes, tomatoes and artichoke hearts) feature frequently as a filling starter.

Boeuf *g*ardian is a spicy beef stew with olives, originally from the Camargue, but served throughout the region.

Many dishes rely on an aromatic blend of wild *h*erbes de Provence – rosemary, savory, marjoram, basil and thyme.

*I*deal gifts to take home include the local *j*ams (confitures). Look out for such unusual flavour combinations as wild apricot and rosemary, or mandarin and thyme.

Fish dishes reign supreme in the Mediterranean, with *l*oup (bass) the most popular catch. Try it grilled au fenouil (over a fire of fennel twigs) and flambéed with aniseed-based pastis.

*M*oules frites (mussels with french fries) are always good value.

Nice's signature dish, the classic salade *N*içoise, is made with tuna, egg, black olives, lettuce and anchovies.

*O*lives, olive oil, herbs, garlic and tomatoes form the basis of Riviera cuisine.

Look out for *p*issaladière (a delicious olive and onion pizza) in the resorts close to the Italian border.

Crystallised fruits, including *q*uince, apricots, melon, pears and figs, are a speciality here. Look out also for quince paste (pâté de coing).

*R*atatouille is a traditional Provençal dish of stewed tomatoes, onions, courgettes, aubergines and sweet peppers. It is served as a meal on its own with French bread, or as a side dish.

A simple treat is *S*occa (a thin pancake made with chickpea flour). Try it in Vieux Nice.

Local black or green olives make tasty *t*apenade (olive paste with capers and anchovies), delicious served on crusty bread.

Don't be put off if you are presented with a plate of shiny, black, seaweed-draped sea *U*rchins (oursins) – they are a great delicacy here!

The tiny village of Tourettes-sur-Loup grows violets primarily for the perfume industry, but you can also find *V*iolettes glacés (crystallised violets) and even violet jams, syrups, oils and liqueurs.

Eleven per cent of France's *W*ine comes from Provence and the Côte d'Azur. Look out for the little-known rosé wines of Draguignan and the Bellet wines of Nice.

Le Louis *X*v (➤ 100), Alain Ducasse's fabled restaurant in Monaco, is the jewel in the crown of gourmet temples on the Côte d'Azur.

From market stalls and local cafés to trendy brasseries and Michelin-starred restaurants, wherever you eat, *y*ou will be served by *Z*ealous gourmands passionate about their food. After all, la cuisine Provençale is among the world's finest regional styles.

Top left: Salade Niçoise

Top right: A market stal! selling locally produced honey

Above: Crystallised fruits, a typical Provençal delicacy

Left: The Moulin á Huile d'Olive Alziari sells local olive oil pressed in Nice

Gardens

The Cote d'Azur is resplendent with flowers, from the extravagant gardens of luxury villas along the coast to the stripy fields of purple lavender and the fragrant wild flowers and herbs of the bucolic hinterland. With 20 per cent of the nation's fruit, vegetables and flowers coming from the Provence–Côte d'Azur region, it's hardly surprising that it's called "the garden of France".

The Riviera's gardens are among the world's most sophisticated, created by wealthy aristocrats during the *belle époque*. Thanks to their lavish horticultural fantasies, tropical succulents, palm trees and exotic flora flourish alongside Mediterranean oleander, cypress, mimosa, olive, rose and jasmine. The results are sweet scented and breathtaking.

Menton, the most temperate town in France, has more than its fair share of semi-tropical gardens, including the extravagant Val Rahmen gardens (avenue St-Jacques). Created in 1925, they contain more than 700 exotic species from every corner of the globe and are maintained by the French National Museum of Natural History. Also in

Above: The Jardin Exotique in Monaco looks over the tiny principality below

Right: Fragrant lavender fields are cultivated in Grasse and throughout Provence

GRASSE

For over 400 years the sleepy, fragrance-filled town of Grasse has been the centre of the French perfume industry, responsible for two-thirds of the nation's production. During the 16th century it was a tannery town. At the time glove-makers began to use local flowers to perfume leather gloves – a fashion made popular by Catherine de' Medici. As a consequence, acres of lavender, mimosa, roses, jasmine and jonquil were cultivated, and Grasse soon became the world's leading perfume centre.

To learn more about the history and alchemy of this ancient industry, the Musée International de la Parfumerie is a treat for the senses, or there are guided tours around the three greatest perfume houses in the world – Fragonard, Galimard and Molinard – which still use old-fashioned methods. Why not create your own scent at Studio des Fragrances Galimard? In a two-hour session, the local "nose" (or nez, ► 14) will evaluate your sense of smell and explain the components of a good perfume. You then blend your chosen "top note", "middle note" and "end note", and receive a 100ml (3.5fl oz) vial of your home-made fragrance for your efforts.

Huge heads of sunflowers, grown both as fodder and for their oil, in the Provençal countryside

LE NEZ

There are 30 major perfumeries in and around Grasse. Each employs a head perfumer, known as *le nez*. There are 300 "noses" in the world, half of whom work in France, and around 50 in Grasse. It is their job to blend the different essences to create new fragrances. A top "nose" produces just three to four perfumes a year.

Menton, Palais Carnolès (3 avenue de la Madone) is the largest citrus fruit garden in Europe.

Monaco and Èze boast cliff-hanging exotic gardens with precipitous sea views. Monaco's Princess Grace Rose Garden is fragrant with the scent of 4,000 rose trees. It is said that Baroness Béatrice de Rothschild dressed her 34 gardeners in sailor suits when they created the luxuriant Ephrussi Gardens (▶ 70–71) in the early 1900s. Her nine gardens are a blaze of colours, perfumes and design. The less-celebrated Rayol Gardens at Rayol-Canadel, near the flowery paradise of Bormes-les-Mimosas (▶ 149), contain rare plants from every continent, and even an "under water garden" snorkelling tour of multicoloured sea plants just offshore. There's another underwater path off Île de Port-Cros (▶ 144–145), France's only offshore national park, while the neighbouring island of Porquerolles (▶ 144, 145) boasts a botanical garden containing over 150 varieties of olive, 200 of fig and the national peach collection. Sadly, tastings are not allowed!

Terraced vegetable gardens on a hillside in the village of Levens

ARTISTS' GARDENS

Fondation Maeght's sculpture garden (▶ 120) is a must-see for all art aficionados, with its playful collection of fountains, statuary, mosaics and mobiles by such luminaries as Miró, Chagall, Braque, Calder, Giacometti and Moore. The amusing gardens of Château de la Napoule are worth a visit too, with their animal-shaped topiary and bizarre "demon" statues created by eccentric American millionaire sculptor Henry Clews in 1919. The most moving artist's garden on the Côte d'Azur is undoubtedly the Renoir Garden – a simple grove of ancient gnarled olive trees where the painter would sit in his wheelchair for hours, his brushes strapped to his rheumatic fingers. The garden today still resembles a Renoir landscape.

Ever since the Lumière brothers
filmed *Train Entering La Ciotat Station* in 1895, the
south of France has been at the forefront of cinematic
development, and many of its towns and villages have
featured in films by the legendary
French directors Pagnol, Truffaut,
Godard and Vadim.

By the "Roaring Twenties" Nice was the
capital of French cinema, with nearly
200 films made at the celebrated
Studios de la Victorine in just one
decade. Actors and actresses flocked to
the Côte d'Azur to make their fortune in
the silent films and then the early
"talkies" in what became known as the
Golden Age of Classic Film.

In 1955 the legendary American film
actress Grace Kelly came here to star
alongside Cary Grant in *To Catch a Thief*
directed by Hitchcock – a story about

Cary Grant and
Grace Kelly in
*To Catch a
Thief* (1955)

thieves stealing from the swankiest hotels on the Riviera.
During the filming she met Prince Rainier III and the rest is
history: she never acted again, but chose to concentrate on
her duties as wife and mother of Caroline, Albert and
Stephanie until her fairy-tale life came to an abrupt end in
a tragic car accident along the Moyenne Corniche (▶ 66) in
1982. (A neighbouring road, the Corniche Littorale from
Nice to Cannes, featured in Frederick Forsyth's classic
1973 film, *The Day of the Jackal*.)

Sex goddess Brigitte Bardot is another glamorous name associated with the Côte d'Azur. She made her screen debut in 1952, aged 18, in *Le Trou Normand*. In that same year she married the celebrated film director Roger Vadim (the first of four marriages). Already a magazine celebrity and pin-up by 1956, her 17th film *Et Dieu Créa La Femme* was a major international success. Her sexy walk as she strolled around St-Tropez made Bardot, Vadim and the port world-famous, and marked the start of a new, permissive era. As *Time* magazine once wrote: "Brigitte Bardot exuded a carefree, naïve sexuality that brought a whole new audience to French films."

Among the best-known movies shot in the region is *Tender is the Night* (1962), based on F Scott Fitzgerald's famous autobiographical novel of the same name. It portrays the reck-

ON LOCATION
Films made in the Provence-Côte d'Azur region include:
Mare Nostrum (1926)
The Magician (1926)
Perfect Understanding (1933)
The Red Shoes (1948)
To Catch a Thief (1955)
Ill Met by Moonlight (1957)
Tender is the Night (1962)
The Day of the Jackal (1973)
Jean de Florette (1986)
Manon des Sources (1986)
Horseman on the Roof (1995)
The Man in the Iron Mask (1998)

Top: Brigitte Bardot in *Et Dieu Créa La Femme* (And God Created Woman, 1956)

Above: Gérard Depardieu in *Jean de Florette* (1986)

less hedonism of the Riviera during the 1920s and '30s, when notorious American socialites F Scott and Zelda Fitzgerald frequented the palatial Hôtel du Cap Eden Roc on Cap d'Antibes.

The prolific Provençal writer Marcel Pagnol had always dreamed of turning his novels into films to pay tribute to his beloved countryside, and in 1935 he founded his own production company and studios in Marseille. His most enduring novel, *L'Eau des Collines* (*The Water of the Hills*), is best known in its adaptation into the two highly acclaimed films *Jean de Florette* and *Manon des Sources*, which tell the moving story of two provincial farmers systematically destroying the happiness of a city man (played by Gérard Depardieu) who moves to Provence in the 1920s to till the land.

Depardieu is just one of many actors resident on the Côte d'Azur, together with Joan Collins, Brigitte Bardot, Jean-Paul Belmondo and countless other megastars of the silver screen. Best venues to spot them include the Cannes Film Festival; the St-Tropez quayside, clubs and beaches; shopping in Monaco; eating out in Mougins or, as in the movies, driving along the Corniches in an open-top roadster.

Jennifer Jones and Jason Robards Jr in *Tender is the Night* (1962)

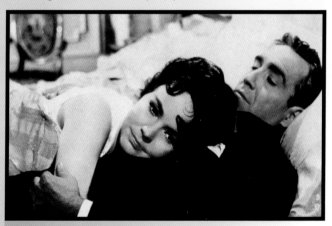

THE CANNES FESTIVAL

The Cannes International Film Festival was founded in 1939, in an attempt to make the Côte d'Azur a rival to Hollywood. Indeed, alongside the Oscars, the Palmes d'Or are the most sought-after awards of international film idols. The outbreak of war led to the postponement of the first festival until 1947, but it has taken place here ever since for two weeks in mid-May, attracting famous faces from all around the world. Cinemas throughout the town screen films from early morning until well into the night. You are unlikely to get tickets unless you are accompanied by Bardot or Bond 007, but just being part of the excitement – star-gazing on the edge of the red carpet – is great fun.

Did You Know?

Fashion designer Jacques Heim and mechanical engineer Louis Reard both claim to have "invented" the bikini on the Côte d'Azur. Launched on the beaches of Cannes in the summer of 1946, it became an instant hit with the local *jeunes filles*, keen to achieve a newly fashionable suntan. Brigitte Bardot, frolicking on the sandy beaches of St-Tropez, popularised the look, sometimes *sans* top in the 1960s, marking the advent of topless bathing.

Nice's tiny AOC wine region called Bellet is little known, largely because the majority of the 1,200 hectolitres (26,400 gallons) produced annually never get beyond the cellars of the Côte d'Azur's top restaurants. The special quality of the wines is attributed to their unusual grape varieties, and the sea and mountain air. The full-bodied red, with its wild cherry bouquet, can be aged up to 30 years. The golden white is reminiscent of Chablis, and the rosé is quite the best accompaniment to local fish specialities.

Coco Chanel introduced Chanel No 5 to the world on the fifth day of the fifth month in 1925, naming the perfume after her lucky number. It was created by one of the great "noses" of Grasse (► 14).

Pétanque, or boules, was invented in the south of France. You can see it taking place in most villages in the region. It is a tactical game – there is skill in deciding whether to posi-

Above: Pétanque was invented in Provence, and is today the nation's most played sport

Right: The beaches of St-Tropez, where women first dared to sunbathe topless

tion your ball near the small wooden ball (the *cochonnet* or "piglet") or to oust your opponent's ball. With a flick of the wrist, players sometimes manage to do both simultaneously.

It takes between 200kg (440lb) and 1,000kg (2,200lb) of rose petals – that's about a million flowers – to obtain 1litre (1.8 pints) of essential oil, and the whole process costs around €20,000. Little wonder perfume is so expensive!

Just inland from Menton, the Parc National du Mercantour – one of France's most beautiful alpine reserves – provides sanctuary for most of Europe's mountain animal species, including wild boar, marmot, chamois, ibex and mouflon (wild sheep).

Ever since the Romans used it to scent their baths, lavender (from the Latin *lavare* "to wash") has been in demand for its sweet smell and soothing qualities, and its scent and colour pervade the *arrière pays* (hinterland). There are two main types of plant: wild mountain lavender, which produces the most precious essences sought after by the makers of great perfumes, and lavendin, a hybrid grown in lower plains, which yields great quantities of inferior essence used in such products as soap, honey and lavender wine.

Auguste Escoffier (*c*1847–1935), the great French "chef of kings and king of chefs" and creator of the *pêche melba*, learned to cook as a boy at his uncle's restaurant in Nice. He spread the renown of French cuisine throughout the world in the early 20th century and many of the country's top chefs have been drawn to the region to perfect the art of Provençal haute cuisine.

The olive tree was introduced to the Côte d'Azur by the Greeks 3,000 years ago. More than 50 varieties of olive tree now grow along this coastal region. Harvesting takes place from November (for the ripe green olives) to January (for the more mature black olives). One tonne of olives produces 10–15 litres (17–26 pints) of oil.

The village of Collobrières (▶ 151), surrounded by cork oak forests in the Massif des Maures, is reputed to have been the first place in France to learn about corkage from the Spanish in the Middle Ages, and cork production is still its major industry. Trees must be at least 25 years old before the cork can be harvested. Huge swathes of the bark are cut and left to stand for a month. They are then dried and boiled to make them more supple, and then individual corks are punched out by machine.

Festivals

Festivals are very much a way of life on the Côte d'Azur, whether seasonal, historic, musical, sporting, culinary, religious or profane. Throughout the year every town and village has a fête, often with traditional costume and lavish processions.

The first major festival of the year is the **Feast of the Epiphany** (6 January) marking the 12th day of Christmas, when the Three Kings are commemorated across the region with crown-shaped pastries.

In February the floral festivals commence. Bormes-les-Mimosas (▶ 149) holds the **Corso Fleuri**, a dazzling procession of floral floats, majorettes and brass bands. Menton (▶ 72–73) has fêted its **lemons** every February since 1934. Legend has it that when Eve was banished from the Garden of Eden, she smuggled out a lemon and brought it here to flourish in the town's acclaimed micro-climate. For two weeks, giant sculptures of oranges and lemons adorn the Biovès gardens, and on Sundays there are lavish parades of citrus-smothered floats, street parties and fireworks.

No one in France takes street-partying quite as seriously as the Niçois during the **Nice Carnival** (www.nicecarnaval.com). It's the biggest pre-Lenten carnival in France, with 18 wild days of daily parades, bands, *batailles des fleurs* ("flower battles"), prestigious balls and concerts leading up to Shrove Tuesday. This event began in 1873 and has followed the same formula annually, from day one, when His Majesty King Carnival (a papier

Nice Carnival

mâché figure) is trumpeted into town on the grandest float, to day eighteen when he is burned on the seashore.

March sees some unusual festivals, including the **Festin des Cougourdons**, a festival of dried, sculpted gourds in Nice, and the **Fête des Violettes** in Tourrettes-sur-Loup (► 164) on the second Sunday of the month, when the village is carpeted with fresh violets.

In April everyone takes to the mountains for the **Ski Grand Prix** marking the end of the season at Isola 2000 (www.isola2000.com), the nearest ski resort to Nice – just 90 minutes by car or bus from the coast.

The next Grand Prix in the region is the thrilling **Monaco Grand Prix** (► 104) in May, the world's most glamorous motor race and the only circuit on public roads, once described by former racing driver Nelson Piquet as trying to ride a bicycle round your living room. From high-octane bling

Top: Monaco Grand Prix

to highbrow art-house movies, the beautiful people of the world are drawn to the **Cannes International Film Festival** (► 17) during May.

May also marks St-Tropez's **bravade** (► 140) – a religious procession devoted to the town's patron, St Torpes, a Roman soldier who converted to Christianity and was martyred by decapitation. His body was placed in a boat with a hungry dog and a cockerel, but miraculously it remained untouched and the vessel was washed up on the spot where St-Tropez stands today.

June is the best time to visit the medieval village of Gorbio (► 74), for the eccentric **Procession dai Limaça** (Snail Procession), when the streets are lit with thousands of tiny lamps made from snail shells to celebrate **Fête-Dieu** (the Feast of God).

The balmy evenings of July and August are filled with music festivals to entertain the masses of holidaymakers, ranging from the **Rencontres de Musique Mediévale** (medieval music festival) in the Abbaye du Thoronet (► 146–147) to the **Nice Jazz Festival**

(www.nicejazzfest.com) in Cimiez (► 34, 51), a week-long festival of jazz, blues, fusion and urban funk. The annual **Jazz-at-Juan** festival at Juan-les-Pins (► 34, 122), also in July, has welcomed the great names in contemporary music since its foundation in 1906, including Louis Armstrong, Miles Davis, John Coltrane and George Benson.

The autumn months contain fewer events than the rest of the year. Highlights include a **Chestnut Festival** during October in La Garde Freinet (► 151–152); and an electrifying firework display for the **Fête du Prince** – Monaco's national day (19 November). On the sporting front, crowds flock to Nice mid-year for the **international triathlon** (cycling, running and swimming) – known by locals as the "Madman's Promenade". But fewer people attend the Christmas Day skinny-dip, the great **Bain de Noël**.

An elaborate display of citrus fruits at the Fête du Citron in the Biovès gardens, Menton

Left: The old fishing village of Le Suquet, Cannes

Finding Your Feet

First Two Hours

Arriving in Nice

By Air

- **Nice-Côte d'Azur** (tel: 0820 423 333; www.nice.aeroport.fr) is the major airport for eastern Provence and lies on the coast 6km (4 miles) west of Nice. Direct flights are available from mainland Europe, but many long-haul destinations require you to change planes in Paris. Terminal 1 serves the majority of international flights, with airlines including British Airways, bmibaby and Aerlingus. Terminal 2 serves Air France, British Midland and easyJet.
- The easiest way to **get into Nice** is by **bus**. Ligne d'Azur runs three bus routes from the airport into central Nice. **Bus 23** runs from Terminal 1, Stand 6, into the heart of the city every 20 minutes. **Bus 98** goes to the **bus station** (*gare routière*) in centre of Nice via the promenade des Anglais. It departs from Terminal 1, Stand 1, or Terminal 2, Stand 5. **Bus 99** goes to the Nice **train station** (*gare SNCF*). It departs from Terminal 1, Stand 1 or Terminal 2, Stand 4. It's 20 minutes by bus to central Nice. To catch any of these routes, you will need to purchase a Ligne d'Azur day pass (€4).
- Purchase **bus tickets and passes** from ticket machines, or at the office opposite the bus stand outside Terminal 2. See www.nice.aeroport.fr or www.lignedazur.com for more information. Remember to **validate** your ticket in the machine on the bus, or you may incur a fine.
- The local **TER** (*Trains Express Régionaux* or Regional Express) **train station**, Nice St-Augustin, is a short walk from Terminal 1. Trains run from here to the *gare SNCF* in central Nice.
- **Taxi** ranks are situated outside both terminals, and a taxi into Nice costs about €25. Have your cash ready (there are ATMs inside the terminals) as taxis accept payment in cash only.
- **Car-rental** desks on the arrivals level are open until 10 pm. After this time you can rent cars from the car-rental zone at Terminal 2, behind the P5 car park. Nice is a 15- to 30-minute drive from the airport on the **N7**.
- A free **shuttle bus** runs between the two terminals every 7 to 10 minutes.

By Train

- Train services within France are run by the state railway company, the Société Nationale des Chemins de Fer (**SNCF**, tel: 08 92 35 35 35).
- Nice is easily reached from Paris in 6 hours on a **TGV** (*Train à Grande Vitesse*) high-speed train – change at Lyon or Marseille. TGVs run five times daily in summer, twice daily in winter. **CORAIL** trains provide regular long-distance services (*Grandes Lignes*) and **TER** provide the local service (*Lignes Régionales*). Nice train station has 11 regular connections from abroad and 20 daily connections with large cities in France.
- A **car-train service** is available between major French cities in which vehicles are conveyed at the same time as their owners, who travel in *couchettes* (sleeping cars). It is advisable to book this service well in advance through SNCF.
- For more **information in English**, and to purchase **rail passes** online, see Rail Europe (www.raileurope.co.uk; or www.raileurope.com in the US).

By Road

- Nice interconnects with major European cities via an extensive **motorway network**. The city is linked by the **A8** (La Provençale) to Aix-en-Provence in the west and the Italian border in the east.
- It takes approximately 9 hours to drive from **Paris to Nice** by motorway.
- From the motorway, **access to the city centre** is via five exits: promenade des Anglais (exit 50), St-Augustin (51), St-Isidore (52), Nice-Nord (54) and Nice-Est (55).
- **Long-distance bus routes** within France are generally slightly less expensive than the trains, but much slower. Eurolines (tel: 0892 695 252; www.eurolines.fr) operates services to Nice.

- **Nice Tourist Offices**
  - ✉ 5 promenade des Anglais ☎ 08 92 70 74 07; www.nicetourism.com
    ◉ Mon–Sat 9–6 (low season); Mon–Sat 8–8, Sun 9–7 (high season).

  - ✉ Gare SNCF, avenue Thiers ☎ 08 52 70 74 07 ◉ Mon–Sat 8–7, Sun 10–5 (low season); Mon–Sat 8–8, Sun 9–7 (high season).

  - ✉ Aéroport Nice Côte d'Azur, Terminal 1 ☎ 08 92 70 74 07
    ◉ Mon–Sat 8–9 (low season); daily 8–9 (high season).

Arriving in Monaco

By Air

- **Access to Monaco** by air is via the International Nice-Côte d'Azur Airport. The 17km (11 miles) from the airport to Monaco can be covered directly by road, or a 7-minute **helicopter** flight. A helicopter departs daily every 20 minutes, and costs about €95 per person each way.
- **Rapides Côte d'Azur** (tel: 08 20 42 33 33; www.rca.tm.fr) runs bus 110 every hour from both airport terminals. It takes about 45 minutes to reach the city centre (€14.70 single, €23 return).
- A **taxi** from the airport will take about 35 minutes, and cost about €75.

By Train

- Monaco is connected with France and the rest of Europe via a **TGV** line that runs between Paris and Monaco (5 hours 45 minutes), and by the slower **TERs**, connecting Monaco with towns and cities in the local area.
- **International rail connections** with Monaco include the Train Bleu, an overnight service from Paris to Ventimiglia, and the Ligure, which runs from Marseille to Milan. The Metrazur stops at all towns along the Côte d'Azur to the Italian border, with more regular services in summer.

By Road

- Monaco is linked to France, Italy, Germany, Switzerland, Belgium and the UK by a network of **motorways**. Coming from Italy, take the Monaco-Roquebrune exit (58); from France, take the Monaco exit (56).
- The three **corniche roads** (➤ 64–67) are the most scenic routes between Nice and Monaco, although the A8 may be faster, especially in summer.

By Sea

- The main harbours are **Condamine** (or Port Hercule) and **Fontvieille**. Both are equipped to handle yachts. Intercontinental liners anchor in Monaco Bay.

- **Monaco Tourist Office**
  ✉ 2a boulevard des Moulins, Monte-Carlo ☎ 04 92 16 61 66;
  www.visitmonaco.com

Arriving in Cannes

By Air

- **Several regular buses** operate between Cannes and Nice-Côte d'Azur
  International Airport, 27km (17 miles) away. Ligne d'Azur bus 200
  departs every 30 minutes from Terminal 2, Stand 3 (€4 day pass).
  Rapides Côte d'Azur (tel: 08 20 432 33 33; www. rca.tm.fr) runs
  bus 210 from both terminals (€12.90 single, €21 return).
- A **taxi** from the airport to Cannes costs about €65.
- A **helicopter** service between the airport and Cannes is available, and
  costs approximately €90 per person one way. It departs every 30 minutes, with a free shuttle between the heliport and the centre of Cannes.
- The smaller **Cannes-Mandelieu Airport**, 8km (5 miles) outside Cannes,
  can be accessed by private planes and charter flights.

By Train

- The **Cannes train station** *(gare SNCF)* in the town centre can be reached
  by TGV, TER and CORAIL services. See www.sncf.com or Rail Europe for
  more information. International trains to Cannes include the Train Bleu
  from Paris to Ventimiglia, and the TEE (Trans Europe Express).

By Road

- Approach Cannes from the **A8** Esterel Côte d'Azur motorway, and take
  the Cannes Est exit (42).

- **Cannes Tourist Office**
  ✉ Palais des Festivals, 1 boulevard de La Croisette ☎ 04 92 99 84 22;
  www.cannes.com

Arriving in St-Tropez

By Air

- The nearest airports are **Toulon-Hyeres** (52km/37 miles), **Nice-Côte d'Azur**
  (65km/40 miles) and **St-Tropez/La Mole** (20km/12 miles). La Mole air-
  field has domestic and international flights, including regular flights to
  Geneva, Bale-Mulhouse, Munich, Paris and Nice.
- A **taxi** from Toulon airport to St-Tropez costs about €85. Sodetrav runs a
  bus service from Toulon airport to St-Tropez (€19.30, www.sodetrav.fr).

By Train

- St-Tropez does not have its own railway station. A **bus service** runs
  between St-Tropez and the railway stations at St-Raphaël and Toulon.

By Road

- From Marseille–Aix **A8 motorway** take the exit at the Cannet des Maures
  junction, then proceed on the D558 for 38km/24 miles.
- From Nice take the **A8 motorway** and exit at the le Muy junction, then
  proceed on the D25 for 40km/25 miles.
- There is a **coach service** from Nice to St-Raphaël with Variose d'Autocars
  (tel: 04 98 11 37 60).

- **St-Tropez Tourist Office**
  ✉ Quai Jean-Jaurès ☎ 04 94 97 45 21; www.ot-saint-tropez.com

Getting Around

You could get around the Côte d'Azur in a helicopter if you were so inclined; but the local train line is very efficient and a number of buses are also available. A car is useful if you plan to explore smaller villages away from the main resorts.

Domestic Air Travel

- **Helicopter** travel is becoming increasingly popular in the area, particularly between Nice airport and glamorous Monaco. Several companies fly between these points, and others along the coast, including Heli Air Monaco (tel: 377 92 050 051; www.heliairmonaco.com) and Azur Helicopter (tel: 04 93 90 40 70; www.azurhelico.com). There are information desks for various companies outside the arrivals of Nice airport, Terminal 1.

Trains

- **High-speed TGV trains** (www.tgv.co.uk) connect Paris with many towns along the Côte d'Azur, including Toulon, Hyères, Les Arcs, Draguignan, St-Raphaël, Antibes, Cannes, Nice, Monaco and Menton.
- **Regional TER trains** (www.ter-sncf.com) connect many towns along the Côte d'Azur to the Italian border. The TER trains are reliable, and avoid the hazards of traffic jams and finding a car park.
- **Bicycles** can be taken onto all suitable trains outside the peak hours (Mon–Fri 7 am–9 am and 4:30 pm–6:30 pm).
- **Tickets** can be bought at stations, but if there is no ticket office or it is closed you can pay the conductor on the train. You must stamp your ticket in the orange machine on the platform before boarding the train at the start of your journey to **validate** it. If the platform doesn't have a validation machine, the conductor will validate your ticket on the train.

Buses

- **Several bus** services connect key towns along the Côte d'Azur, but reaching smaller villages can be problematic.
- On Sundays and official holidays, services are **often limited**.
- Timetables are available at the bus station or through bus company offices. The **bus station** (*gare routière*) is usually situated at the central town square, close to the railway station (*gare SNCF*).
- **Tickets** can usually be bought on board, but may also be available from kiosks (*tabacs*) around the town. Remember to validate your ticket in the machine on the bus.
- **Ligne d'Azur** (tel: 08 10 06 10 06; www.lignedazur.com) is the city bus service for Nice and the surrounding area, including the airport. The bus station is at boulevard Jean Jaurès. The long-distance bus station (*gare routière*) is next door.
- **Ligne d'Azur bus tickets** can be bought on the bus; at Bel Canto, 29 avenue Malausséna (Mon–Sat); at the Grand Hotel, 10 avenue Felix Fauré (Mon–Sat), and at various *tabacs* around Nice. Single tickets: €1.30; multi tickets: €20 (17 trips) or €10 (10 trips); day passes: one day €4, seven days €15.
- **Compagnie des Autobus de Monaco** (www.cam.mc) serves Monaco, with six routes covering the principality. Routes 1 and 2 are most useful for visitors, linking Monaco Rock with Monte-Carlo.

- **Tickets** can be bought on the bus and are available as singles, in packs of four or eight, or as a day pass.
- In Cannes, **Bus Azur** run services (6 am–8:30 pm) covering the city and surrounding towns. Information can be found at the **bus station** in place Cornut Gentille, next to the town hall (tel: 0825 825 599). **Sillages** runs services from Cannes north into the hills around Grasse (tel: 0800 095 000/04 93 64 88 84; www.sillages-stga.tm.fr).
- **Bus Azur** €1.30 for a single ticket, and packs of ten or weekly passes are also available for about €10. You can buy single tickets on the bus, but all others must be purchased from the bus station.
- St-Tropez does not have a bus service within the town itself. **Sodetrav** (tel: 08 25 00 06 50; www.sodetrav.fr) buses run around the Golfe de St-Tropez from the town's *gare routière*, just outside the parking du Port. They also provide services to markets in the area and to the rail stations at Toulon and St-Raphaël. Tickets can be bought on the bus.
- **Raphaël Bus** (tel: 04 94 83 87 63) runs services within St-Raphaël and along the Corniche de l'Esterel between St-Raphaël and La Trayas.

Tram

- The construction of a tramway is currently underway in **Nice**. The tramway project encompasses three lines, the first of which is due to open in 2007, the second in 2010, and the third in 2015. See www.tramway-nice.org (in French).

Taxis

- **Taxis** charge a pick-up fee and then charge per kilometre (0.6 mile) driven, plus extra for items of luggage and travel in the evening or on Sundays. All taxis use a **meter** (*compteur*), and taxi stands in towns and cities are marked with a square blue sign. If you phone for a taxi, the meter will be set the moment it sets off to pick you up.
- Some taxis accept bank cards, but most will **accept cash only**. It is usual to give a tip of around 10 per cent.

Driving

- Summer brings many tourists to the Côte d'Azur, and subsequently drivers who are unfamiliar with the roads. At this time of year **traffic jams** are a problem, particularly on the coast. The situation worsens on weekends, when locals and tourists alike head to the beach. Traffic towards Nice and St-Tropez is particularly heavy.
- An excellent system of motorways/expressways (*autoroutes*, marked A on maps and road signs) fans out from Paris, making it fairly straightforward to drive between destinations. **Tolls are charged** on most *autoroutes*, so have some cash to hand as foreign credit cards are not always accepted. Driving from Paris, take the A6 to the Alps and the Riviera.
- There's a comprehensive network of other roads across the country, including main highways (*route nationale*, marked N), lesser highways (*route départementale*, marked D) and minor country roads. Surfaces are generally good at all levels.
- If **bringing your own car** to France, you must always carry the following documentation in addition to your passport: a full, valid national driver's licence, a certificate of motor insurance and the vehicle's registration document (plus a letter of authorisation from the owner if it is not registered in your name). Third-party motor insurance is the **minimum requirement**, but fully comprehensive cover is strongly advised. Check that your **insurance** covers you against damage in transit, and that you have ade-

quate **breakdown cover** (for information contact the AA, tel: 0800 444 500; www.theAA.com, or your own national breakdown organisation). You must also display an **international sticker** or distinguishing sign plate on the rear of the car by the registration plate. **Headlights** of right-hand-drive cars must be adjusted for driving on the right.

Renting a Car

- Cars may be rented by drivers **over 21** who have held a full driver's licence for a year, but some companies require a minimum age of 25. The average **maximum age** limit is 70, and you will be requested to show your licence and passport or national ID card.
- Most major **car rental firms** such as Europcar, Avis and Hertz have outlets at airports, main railway stations and in large towns and cities throughout France. Most will let you return your car to other cities and even countries, but agree this ahead; there may be a surcharge.
- Due to high taxes, renting a car in France can be **expensive**. Fly-drive packages arranged through a tour operator or airline could be less expensive. SNCF has train and car-rental deals from mainline stations.
- Most rental cars in France are **manual**, so if you want an automatic, make sure you specify this and reserve ahead.
- Most **rental agreements** will include: unlimited mileage, comprehensive insurance cover, theft protection and 24-hour emergency roadside assistance, although some agencies may charge you mileage above a certain distance.
- Make sure you have **adequate insurance** and are aware of what you are covered for in the event of an accident. Be aware that low-cost operators may have an extremely **high excess charge** for damage to the vehicle.

Driving Know-How

- Drive on the **right-hand side** of the road (*serrez à droite*).
- Drivers must be **18 or over**, and you'll need to be over 21 to rent a car.
- **Speed limits** are 50kph/31mph on urban roads, 90kph/56mph outside built-up areas (80kph/49mph in rain), 110kph/68mph on dual carriageways/divided highways and non-toll motorways (100kph/62mph in rain), and 130kph/80mph on toll motorways (110kph/68mph in rain). Visiting drivers who have held a licence for less than two years must follow the wet-weather limits **at all times**, even when it's dry. Drivers from within the EU who **exceed the speed** limit by more than 25kph/15mph may have their licences confiscated by the police on the spot.
- At roundabouts/traffic circles, *Cédez le passage* or *Vous n'avez pas la priorité* signs indicate that traffic already on the roundabout has priority.
- **Do not overtake** where there is a solid single line in the centre of the road.
- **The blood alcohol limit** is 0.5 percent (US blood alcohol content 0.05).
- **Fuel** comes as unleaded (95 and 98 octane), lead replacement petrol (LRP or *supercarburant*), diesel (*gasoil* or *gazole*) and LPG. Many filling stations **close on Sundays** and at 6 pm during the week.
- The **French highway code** is available at www.legifrance.gov.fr. For information on road signs, see www.permisenligne.com

Admission Charges
The cost of admission for museums and places of interest mentioned in the text is indicated by the following price categories:
Inexpensive under €5   **Moderate** €5–8   **Expensive** over €8

Accommodation

There is a wide variety of accommodation available on the Côte d'Azur. Despite having some of the most exclusive and expensive accommodation in France, you will also be able to find more affordable options. Accommodation ranges from hotels through to authentically French *chambres d'hôte* (B&Bs), *gîtes*, *auberges* and ubiquitous campsites.

Types of Accommodation

Hotels

■ Hotels in France are regularly inspected and are **classified into six categories**: no star, 1*, 2*, 3*, 4* and 4*L (Luxury). They must display their rates (including tax) both outside the hotel and in the rooms. Charges are usually per room rather than per person, and breakfast is generally charged separately. If you're travelling with a family on a budget, note that for a little extra, many hotels will put another bed in your room.

■ International chain hotels and motels are the easy option, but there are far more interesting options available at similar prices. If you're travelling on a budget, some of the best accommodation are the small family-run inns and hotels known as **Logis de France**. All have a basic standard of comfort, and some are in particularly quaint or charming locations. Most have their own restaurant, serving good local food. By prior arrangement, luggage can be transported between Logis for you – very useful if you're planning a hiking break. As well as star gradings, Logis also have their own chimney symbol of classification. Find them listed on the website www.logis-de-france.fr, or get a complete list from the tourist office.

■ There are some great **luxury hotels** if you want to treat yourself. The traditional *belle-époque* hotels of the Riviera have a cachet which is hard to beat. For something with a more modern twist, look at designer hotels such as Hi Hôtel in Nice (► 54), where organic food and hammams are part of the fun. In most luxury hotels, health and beauty treatments are provided in state-of-the-art spas. Smaller, but no less expensive, are the boutique hotels, with just a few rooms styled by fashion gurus.

Bed-and-Breakfast

■ *Chambres d'hôtes*, also known as *maisons d'hôtes* at the upper end of the scale, give a taste of life in a real French household, and may offer accommodation anywhere from a farm to a château.

■ **Breakfast** usually includes home-made treats, such as fresh croissants and jams. Some families also offer a *table d'hôtes* option, an arrangement that allows you to have (an often gourmet) dinner with the family.

■ Many of the best are affiliated to the **Gîtes de France** organisation, which grades them with one to four ears of corn (*épis*) according to the level of comfort and facilities. The AA publishes its *Bed and Breakfast in France* guide in conjunction with **Gîtes de France.** A further guide to B&B accommodation across France is **Maisons d'Hôtes de Charme**, available in print or online (www.guidesdecharme.com), listing upmarket options in particular. Tourist offices can also inform you of local availability.

Self Catering

■ *Gîtes* are self-contained cottages, villas and apartments, often with swimming pools, widely available all across France. They offer

- particularly good value for families, providing simple and decent accommodation (bring or rent your linen), with a certain rustic charm. They are usually rented by the week or fortnight.
- Many of the most charming *gîtes* are administered through the **Gîtes de France** organisation, which inspects and grades them according to comfort and facilities (www.gites-de-france.fr). Tourist offices also generally hold this information for their area.

Youth Hostels and Budget Options

- **Budget beds** are available at a number of youth hostels (*auberges de jeunesse*) along the Cote d'Azur. Most will charge a small **extra fee** if you are not a member of **Hostelling International** (www.hihostels.com) in your home country. For a list of youth hostels available in the area, contact the French federation of youth hostels, Fédération Unie des Auberges de Jeunesse (tel: 01 48 04 70 40; www.fuaj.org).
- A growing number of budget hotels and **cheap deals** can be booked **online** though sites such as Octopus Travel and Expedia.

Camping

- Sites are **inspected and graded** with a star system like that of the hotels, and range from basic (electricity, showers, lavatories) to luxurious, with swimming pools and other family sports activities, restaurants and bars, and kids' clubs. You don't even have to take your own tent – many have pre-pitched tents and mobile homes on site, complete with cooking equipment, fridges and beds.
- Campsites can become very crowded, particularly during July and August. It is a good idea to **book well ahead** during the high season, which runs from April to October. Contact the National Federation of Campsites (tel: 01 42 72 84 08; www.campingfrance.com).
- Camping or overnight parking of caravans and motorhomes is **not permitted** on the beach or at the roadside. Check with the local town hall first if you plan on *camping sauvage* (away from official campsites), as it is often forbidden, especially in areas at risk of forest fires.
- If you haven't booked and need to find a campsite, the **local tourist office** should be able to advise you, and in case of an emergency, police stations can also let you have a list of local campsite addresses.

Finding a Room

- It is essential to **reserve your accommodation** well in advance for July and August, when it is almost impossible to find accommodation if you haven't booked ahead. Local tourist offices can tell you where rooms are available, and will be able to provide you with a list of accommodation with prices. In villages without a tourist office, you're likely to find the greatest concentration of hotels in the main square or centre of town.
- When you **check in**, you'll need to complete a registration form and show your passport. Ask to see the room first, especially in cheaper accommodation, where payment is often taken in advance.

Seasonal Rates

- Along the Côte d'Azur, **higher prices** may be charged between April and October, and will certainly be charged during July and August, when holidaymakers from all over France make for the coast.

Prices

Expect to pay per double room per night

€ under €80   €€ €80–€150   €€€ over €150

Food and Drink

The French create superb gastronomic feasts, and take enormous pride in
their food. Eating out is one of the best ways to experience French culture
and hospitality. Try the local dishes and order in French, it's part of the fun.

Eating

- You'll find a decent **restaurant** or several in every town, where the glasses
  are polished and the linen and waiters starched. Expect to **reserve your
  table in advance, dress smartly, and allow plenty of time** for the full gastronomic experience. Michelin stars and Gault et Millau *toques* help to
  identify the top eating places. Top restaurants have a *menu dégustation*
  with selected signature dishes and accompanying wines at a fixed price.
- **Brasseries** and **bistros** are **informal** establishments where you can sample
  traditional local dishes, such as bouillabaisse. Brasseries are generally
  open longer hours than other restaurants, and bistros tend to be small
  and friendly family-run restaurants with a modest wine list.
- Anything described as **Provençal** style means it is cooked with olive oil,
  garlic, tomatoes, onion and herbs. **Niçois** style involves olive oil, garlic,
  tomatoes, onion, herbs, olives, capers, anchovies and tarragon.
- Lunchtime menus tend to offer the **best value**, when a *menu du jour*
  (daily menu) of two or three courses with wine costs much less than an
  evening meal. *Prix fixe* (set price) three- or four-course meals also offer
  good value.
- Restaurants mostly keep to **regular opening hours,** noon–2:30 and
  7:30–10, although some may stay open longer in summer. They sometimes close for Sunday dinner and all day Monday, and some close com-
  pletely between November and Easter.
- **Service** should be **included in the bill** (*l'addition*) – look for the words
  service compris, or *s.c.* If the service is exceptional, you could leave
  your loose change in a bar, or a tip of around 5 per cent in a restaurant.
- All restaurants are required by law to have a **non-smoking** (*non-fumeur*)
  section.

Drinking

- In cafés you will be charged more for your drink if sitting outside. Locals
  tend to **stand at the bar** where it is cheaper. Cafés and bars serve coffee,
  soft drinks, alcohol, snacks and often herbal and traditional teas.
- Cafés and bars can open as early as 7 am **to serve breakfast**, and close
  any time between 9 pm and the early hours of the next morning.
  Licensing hours vary according to the individual establishment.
- A *carafe d'eau* (tap water) is usually supplied **free of charge** when you
  order food at restaurants and cafés. Bottled water (*eau*) comes as
  gazeuse (carbonated) or *non-gazeuse* (still). Beer (*bière*) is usually the
  light European lager. White and red wine (*vin blanc, vin rouge*) is widely
  available, and it is worth seeking out the local wines. If in doubt, try the
  house wine (*vin ordinaire* or *vin de table*).
- The **legal age** for drinking alcohol is 16. Children aged 14 to 16 may
  drink wine or beer if accompanied by an adult.

Prices
Expect to pay per person for a three-course meal, excluding drinks:
€ under €25   €€ €25–€60   €€€ over €60

Shopping

The towns along the Côte d'Azur offer all kinds of shopping, from the chic boutiques of Monaco to the atmospheric local markets in every town. Any purchase is an indulgence, whether you're buying haute couture or choosing the chocolatiest cake in a *pâtisserie*, but this glamorous stretch of coastline is hardly the place for self-dicipline.

Where to Go

■ **Markets** (*marchés*) are a quintessentially French experience, and a wonderful way to sample the local produce and atmosphere. Large cities hold markets daily, and smaller towns will have at least one a week. They generally operate from around 7 am to noon. There are also *marché nocturnes* (night markets) at cours Saleya in Nice and at Frejus Plage most evenings in the summer. The people selling the food are usually the people who made it too, and they can tell you all about their produce. In addition to food markets, there are often markets selling books, antiques, flowers, glassware and pottery.

■ Food shops usually open from Tuesday to Saturday, between 7 or 8 am and 6:30 or 7:30 pm, and may close for lunch. Some may open on a Monday afternoon, and most bakeries open on Sunday morning. With the exception of supermarkets, **food stores** tend to specialise in one kind of product, and in each town you will find a *boulangerie* (bakery), *pâtisserie* (pastry/cake shop), *fromagerie* (cheese shop), *boucherie* (butcher), *charcuterie* (delicatessen) and *poissonnerie* (fishmonger).

■ **Supermarkets** and **hypermarkets** generally open from 9 am to 9 or 10 pm, Monday to Saturday; the main names include Carrefour, Auchan, Champion and E Leclerc. Here you will find the *boulangerie, boucherie* and *charcuterie* under one roof.

■ Boutiques selling **fashion**, shoes and lingerie, designer babywear and maternity clothes are in abundance. The most upmarket of these are in Monaco, Nice and St-Tropez. Department stores (*grand magasins*) can also be found in the larger cities.

What to Buy

■ Provence is known for its excellent **produce**: fresh herbs, olive oil, lavender, honey, garlic, truffles and wine are among its specialities, and any market in the Côte d'Azur will have a proliferation of these. Locally, snaffle up delicious *marrons glacés* (glazed chestnuts) in Collobrières, drench yourself in **perfume** from Grasse, and buy quality **glassware** from Biot, *faïence* (fine glazed ceramics) from Moustiers-Ste-Marie, **sculpture and art** from St-Paul-de-Vence and haute couture from Monaco.

■ The village of **Grasse** is famous for its perfume, made from flowers grown on the nearby hillsides. This is where most of the best-known **French perfume** originates. You won't find Chanel or Dior here, but there is plenty of the less expensive, but high-quality local perfume to try.

■ **Biot** is well known for the ceramics and glassware it produces. You can visit a glass-blowing workshop to see the wares being made.

■ There are various options for buying **wine**. Hypermarkets usually stock an excellent range of French wines at a good price.

■ Experience a shopping spree of the highest order in **Monaco**, where the biggest names in fashion display their latest offerings at the sweep of **luxury stores** along the avenue des Beaux-Arts.

Entertainment

Whether you are interested in classy casinos, chic nightclubs or film and jazz festivals, this area has a wealth of entertainment, encompassing everything from hedonistic nightspots to humble village festivals.

Music

- **Jazz** aficionados flock to the area in July when the Côte d'Azur hosts two of Europe's major jazz festivals, which generally overlap, allowing you to sample the best of both. **Jazz à Juan** (► 22, 122) attracts some of the greatest names in jazz and swing to the pine groves of Antibes–Juan-Les-Pins, while the lively **Nice Jazz Festival** (► 22, 51) takes place in Nice's Cimiez gardens over two weeks .
- Menton hosts an annual **chamber music** festival (► 73) in August in the baroque square of the Parvis de la Basilique St-Michel Archange, in the heart of the Old Town.
- Cannes holds a **classical music** festival, Nuits Musicales du Suquet (Suquet Musical Nights), over ten days in mid-July.
- **Sacred music** is performed at summer concerts in the Cimiez monastery and in churches in Nice.

Film

- Hollywood descends upon Cannes in May, during the annual 12-day **film festival** (► 17). The biggest screenings and parties are strictly invitation only affairs, but there are some public screenings as well.

Nightlife

- A lively **club scene** thrives in the major resorts along the coast. Tourist offices, music stores and cafés will have flyers. Clubs often don't get started until midnight, and stay open until dawn. Dress well to make it past the bouncers-cum-fashion-police at the door, and be prepared to pay an extortionate amount for your drinks. The admission charge usually includes your first drink.
- The inextricably linked **café-bar** is the place for a drink in the evening, particularly in smaller towns. Every bar worth its salt will have tables outside during the summer, and the most popular are those where the clientele can watch the world go by as evening turns to night. In cities, bars open as early as 7 am to serve breakfast and stay open until the early hours of the morning. Out of season and out of the cities, bars may close as early as 9 pm.
- An evening at Monte-Carlo's **casino** (► 93–95) is part entertainment, part spectator sport: a great place to blow your savings, or at least watch the drama unfolding around the high rollers. Be prepared for an **admission fee** and dress well, or be restricted to playing the poker machines. Tables open around 8 pm and close around 4 am. Only foreigners (over 18) are allowed to play, so you'll need your **passport**. Locals, even the royals, are barred from gambling.
- There is a vibrant **gay bar and club scene** in Nice and St-Tropez (www.gay-provence.org). Check out local listings magazines for details.

Sport

- Motor racing fans will look forward to Monaco's glamorous **Grand Prix** which takes place in May (► 104).

Nice

Getting Your Bearings

Nice is France's main tourist centre, the most visited city after Paris and the Côte d'Azur's largest, most vibrant resort. Friendly and informal, it radiates a unique atmosphere that is hard to define, although many have tried, labelling it the "Queen of the Riviera", "Capital of the Côte d'Azur", "Nizza la Bella", "The Big Olive" and "Mediterranean Chicago". "Nice" just doesn't seem to cover it.

Over the centuries the city has enjoyed a colourful history. Founded by Greeks and settled by Romans, it thrived in the Middle Ages under the Counts of Provence who were followed by the Italian Dukes of Savoy. Unified with France only as recently as 1860, it still retains a strong Italianate character and is a seductive mix of the best of France and Italy, with its own dialect (*lenga nissarda*) and delicious cuisine. Nice is also blessed with more museums and galleries than any French town outside Paris. Its Mediterranean charm has long provided inspiration to artists, with its pastel-painted buildings and terracotta roofs, cradled by the vine-clad foothills of the Maritime Alps and fringed by a vivid blue sea bathed in magical, incandescent sunlight. Even the palatial hotels, designer boutiques and crowded terrace cafés exude a carefree *joie de vivre*. No wonder Nice has been voted the city where the French would most like to live. As Sandy Wilson remarked in his musical comedy *The Boy Friend* (1954): "Other places may be fun, but when all is said and done, it's so much nicer in Nice."

★ Don't Miss

At Your Leisure

Page 35:
Vieux Nice

Above:
Shopping in Nice

Opposite:
An overview of Nice and the azure Baie des Anges

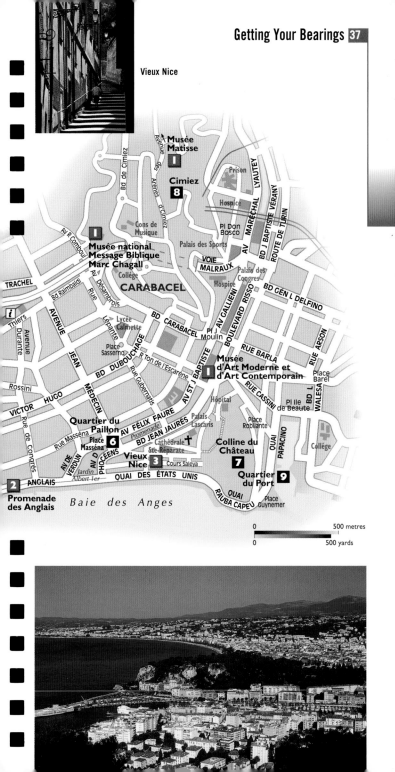

Vieux Nice

Musée Matisse 1

Cimiez 8

Prison

Hospice

Pl Don Bosco

Palais des Sports

Cons de Musique

Musée national Message Biblique Marc Chagall 1

VOIE MALRAUX

Palais des Congrès

Collège

CARABACEL

Hospice

BD GÉN L DELFINO

TRACHEL

Lycée Calmette

Pl J Moulin

RUE BARLA

Place Sasserno

RUE CASSINI

Musée d'Art Moderne et d'Art Contemporain 1

Place Barel

Quartier du Paillon 6

Hôpital

Place Robilante

Place de Beauté

Collège

Place Masséna

Palais Lascaris

Cathédrale

Colline du Château 7

Vieux Nice 3

Cours Saleya

Ste-Réparate

Quartier du Port 9

ANGLAIS 2

Jardin Albert Ier

QUAI DES ÉTATS UNIS

Place Guynemer

Promenade des Anglais

Baie des Anges

| 0 | 500 metres |
| 0 | 500 yards |

This two-day itinerary is a must for art lovers,
photographers and everyone who wishes to visit some of
the greatest sights that Nice has to offer, from world-class
museums and galleries to top restaurants, the gracious
seaside promenade and the mouthwateringly colourful
market of Vieux Nice.

Nice in Two Days

Day One

Morning
Start the day at **cours Saleya** (left, ➤ 46) one of France's best fruit, vegetable and flower markets, where the air is fragrant with lavender, mimosa, olives, *socca*, strawberries, citrus fruits and *herbes de Provence*. Then explore the dark, narrow alleys of atmospheric **🄳 Vieux Nice** (➤ 46), with its lively cafés, flower-festooned squares, small boutiques and galleries.

Lunch
The lively, narrow streets of Vieux Nice are full of tiny restaurants. For a light bite, Lou Pilha Leva (➤ 55) serves Niçois fast-food enjoyed *toute ensemble* with local shoppers on outdoor benches. For dessert, Fenocchio (➤ 55) sells the best ice cream on the Côte d'Azur.

Afternoon
Set off to the stylish residential district of Cimiez, to the remarkable **🄸 Musée Matisse** (below, ➤ 40–41), housed in a handsome 17th-century villa in an olive grove, with works spanning the artist's entire life. Near by, the **🄸 Musée national Message Biblique Marc Chagall** (➤ 41–42) is also well worth a visit, with its series of monumental canvases and dazzling stained-glass windows evoking biblical scenes.

Evening
Reserve a table at Aphrodite (➤ 54–55) to experience Niçois cuisine at its best, then while away the balmy evening sipping chilled Provençal wines on the café terraces lining the cours Saleya.

Day Two

Morning
Stroll along the fashionable palm-lined waterfront – the **2** promenade des Anglais (➤ 44–45) – past exuberant mansions and follies created by English lords and Russian aristocrats, and the world famous Hôtel Négresco (right), built in the classic wedding cake-style architecture of Nice's heyday, the *belle époque*.

A short uphill detour from the seafront leads you to the **8** Musée des Beaux-Arts (➤ 42), with its impressive fine arts collection from the 17th to the 20th centuries.

Lunch
Return to the city centre for a platter of Nice's finest shellfish at Le Grand Café de Turin (➤ 55).

Afternoon
Just a stone's throw away, **6** Musée d'Art Moderne et d'Art Contemporain (left, ➤ 42–43) show-cases works of the "Nice School", 20th-century multi-media iconoclasts whose extraordinary constructions spoof society and the precious highbrow world of art. Alternatively, climb **7** Colline du Château (Castle Hill, ➤ 50–51) for sweeping views over the bustling **9** Quartier du Port (➤ 52) and the curvaceous, glittering Baie des Anges.

Evening
Get tickets for the Opéra de Nice (➤ 58), a rococo extravaganza in red and gold, and home of the Nice Opera, the Philharmonic Orchestra and the Ballet Corps. Round off a perfect evening with a sumptuous meal at La Petite Maison (➤ 56) near by.

❶ Nice Museums

The quality of light and intense colours of the Côte d'Azur have long attracted artists to this part of France. As a result, Nice has a strong artistic heritage, and the largest number of galleries and museums of any French city outside Paris. Some of the best include the Musée des Beaux-Arts, featuring fine art from the 17th to the 19th centuries within a grand villa; the Musée d'Art Moderne et d'Art Contemporain, a legacy of the French and American avant-garde artists drawn to the area in the 1960s; and the individual galleries of Matisse and Chagall, who both lived here and left behind important collections of their works.

Musée Matisse

Henri Matisse (1869–1954), who spearheaded the fauvist movement in the early 20th century, wintered in Nice from 1917 until his death in 1954, and bequeathed his entire personal collection to the city. Together with a second, even bigger, donation from his wife in 1960 (including more than 100 personal effects from his studio in the nearby **Hôtel Regina**), it formed the basis of an extensive collection that celebrates the life, work and influence of this great artist.

The Musée Matisse is in Les Arènes park, set in the middle of a large olive grove in the **Cimiez** district of Nice (▶ 51). The museum incorporates the striking red 17th-century villa where Matisse actually lived, which houses the permanent collection, and a modern underground building where three temporary exhibitions are held each year.

Left to right:
Musée Matisse

Musée national Message Biblique Marc Chagall

Musée d'Art Moderne et d'Art Contemporain (MAMAC)

The permanent collection allows visitors an overview of Matisse's entire working life, starting with copies of Old Master paintings that he made during his apprenticeship, through an era of sober, dark-toned paintings of the 1890s (including his first personal painting, *Nature Morte aux Livres*, and *Intérieur à l'Harmonium*) and his impressionist and fauvist phases (*Jeune Femme à l'Ombrelle* and *Portrait of Madame Matisse*). The bright colours and simple shapes of his maturity are best portrayed in his decorative, post-war paper cut-outs, silk-screen hangings and works such as *Nature Morte aux Grenades* and the well-known *Nu Bleu IV* (*Blue Nude IV*).

The museum also boasts all the bronze sculptures that Matisse ever made, and the world's largest collection of his drawings and engravings, including his illustrations for Irish writer James Joyce's novel *Ulysses*, and his powerful sketches and stained-glass models for the remarkable Chapelle du Rosaire at Vence (► 125). Matisse is buried in the nearby **Cimiez cemetery**.

TAKING A BREAK

There is a café in Les Arènes park near Musée Matisse. Alternatively, pack a picnic with supplies from the cours Saleya market and enjoy it in the park.

Musée national Message Biblique Marc Chagall

Down a side-road at the foot of Cimiez hill, this striking modern museum was especially designed by André Hermant to exhibit Chagall's "Biblical Message", a series of 17 monumental canvases created between 1954 and 1967, vividly evoking the Garden of Eden, Moses and other biblical themes. Other works were donated to the museum after Chagall's death in 1985, making this the largest and most important permanent collection of his work.

Chagall was a highly individualistic Russian-Jewish painter who drew his main themes from the Old Testament and Russian-Jewish folklore. Born in Vitebsk (in present-day Belarus) in 1887, he spent the war years in America, before moving permanently to St-Paul-de-Vence in 1950. He opened the museum here himself in 1973.

Known for his dreamlike paintings featuring violin-playing goats and people floating in the sky, Chagall's paintings here are vast and expressive canvases vividly portraying biblical stories (*messages bibliques*) and Jewish subjects, including his childhood *shetel* (Jewish village) home. Also in the collection are Chagall's mosaic of Elijah, reflected in a pool, and beautiful blue stained-glass panels depicting the creation of the world.

Musée des Beaux-Arts

This prestigious museum of fine arts is housed in a handsome 19th-century mansion, once home to a Ukranian princess, at the western end of the beach. The collection here began with a donation by Napoléon II, and focuses on European fine arts of the 17th to the 19th centuries. Highlights include paintings of the Riviera by Edgar Degas, Alfred Sisley and Raoul Dufy, sculptures by Auguste Rodin and paintings by 17th-century Italian Old Masters.

La Musique (1900), Jules Chéret

The main attraction of the museum is a collection of works by the impressionist café-society artist **Raoul Dufy** (1877–1953), moved from the former Musée Dufy on the waterfront because the salt air was affecting the paint. Of particular note are the early fauve works, the 1908 *Bâteaux à l'Estaque* (a cubist painting predating cubism), and a handful of colourful Nice scenes.

One gallery is given over to 18th-century Niçois artist Carle Van Loo (1705–65), and the main staircase is adorned with the works of Jules Chéret (1836–1932), a popular *belle-époque* lithographist, who introduced colour advertising posters to France in 1866.

The École Française is well represented, with works by Degas, Boudin and Sisley. There are also important impressionist and post-impressionist works by Bonnard, Vuillard and Van Dongen (including his famous *Tango of the Archangel* – which evokes the Roaring Twenties on the Riviera).

Musée d'Art Moderne et d'Art Contemporain

This remarkable museum traces the history of French and American avant-garde from the 1960s. Nice was at the centre of *nouveau realisme* – the French counterpart to pop art – in the 1960s, and the collection at the Musée d'Art Moderne et d'Art Contemporain (MAMAC) includes works by the movement's most prominent artist, Yves Klein, as well as that of other artists from the time who lived and worked in the town, such as pop artists Andy Warhol and Roy Lichtenstein.

The MAMAC building, designed by Yves Bayard and Henri Vidal, is itself a bold piece of modern art, with four octagonal, grey-marble towers linked together by glassed-in walkways.

Collections are exhibited in rotation and reflect the main avant-garde art movements of the last 40 years in France and the US. The primary focus is on French *noveau realisme* and the artists of the second École de Nice, such as Rayasse, César, Arman, Ben, Tinguely and Yves Klein. Many of their works parody society and the highbrow art world. Also look out for artworks from the support-surface movement (where artists sought to reduce painting to its materialistic reality, concentrating on the frame and the texture of the canvas), and a collection of Christo's drawings and wrapped "packages" from the 1960s. American abstraction, minimalism and pop art are also represented.

The **rooftop terrace** of MAMAC has unsurpassed views of Nice, as well as Klein's *Mur de Feu* (*Wall of Fire*) which is illuminated on special occasions.

TAKING A BREAK

Have a coffee in MAMAC's **Café des Arts** or a seafood lunch near by at **Le Grand Café du Turin** (➤ 55). For a cheap bite, you'll find locals lining up for a snack at **Specialities Niçoises** on rue Pairolière (➤ 56).

Musée Matisse
➕ 184 off C3 ✉ 164 avenue des Arènes
☎ 04 93 81 08 08; www.musee-matisse-nice.org ⏰ Wed–Mon 10–6 💰 Inexpensive, under 18 free; free on 1st Sun of month
🚌 15, 17, 20, 22, 25. Bus 15 free between Matisee and Chagall museums, ticket available from musuem sales desk

Musée Marc Chagall
➕ 184 C3 ✉ Avenue Docteur Ménard
☎ 04 93 53 87 20; www.musee-chagall.fr
⏰ Wed–Mon 10–6, Jul–Sep; Wed–Mon 10–5, Oct–Jun 💰 Moderate, under 18 free; free on 1st Sun of month 🚌 15 (free between Chagall and Matisse museums)

Musée des Beaux-Arts
➕ 184 off A1 ✉ 33 avenue des Baumettes ☎ 04 92 15 28 28 ⏰ Tue–Sun 10–6 💰 Inexpensive, under 18 free
🚌 3, 6, 9, 10, 11, 12, 22, 23

Musée d'Art Moderne et d'Art Contemporain (MAMAC)
➕ 184 D2 ✉ Promenade des Arts
☎ 04 93 62 61 62; www.mamac-nice.org
⏰ Tue–Sun 10–6 💰 Inexpensive, under 18 free; free to all on 1st and 3rd Sun of month 🚌 1, 2, 3, 4, 5, 6, 7, 8, 9, 10, 14, 16, 25, 30, 88, 89

NICE MUSEUMS: INSIDE INFO

Top tips The **Nice Museum Pass** (*Carte Musées Ville de Nice*) provides entrance to many of the galleries and museums in Nice (€6 for 7 days). If you plan to visit other galleries in the area, the **Riviera Museum Pass** (*Carte Musées Côte d'Azur*) covers 65 museums, monuments and gardens in the region (€10 for 1 day, €17 for 3 days, €27 for 7 days). Passes are available at the sales desk of museums, FNAC stores and some tourist offices.
• *Carte Musées Ville de Nice* includes: Anatole Jakovsky International Museum of Naïve Art; MAMAC; Asian Arts Museum; Archaeology Museum and Cimiez site; Fine Arts Museum; Marc Chargall Museum; Matisse Museum and the Terra Amata Human Palaeontology Museum.
• For a full list of museums covered by the *Carte Musées Côte d'Azur*, visit http://www.infografix.biz/diversweb/cmca or ask at the local tourist office.
• Municipal galleries are **free to all** on the 1st and 3rd Sundays of every month.

Hidden gems Two of the lesser-known museums, but well worth seeking out, are the **Asian Arts Museum** (405 promenade des Anglais) and the **Anatole Jakovsky International Museum of Naïve Art** (avenue de Fabron).

Promenade des Anglais

BLUE BE

The elegant promenade des Anglais and the opulent buildings of the *belle époque* (beautiful era) that line it have an air of sophistication reminiscent of the halcyon days of Nice, when it was a haven for the European aristocracy in search of a more agreeable climate. The lavish architecture and sparkling blue bay continue to draw people today, with runners, rollerbladers and walkers all coming here to enjoy the fresh sea air and the wonderful view.

Originally the promenade was a simple coastal path only 2m (6 feet) wide. Today it is a broad, noisy, seafront road, and the white wedding-cake-style architecture of the luxury *belle-époque* **hotels**, such as the stately Négresco, are juxtaposed with ugly concrete apartment blocks. Despite all this, the promenade is still an attractive spot for a stroll, and on fine days is full of people sauntering, sitting in the sun or rollerblading.

The wide promenade follows the brilliant azure coastline for 6km (4 miles), and will take a few hours to walk all the way up and back, although it is also possible to rent bicycles or rollerblades to cover the distance (➤ 52 For Kids). Benches along the length of the promenade are prime places, so sit back and enjoy the view of the glittering ocean, or the people passing by. To the north lies a web of busy pedestrianised streets, brimming with restaurants, bars and chic boutiques. The promenade des Anglais officially ends at the Jardin Albert Ier, but the walkway can be followed as far east as quai des États-Unis, and around quai Rauba-Capéu to Vieux Port.

Hôtel Négresco

Of the many splendid *belle-époque* buildings along the promenade des Anglais seafront, the best known is the magnificent domed Hôtel Négresco (➤ 54).

The hotel was built in 1912 for the Romanian Henri Négresco, once a gypsy-violin serenader, who went bankrupt eight years later. Nevertheless, it remains a famous Riviera landmark, a National Historic Monument and one of France's most magnificent hotels, and its guest list is legendary, including Churchill, Chaplin, Piaf, Taylor and Burton, Picasso, Dali and the Beatles. The American dancer Isadora Duncan died outside the hotel in 1927, when her trailing scarf caught in the wheel of her Bugatti and broke her neck.

From the outside the pink-and-white turreted façade resembles a wedding cake more than a hotel. You may have trouble finding the main entrance because it is in a small back street. Incidentally, the whole hotel was built backwards to protect guests from the then unfashionable sun.

Since 1957 the hotel has been privately owned by Madame Augier, who resides in the hotel's cupola and dines each night in its Michelin-starred Chantecler restaurant (➤ 55). Still functioning as a hotel in the traditional sense, the Négresco is also an eclectic museum of modern art and décor. The interior is full of surprises, ranging from the world's largest Aubusson carpet to gaudy, gold, glittery bathroom suites. The décor is inspired by the royal palace at Versailles, and the lavatories are more lavishly ornamented than any others you are likely to see. In La Rotonde restaurant (➤ 56), meals are served in the original cabins of an 18th-century merry-go-round. Perhaps not the most reasonably priced hotel in Nice, but the Négresco is certainly unique.

Left:
Holidaymakers
stroll past
national flags
flying along the
promenade des
Anglais

The promenade
is popular with
rollerbladers

Below: The
Hôtel Négresco

TAKING A BREAK

Inside the Négresco, **Le Chantecler** (➤ 55) or the more affordable **La Rotonde** (➤ 56) make for memorable dining.

Promenade des Anglais
➕ 184 B1 ✉ Promenade des Anglais 🚍 52, 59, 60, 62, 94, 98, 99

Hôtel Négresco
➕ 184 A1 ✉ 37 promenade des Anglais ☎ 04 93 16 64 00
🚍 52, 59, 94, 98, 99

PROMENADE DES ANGLAIS: INSIDE INFO

Top tips Extend your stroll to include the road leading around the headland towards the port in the east. Known in the local dialect as **quai Rauba-Capéu** or "Hat Thief", this windy spot is a great place to watch the sun set.

Exploring further Stairs and an elevator lead from the quai des États-Unis to Colline du Château (➤ 50) above, from where there are wonderful **views** of the whole city.

③ Vieux Nice

The best way to discover Nice is to get lost in the tangle of
dark, narrow streets that make up historic and atmospheric
Vieux Nice (Old Nice). Also known as the Vielle Ville (Old
Town), this is most colourful part of the city, full of life,
festooned with flowers and laundry, and brimming with
cafés, hidden squares and bustling markets.

In this jumble of lanes there are the usual bars, restaurants and souvenir
shops, but you can also stumble across side-streets leading into quiet,
undiscovered corners. In the back streets, designer boutiques, atmospheric
galleries and intimate Niçois restaurants rub shoulders with no-nonsense
workers' cafés and run-of-the-mill stores catering for the daily needs of the
locals. The **rue du Marché**, **rue de la Boucherie**, **rue du
Collet** and **rue Pairolière** have the atmosphere of a covered
market, with food stalls full of tempting produce. For early
risers, a visit to the pungent **fish market** on place St-François
is an interesting and rewarding experience.

At the heart of Vieux Nice is **cours Saleya**, buzzing day
and night with alfresco restaurants, bars, and the vibrant fruit,
vegetable and flower markets that take place here each day.
Near by are two interesting small baroque churches: the
Église de l'Annonciation, one of the oldest churches in Nice;
and the **Chapelle de la Miséricorde**, which is noted for its
elaborate rococo interior.

Vieux Nice also has several quirky art galleries, including
the **Galerie de la Marine** and the vaulted **Galerie des
Ponchettes**, which was formerly used as an arsenal for the
Sardinian navy then as a fish market until Matisse persuaded
the local authorities to renovate it in 1950. Both stage
temporary exhibitions, changing every three months.

Cours Saleya
This spacious, sunny square is the scene of one of France's
best fruit, flower and vegetable markets, taking place here
every morning, except Monday, which is reserved for antiques
dealers. The colourful stands overflow with locally grown produce,
including flowers, olives, honey, tomatoes, aubergines, citrus fruits and *herbes
de Provence* – the tastes, fragrances and colours of Provence and Italy are a
veritable feast for the senses.

Arrive at dawn and you will find the Riviera's top chefs choosing their
plats du jour (dishes of the day) from the tempting food displays. During
the day it is fun to watch the world go by from the pavement terraces of the
bars and restaurants that line the famous market, or to try a light snack from
the market stalls. Look out for *pissaladière* (onion tart with anchovy and
olives) and *beignets de courgettes* (frittered courgette flowers) or visit Madame
Thérèse's stall for the best *socca* (traditional Niçois chickpea pancake) in
town. At night cafés and restaurants come into their own, making this one
of Nice's most animated nightspots.

Top: Shopping for fruit and vegetables in the cours Saleya

Above: Cathédrale Ste-Réparte in place Rosetti, Vieux Nice

Cathédrale Ste-Réparate

In place Rosetti, the main square of Vieux Nice, is the lovely baroque Cathédrale Ste-Réparate, built by local architect Jean-André Guibera in 1650 and dedicated to the city's patron saint.

The building is dominated by an 18th-century bell tower and a magnificent emerald dome of Niçois tiles. The carefully proportioned façade, with its arcaded entrance, decorative niches and medallions, dates from 1825 and has recently been enhanced with colour.

Inside, visitors are confronted by a profusion of baroque marble, stucco and gilt. Note the ornate marble high altar and choir balustrade, the walnut panelling in the sacristy, acquired from Nice's Dominican convent, and the painting *Dispute du Saint-Sacrement* in the right transept, attributed to the Raphaël School.

Palais Lascaris

In a narrow back street at the heart of the Old Town, behind a façade of ornate balconies and pilasters adorned with garlands of flowers, lies the beautiful Palais Lascaris. This Genoese-style palace was originally four separate houses, bought in 1648 by the powerful Lascaris-Ventimiglia family. The city of Nice purchased the property in 1942 and has since restored this noble building.

In the entrance hall the family coat of arms is engraved on the ceiling, bearing the motto "Not even lightning strikes us". On the ground floor there is a reconstruction of a pharmacy dated 1738, with an unusual collection of porcelain vases. A grandiose balustraded staircase, decorated with 17th-century paintings and statues of Mars and Venus, leads to sumptuous reception rooms containing elegant chandeliers, Flemish tapestries, 17th- and 18th-century furniture, ornate woodwork and a *trompe-l'oeil* ceiling.

TAKING A BREAK

For simple, inexpensive, local food, **Bar René Socca** (► 55) at the top of the Old Town is a friendly place for a light meal or to sample the local specialities. For dinner, just around the corner from Bar René, **La Table Alziari** (4 rue Francois Zanin, tel: 04 9380 3403), owned by the respected Alziari family of olive-oil fame, serves traditional Provençal food.

✚ 184 C1
Cours Saleya Market
✚ 184 C1 ✉ Cours Saleya ⊙ Fruit and vegetable market: Tue–Sun 6 am–1 pm. Flower market: all day except Sun pm. Flea market: Mon am 🚌 All buses go to the *gare routière*, near Vieux Nice

Cathédrale Ste-Réparte
✚ 184 D1 ✉ Place Rossetti ☎ 04 93 92 79 10
⊙ Daily 9–12, 2–6 🕯 Free
❓ No shorts or sleeveless shirts

Palais Lascaris
✚ 184 D1 ✉ 15 rue Droite ☎ 04 93 62 72 40
⊙ Wed–Mon 10–6. Closed Tue 🕯 Free

Galerie de la Marine
✚ 184 C1 ✉ 59 quai des États-Unis ☎ 04 93 91 92 90
⊙ Tue–Sat 10–12, 2–6, Sun 2–6. Closed Mon and public hols 🕯 Free

Galerie des Ponchettes
✚ 184 C1 ✉ 77 quai des États-Unis ☎ 04 93 62 31 24
⊙ Tue–Sun 10–6. Closed Mon and public hols
🕯 Free

Palais Lascaris, Vieux Nice

VIEUX NICE: INSIDE INFO

Top tips When selecting your fruits and vegetables at cours Saleya, use a **tin** given to you by the vendor. To really look like a local, take along a basket or your own shopping bag.
• Get to cours Saleya **in the morning** when people are out buying food from the market. For **a cheap breakfast**, buy some pastries and fresh fruit and grab a coffee from one of the cafés along the street.

At Your Leisure

The interior takes the form of a Greek cross and is brimming with precious icons, frescoes and treasures. The lavish **iconostasis** separating the sanctuary from the nave features a striking icon of Our Lady of Kazan, painted on wood and set amid a riot of silver and precious stones. The church still conducts regular services in Russian.

🚪 184 A2 ✉ Avenue Nicolas II ☎ 04 93 96 88 02 🕐 Daily 9:30–12, 2:30–5:30 (6 pm in summer) Closed Sun am 🎟 Free. Group of 10 or more: inexpensive ❓ No shorts or sleeveless shirts

4 Cathédrale Orthodoxe Russe St-Nicolas

This magnificent pink-and-grey Russian Orthodox church, crowned by six gleaming, green, onion-shaped cupolas, was built by Tsar Nicolas II in 1903 in memory of Alexander II's son Nicolas, who is buried in the grounds. The young, consumptive Tsarevich Nicolas was brought to Nice in search of good health in 1865, but to no avail. The luxurious villa in which he died was later demolished to construct the cathedral and a mortuary chapel.

5 Musée Masséna

This museum of art and history is situated in the **Palais Masséna,** which was built in 1901 by Prince Victor Masséna, the great-grandson of Nice-born Marshal Masséna, Napoléon's ruthlessly ambitious military genius. The building was bequeathed to the city of Nice on the condition that it became a museum devoted to regional history.

The wide-ranging historical exhibits include paintings by members of the early Nice School, a library containing over 10,000 rare books and manuscripts, and a fearsome collection of 15th- and 16th-century weaponry. A section reserved for local traditions includes a display of regional costumes, furniture, *faïence* pottery and craftwork.

🚪 184 B1 ✉ 35 promenade des Anglais and 65 rue de France ☎ 04 93 88 11 34 🕐 Closed for restoration until mid-2007 🚌 52, 59, 94, 98, 99, 60, 62

Colourful cupolas adorn Nice's Russian Orthodox church

6 Quartier du Paillon

The once fast-flowing and often dangerously high River Paillon was canalised in the 1830s and began to vanish under the pavements. It now trickles below Nice's showcase gardens – lush Jardins Albert Ier, fountain-filled place Masséna, leafy place Général Leclerc and the delightful hanging gardens of the promenade du Paillon.

The Paillon district's main focal point is **place Masséna**, a stately 19th-century square of red-ochre buildings built across the path of the river. Many important streets fan out from here, notably **avenue Jean Médecin** (Nice's main shopping street) and **rue Masséna** (a lively pedestrian zone). A balustraded terrace and steps to the south lead to the Old Town. To the north the covered course of the river provided space for several grand civic projects built during the last 25 years: a row of cultural complexes including the MAMAC building, the **Théâtre de Nice** and the **Acropolis** convention centre, a monumental eyesore of concrete slabs and smoked glass.

Théâtre de Nice
🏠 184 D2 ✉ Promenade des Arts
☎ 04 93 13 90 90 🚌 All buses

Colourful fishing boats line Nice's port, overlooked by apartment buildings

Acropolis
🏠 184 D2 ✉ 1 esplanade Kennedy
☎ 04 93 92 83 00 🚌 All buses

7 Colline du Château

The seafront promenade ends at Colline du Château (Castle Hill). Surprisingly, there is no château here, but a high headland rising up between the beach area and the port. The hilltop is a park with cool, shady gardens and fantastic views over the crowded port (▶ 52), colourful Vieux Nice below, and the voluptuous curve of the Baie des Anges.

It was on this imposing site that Nice originated as the ancient Greek acropolis of Nikaïa. Archaeologists have discovered Roman and medieval remains, although the medieval fortress and other buildings that stood here were destroyed by the French in the early 18th century, when Nice belonged to Savoy.

The best approach is up the steps from **quai des États-Unis**, or by elevator from nearby **Tour Bellanda**. Descend eastwards along montée Eberlé and rue Catherine Ségurane to the elegant, arcaded **place Garibaldi**, which is named after the great 19th-century Niçois revolutionary Giuseppe Garibaldi (hero of Italy's unification), who lies buried in a cemetery at the top of the hill.

its original Roman walls, now hosts open-air concerts, including jazz. Beside the park, the small, modern **Musée d'Archéologique** displays objects found here and elsewhere in Nice and illustrates the city's history from the Bronze Age to medieval times.

Near by is the **Musée Matisse** (➤ 40). Both museums back on to an old olive grove that is the venue for the international **Nice Jazz Festival** (➤ 22) in July.

At the eastern end of the grove is the **Monastère Franciscain de Cimiez** (Franciscan Monastery) and the church of Notre-Dame-de-l'Assomption. The Franciscans have used the church and monastery since 1546. Inside are two masterpieces by Louis Bréa, a leading painter of the Nice School, and an impressive carved altarpiece. Dufy and Matisse lie buried in the adjacent cemetery overlooking Nice.

A statue of Queen Victoria, a frequent visitor to Nice, set in one of the city's parks

➕ 184 D1 ✉ Colline du Château
☎ 04 93 85 62 33 💷 Free ❓ Elevator operates Jun–Aug daily 9–8; Apr–May, Sep 10–7; Oct–Mar 10–6; inexpensive

8 Cimiez

Cimiez is a district of luxury villas and palatial residences on the low hills overlooking the city. A monument dedicated to Queen Victoria outside her favourite winter residence, the **Hôtel Regina**, serves as a reminder that Cimiez was frequently visited by royalty in the past. It is still considered to be Nice's smartest residential quarter.

The Cimiez district is the site of **Roman Nice**. As early as 140 BC the Romans built a town on the hills of Cimiez called Cemenelum which, by the end of the second century AD, had 20,000 inhabitants. There are Roman ruins and a museum at the Parc des Antiquités, an archaeological site now laid out as a pleasant little park, and known locally as **Les Arènes**.

The remains of a small amphitheatre (Arènes) were excavated here. The oval arena itself, still within the ruins of

➕ 184 off C3
Site et Musée d'Archéologique
✉ 160 avenue des Arènes (entrance: avenue Monte-Croce)
☎ 04 93 81 59 57 🕐 Wed–Mon 10–6.
💷 Moderate; free on 1st and 3rd Sun of month 🚌 15, 17, 20, 22, 25

Monastère Franciscain de Cimiez
✉ Place du Monastère, avenue Bellanda
☎ 04 93 81 00 04 🕐 Mon–Sat 10–12, 3–6. Closed Sun and public hols
💷 Free 🚌 15, 17, 20, 22, 25

Monastère Franciscain (Franciscan Monastery) in Cimiez

9 Quartier du Port

For centuries there was no port at Nice. Local boats simply moored in the lee of the castle rock, while larger ships anchored in the harbour at Villefranche. It was only in 1750 that Charles-Emmanuel III, Duke of Savoy, saw the potential trading benefits, and excavated a deep-water port at the mouth of the Lympia River.

Today the port is busy with craft of all kinds, from tiny traditional fishing barques to car ferries from Corsica. It is flanked by striking red-ochre, 18th-century buildings and the neoclassical church of Notre-Dame-du-Port. You will also find some popular restaurants in this part of town.

The port is best approached via a windy headland, **quai Rauba-Capéu**, past a colossal monument commemorating the 4,000 Niçois who died during World War I. On a hill to the east of the port, the **Musée de Terra Amata**, built on the site of an excavated fossil beach, documents prehistoric life in the region.

✚ 184 D1
🚌 1, 2, 7, 9, 10, 14, 20, 30, 81

Musée de Terra Amata
✉ 25 boulevard Carnot
☎ 04 93 55 59 93 🕐 Tue–Sun 10–6.
Closed Mon and some public hols
🚌 81, 100

For Kids

• Kids will love cycling or rollerblading along the promenade des Anglais. **Rent cycles and blades** from Nice à Location Rent (12 rue de Belgique, tel: 04 93 82 42 71, www.nicealocationrent.com) or Roller Station (49 quai des États-Unis, tel: 04 93 62 99 05).

• In December, part of the place Masséna is converted into an **outdoor ice-skating rink**. Skates can be rented opposite the rink. There is also a permanent **indoor ice-skating rink** *(patinoire)* at the Jean Bouin Palais de Sports Centre (place Don Bosco) just north of MAMAC.

• **Colline du Château** has plenty of room for children to run around, and a good-sized playground.

• The **beach** is a good place to cool off in the hot weather, and has a pebbly seashore, perfect for skimming stones.

Where to... Stay

Prices
Expect to pay per double room, per night
€ under €80   €€ €80–€150   €€€ over €150

Hôtel Armenonville €€
A 20th-century mansion with a lovely flower garden is the setting for this two-star hotel. Some rooms are particularly pleasant, with terraces looking out over the garden below. All rooms are bright and clean, with charming touches of antique furniture and art nouveau around the hotel. Breakfast can be served in the garden.
➕ 184 A1 ⊠ 20 avenue des Fleurs
☎ 04 93 96 86 00;
www.hotel-armenonville.com

Hôtel Acanthe €
Simple, one-star budget accommodation in a great position opposite the Jardins Albert 1, situated close to Vieux Nice and the promenade des Anglais. Serves a basic continental breakfast.
➕ 184 C1 ⊠ 2 rue Chauvin
☎ 04 93 62 22 44;
www.hotel-acanthe-nice.cote.azur.fr

Auberge de Jeunesse de Nice €
This youth hostel in the wooded hills of Mont Boron has beautiful views of Nice. Accommodation is in dormitories with six to eight beds. There is a communal room with a TV, kitchen, laundry service and internet access. The hostel is 10km (6 miles) from the city and the beach. Breakfast is included. Credit cards are not accepted.
➕ 180 C3 ⊠ Route Forestière du Mont-Alban ☎ 04 93 89 23 64;
www.fuaj.org

Le Beau Rivage €€€
The artistically inclined visitor will appreciate this elegant hotel, which was a home to the artist Henri Matisse for two years, and also the place where Russian playwright Anton Chekhov wrote *The Seagull*. The hotel has been refurbished and is placed strategically on the waterfront, near the opera house and the Old Town.
➕ 184 C1 ⊠ 24 rue St-François-de-Paule ☎ 04 92 47 82 82;
www.nicebeaurivage.com

La Belle Meunière €
A popular, inexpensive hotel situated near the train station, with friendly service, in addition to private parking and a small garden for breakfast.
➕ 184 B2 ⊠ 21 avenue Durante
☎ 04 93 88 66 15

Hôtel de la Buffa €€
A well-positioned, two-star hotel, close to the promenade des Anglais and the sea. The early 20th-century building has an inviting interior and bedrooms decorated with Provencal fabrics. Rooms facing onto the street have double glazing, and there's private parking.
➕ 184 B1 ⊠ 56 rue de la Buffa
☎ 04 93 88 77 35;
www.hotel-buffa.com

Hotel Comte de Nice €
A sparkling-clean budget option, a bit away from the Old Town, but close to the train station. This friendly hotel provides the sort of mint-on-your-pillow special touches that you might expect from a place with a few more stars. Rooms and apartments available. Rooms can be hot in summer, but it is otherwise a very comfortable place to stay.
➕ 184 B3 ⊠ 29 rue Dijon
☎ 04 93 88 94 56;
www.hotelcomtedenice.com

Where to...
Eat and Drink

Prices
Expect to pay for a three-course meal for one, excluding drinks and service
€ under €25   €€ €25–€60   €€€ over €60

Hi Hôtel €€–€€€

This modern designer hotel has quirky furnishings, an organic 24-hour canteen, a hammam (Turkish bath) and a pool on the roof. Yoga classes and massage are available. A new take on luxury.

➕ 184 A1 ⊠ 3 avenue des Fleurs
☎ 04 97 07 26 26;
www.hi-hotel.net

Hôtel Négresco €€€

Built in 1912, the Negresco and its signature dome have landmark status. The interior is an ode to fine art, from the Renaissance to the modern. The sumptuous rooms maintain an atmosphere of the Côte d'Azur from its early 20th-century heyday. The hotel has a private beach, and a certain element of rich kitsch unlikely to be experienced elsewhere.

➕ 184 A1 ⊠ 37 promenade des Anglais ☎ 04 93 16 64 00;
www.hotel-negresco-nice.com

Palais de la Méditerranée €€€

After 25 years of closure, this luxury seafront hotel has undergone a major facelift. Behind its magnificent art deco façade are 188 lavish rooms, a pool and a spa.

➕ 184 B1 ⊠ Promenade des Anglais
☎ 04 92 14 77 00;
www.lepalaisdelamediterranee.com

Hôtel Windsor €€

This eccentric hotel, just five minutes' walk from the sea, is kept under the watchful eye of a protective Buddha enshrined in the reception area. The hotel has a hammam, Thai-style lounges, an exotic garden with pool, and massages available on request. The rooms have been personalised by contemporary artists. There is also a somewhat less exotic English-style pub.

➕ 184 B1 ⊠ 11 rue Dalpozzo
☎ 04 93 88 59 35;
www.hotelwindsornice.com

L'Acchiardo €

One of the few authentic café bar/restaurants remaining in Vieux Nice, serving simple, nourishing dishes at reasonable prices, and probably the best fish soup in Nice.

➕ 184 D1 ⊠ 38 rue Droite
☎ 04 93 85 51 16
🕔 Closed Sat–Sun

L'âne Rouge €€€

This Michelin-starred restaurant has a menu full of exciting flavours, but the seafood dishes are particularly creative and tantalising. The wine list includes an excellent range of the best local vintages. The restaurant itself is warm and inviting, with beamed ceilings and a large fireplace. Sit on the flower-filled terrace in summer to enjoy the view of the port.

➕ 184 D1 ⊠ 7 quai des Deux-Emmanuel ☎ 04 93 89 49 63
🕔 Fri–Tue 12–2:30, 7:30–10, Thu 7:30–10. Closed Feb

Aphrodite €€

The imaginative culinary creations of young chef David Faure are a seductive blend of classic French and local cuisine. His delectable desserts would grace any modern art gallery.

184 C2 ✉ 10 boulevard Dubouchage ☎ 04 93 85 63 53 ⊘ Closed Sun, Mon

Auberge de Théo €

This friendly, trattoria-style restaurant in Cimiez serves delicious pizzas and salads.

184 off C3 ✉ 52 avenue Cap de Croix ☎ 04 93 81 26 19 ⊘ Closed Mon, Sun pm

Bar René Socca €

Run by the same family as Specialities Niçoises across the road (▶ 56), this friendly bar has plenty of atmosphere, and is a relaxing place for a drink after exploring the Old Town.

184 D2 ✉ 2 rue Miraheti (corner of rue Miraheti and rue Pairolière) ☎ 04 93 92 05 73 ⊘ Tue–Sun 9–9

Le Chantecler €€€

Nice's leading restaurant – a bastion of French gastronomy housed within the Negrésco and a truly memorable dining experience.

184 A1 ✉ Hôtel Négresco, 37 promenade des Anglais ☎ 04 93 16 64 00 ⊘ Wed–Sun 12:30–2, 7:30–10. Closed Jan

Chez Simon €€

This restaurant, once an inn, has been run by the same family for five generations. A traditional atmosphere pervades the restaurant, and the dining room has beamed ceilings, wicker chairs and a plough-wheel candelabrum. In fine weather sit outside on the terrace, where you can dine while watching a game of pétanque. The Provençal cuisine includes stuffed mutton, tripe and hake.

180 C3 ✉ St-Antoine-de-Ginestière ☎ 06 20 04 93 86 51 62; www.restaurantchezsimon.com ⊘ Daily 12:30–2, 7:30–10. Closed Sun dinner and Mon in low season, and 2 weeks in Nov and Feb

Chez Thérèsa €

Something of a local institution, Chez Theresa is the place to try a speciality of the area, socca – crêpes made from chickpea flour and olive oil – best eaten with a sprinkling of pepper. In addition to this hole-in-the-wall establishment in the Old Town is another stall at the cours Saleya market (Tuesday to Sunday).

184 D1 ✉ 28 rue Droite ☎ 04 93 85 00 24

L'Estocaficada €€

The regional dishes in this atmospheric bistro are made from ingredients straight from the market, and are ideal for a snack or a full-blown meal, washed down with a reasonably priced Provençal wine.

184 off A1 ✉ 2 rue de l'Hôtel de Ville ☎ 04 93 80 21 64 ⊘ Closed Sun–Mon

Fennochio €

Don't miss the best ice creams on the Cote d'Azur, in imaginative flavours ranging from lavender and olive to tomato and basil.

184 C1 ✉ 2 place Rosetti ☎ 04 93 80 72 52

Flo €€

A brasserie-style restaurant in a converted art deco theatre with the kitchen in full view on the stage. Late-night menu up to midnight.

184 C2 ✉ 4 rue Sacha Guitry ☎ 04 93 13 38 38 ⊘ Daily

Le Grand Café du Turin €€

This cosy café serves Nice's best shellfish. Order oysters by the dozen, coquillages by the kilo or, if you're feeling really brave, a plateful of sea urchins (oursins).

184 D2 ✉ 5 place Garibaldi ☎ 04 93 62 29 52 ⊘ Daily

Lou Pilha Leva €

Lou Pilha Leva in the local patois means "you take away". At the heart of Vieux Nice, this hole-in-the-wall serves piping hot plates of socca, pissaladière, beignets, farcis, pizza and other Niçois specialities. Ideal for a snack lunch, with large trestle tables that provide the perfect opportunity to chat to the locals.

⊞ 184 D1 ☒ 10 rue du Collet
☎ 04 93 13 99 08 ⓒ Daily 8 am–11 pm (8 pm in winter)

La Maison de Marie €€

A good place for a romantic candlelit meal in the evening, this restaurant is centrally situated, yet sheltered from the hustle and bustle of rue Masséna by a peaceful, paved courtyard. In fair weather a couple of tables are set out on the terrace. The menu includes such Mediterranean treats as sardines stuffed with pine nuts, and lamb with a herb crust.
⊞ 184 B1 ☒ 5 rue Masséna
☎ 04 93 82 15 93;
www.lamaisondemarie.com
ⓒ Daily 12–2, 7–11

La Mérenda €€

An irresistible menu of Niçois specialities lovingly prepared by Dominic le Stanc, former chef of the Hôtel Négresco's famous Chantecler restaurant, and a name synonymous with the very best in Provençal cuisine. Le Stanc left the Chantecler to run this tiny rustic restaurant with his wife. With only 12 tables and no telephone, booking a place can be difficult, but the food is worth the effort.
⊞ 184 C1 ☒ 4 rue de la Terrace
ⓒ Closed Sat–Sun and public hols

La Petite Maison €€€

An upmarket and fashionable, but often crowded, place to dine, this restaurant near the Opéra de Nice offers local market-fresh dishes. For a selection of local delights try the Niçois platter; the desserts are delectable too. Book ahead.
⊞ 184 C1 ☒ 11 rue St-François-de-Paule ☎ 04 93 92 59 59
ⓒ Closed Sun

La Rotonde €€

La Rotonde is the Riviera's most original brasserie. A circular restaurant with kitsch merry-go-round décor, complete with flashing lights, automata and painted wooden horses. Under the roof of the famous Hôtel Négresco, but more reasonably priced than the hotel's prime restaurant, Le Chantecler.
⊞ 184 A1 ☒ 37 promenade des Anglais ☎ 04 93 16 64 00
ⓒ 7 am–11 pm

Le Safari €€

This bistro in Vieux Nice is hugely popular and in good weather, its terrace bulges with people. On offer are authentic local specialities (salad of chopped fresh artichokes with olive oil and lemon, crudités with warm anchovy sauce) and a great choice of freshly baked pizza.
⊞ 184 C1 ☒ 1 cours Saleya
☎ 04 93 80 18 44;
www.restaurantsafari.com
ⓒ Daily 12–2:30, 7–11

Specialities Niçoises

At the back of Vieux Nice, on lively rue Pairolière, you'll find the locals queuing up outside Specialities Niçoises for socca and other local treats. There are some tables outside, or you can take your food into Bar René Socca (► 55) opposite, run by the same family.
⊞ 184 D2 ☒ rue Miraheti (corner of rue Miraheti and rue Pairolière)
☎ 04 93 92 05 73 ⓒ Tue–Sun 9–9

Terres de Truffes €€

This is a unique restaurant specialising in seasonal truffles. Even the desserts are made with these precious gastronomic jewels. A carefully selected wine list complements the menu.
⊞ 184 C1 ☒ 11 rue St-François-de-Paule ☎ 04 93 62 07 68
ⓒ Daily 10 am–11 pm

La Zucca Magica €

Vegetarians and non-vegetarians alike should take advantage of the excellent vegetarian fare at this restaurant beside the city's Old Port. Excellent value and a lively atmosphere. The dishes are rich and delicious, and the staff friendly.
⊞ 184 D1 ☒ 4 bis, quai Papacino
☎ 04 93 56 25 27 ⓒ Tue–Sat

Where to... Shop

Avenue Jean Médecin is the main shopping street in Nice, where you'll find big department stores. There are little boutiques and galleries scattered around Vieux Nice, but the highlight of shopping here is the lively market at cours Saleya.

MARKETS

The **Marché Saleya** (cours Saleya, open Tue–Sun 7 am–1 pm) is a fruit and vegetable market with the best of Provençal produce, including locally grown olives, tomatoes and basil. Keep your cash handy, as credit cards are not accepted at the market stalls. The **Marché aux Fleurs** also takes place here daily, Nice's colourful flower market, and on Mondays the **antiques market**

takes its place (open 8–5). In summer, an **arts and crafts** market is also held here (open Tue–Sun 6 pm–midnight, Jun–Sep), selling Provençal handicrafts, and crafts from other regions of the world.

PROVENÇAL GIFTS

Scents from the Grasse perfumeries can be found at **Parfums Poilpot** (10 rue St-Gaëtan, tel: 04 93 85 60 77), a tiny perfumery with a wide range of local perfumes. *Faïence*, the famous white pottery with delicate, hand-painted designs from the tiny Provençal village of Moustiers-Ste-Marie, can be found in Nice at **Fayences de Moustiers** (18 rue du Marché, tel: 04 93 13 06 03).

FOOD AND DRINK

Buy freshly pressed olive oil from **Moulin à Huile d'Olive Alziari** (14 rue St-François-de-Paule, tel: 04 93 85 76 92, open Tue–Sat 8:30–12:30, 2:15–7), an old family shop that

presses its own olive oil and sells *olives de Nice* by the kilo. The olive oil on sale here comes from a mill in Nice's northwest corner, which you can visit by appointment.

Chocolats Puyricard (40 rue Pastorelli, tel: 04 93 85 34 30) produces handmade chocolates almost too good to eat. Puyricard's are considered the finest chocolates in France and are well worth seeking out. The tiny **Pâtisserie Cappa** (7–9 place Garibaldi, tel: 04 93 62 30 83) has a selection of mouthwatering cakes and pastries. Try the *tourte de blettes*, a local tart with apples, raisins, pine nuts and rum. **Espuno** (35 rue Droite, tel: 04 93 80 50 67) is one of France's premier bakeries and makes an excellent *fougasse* (a type of bread cooked in hot ashes). **Maison Auer** (7 rue St-François-de-Paule, tel: 04 93 85 77 98) is a traditional maker of crystallised fruit, and a good place to sample this local speciality.

For wine, **Caprioglio** (16 rue de la Préfecture, tel: 04 93 85 66 57)

in Vieux Nice has a price range to suit all purses – from *vin de table* (stored in giant orange tanks) to the top French *crus*. **Domaine Massa** (596 chemin de Crémat, tel: 04 93 37 80 02) is an old farm hidden in the sun-soaked hills behind Nice that cultivates two distinctly Niçois products – carnations and Bellet wine. Phone in advance for a tasting.

ART AND PHOTOGRAPHY

There are many boutique galleries in Vieux Nice. **Galerie Boutique Ferrero** (2 rue du Congrès, tel: 04 93 88 34 44) specialises in modern, expensive art. **Atelier Galerie Dury** (31 rue Droite, 04 93 62 50 57) has contemporary artworks by Christian Dury.

The photography of **Jean-Louis Martinetti** (17 rue de la Préfecture, tel: 04 93 85 61 30) makes a wonderful souvenir. His artistic shots capture the essence of the area.

Where to...
Be Entertained

NIGHTLIFE

There are a number of good wine bars in Vieux Nice, but many close by midnight. A few stay open later, including **Le Staccato** (4 rue du Pont Vieux, tel: 04 93 13 84 35) which is open until 2:30 am and hosts live jazz in its cosy cellar during winter.

Nocy-Be (4–6 rue Jules Gilly, tel: 04 93 85 52 25, open Mon–Fri 5–12:30, Sat–Sun 4–12:30) is a chic Morrocan café in Vieux Nice, with low lighting, floor cushions and as many different kinds of tea as you could hope for. Pastries, flavoured tobacco and cocktails are also on the menu. Settle in for an evening or drop by for an aperitif. Nice's largest indoor nightclub, **L'Odace** (29 rue Alphonse Karr, tel:

04 93 82 37 66, open midnight–4 am), draws crowds of all ages for its guest DJs and popular sounds, ranging from house to R&B. Free breakfast is served at 4 am. In the Old Port, **Le Guest** (5 quai des Deux Emmanuels, tel: 04 93 56 83 83, open 11:30 pm–5 am) is an established Niçois nightspot with tropical guerrilla décor.

La Suite (2 rue Bréa, tel: 04 93 92 92 91, open Mon–Sat 10:30 pm –2:30 am) is a trendy after-dinner venue with theatrical baroque décor, where cocktail evenings and fancy-dress theme nights are popular.

L'F (6 place Charles-Félix, tel: 04 93 85 74 10, daily 8 am–3 am) is a café with one of Nice's best terraces (heated in winter) and a 1940s interior.

Nice's **Casino Ruhl** (promenade des Anglais, tel: 04 97 03 12 22) still has all the requisite glitz and glamour, as well as dinner cabarets and private gaming rooms.

CINEMA

Cinémathèque (Acropolis, 3 esplanade Kennedy, tel: 04 92 04 06 66, open Tue–Sat 2–10, Sun 3–5, Oct–Jun) shows original old films, as well as the latest releases. **Cinema Rialto** (4 rue de Rivoli, tel: 0836 680 041, open 11–11) is one of the few cinemas in Nice to show films in their original language.

FESTIVALS

The **Nice Carnival** (▶ 20) and **Nice Jazz Festival** (▶ 22) are two of the biggest in town.

MUSIC AND THEATRE

The **Auditorium du Conservatoire national de region** (24 boulevard de Cimiez, tel: 04 92 26 72 20, open Mon from 6 pm, except school hols) has open rehearsals every Monday. The standard is high and entry is free. The **Opéra de Nice** (4–6 rue St-François-de-Paule, tel: 04 93 13 98 53, open Tue–Sat) stages opera, classical music and ballet in an Italianate theatre with majestic frescoes and chandeliers.

Comedy shows and philosophical debates are staged at the **Bar des Oiseaux** (5 rue St-Vincent, tel: 04 93 80 27 33, open Tue–Fri 12–3, 7 pm–1 am; Sat 7 pm–1 am). Comedy is also performed at **Le Bouff' Scène** (2 rue Caissotti, tel: 04 93 55 54 78, open Thu–Sun 9 pm–midnight).

Théâtre de la Traverse (2 rue François-Guisol, tel: 04 93 55 67 46) has fringe theatre in its intimate space adjoining its bookstore. More mainstream theatre can be seen at **Théâtre National de Nice** (Promenade des Arts, tel: 04 93 13 90 90), with classic and contemporary plays and dance on the bill.

Around Nice

Getting Your Bearings

The dramatic stretch of azure coast between Menton and Nice, with its chic towns, glorious beaches and backdrop of snow-capped mountains, was the original piece of coastline to which the name "Riviera" was applied, when it first became fashionable as a winter destination in the 19th century. The towns here still evoke *belle-époque* grandeur.

Today the resorts of this incredible stretch of coastline have virtually fused together into one giant, bustling megalopolis from Menton to Cannes. But each resort has managed to maintain its identity: genteel Menton, an old Italo-Provençal resort of art nouveau villas and citrus trees on the Italian border, is considered by many to be the most attractive town on the Côte d'Azur; Cap Ferrat – the "Peninsula of Billionaires" – with its sumptuous villas amid subtropical foliage, is arguably the most desirable address on the Riviera; while jet-setting Monaco (➤ 83–104) is its most sophisticated holiday playground.

The resorts are linked by three famous cliff roads, called Les Corniches, which hug the contours of the coast at varying levels, traversing the most mountainous stretch of the Côte d'Azur with their hair-raising bends, sudden tunnels and breathtaking views. Two medieval hilltop villages dominate the coast here: La Turbie with its massive Roman monument, and picturesque Èze, clinging to a mountaintop 427m (1,400 feet) above sea level, with dizzying views of the coast. By contrast the interior is surprisingly unpopulated, with its fertile valleys and ancient villages clinging to the hillsides – a perfect retreat from the touristic frenzy of the coast.

Page 59:
Roquebrune-
Cap Martin

Opposite:
Augustus'
Trophée des
Alpes towers
above La Turbie

Below: The sea
and coastline
from Èze's lofty
Jardin Exotique

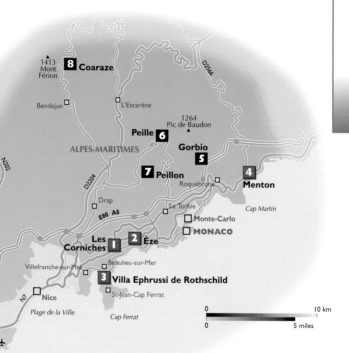

1413 Mont Férion

8 Coaraze

Bendejun

L'Escarène

1264 Pic de Baudon

Peille 6

ALPES-MARITIMES

Gorbio 5

4 Menton

7 Peillon

Roquebrune

Drap

Cap Martin

E80 A8

La Turbie

Monte-Carlo

MONACO

Les Corniches 1 2 Èze

Villefranche-sur-Mer

Beaulieu-sur-Mer

3 Villa Ephrussi de Rothschild

St-Jean-Cap Ferrat

Nice

Plage de la Ville

Cap Ferrat

N202

N7

0 — 10 km
0 — 5 miles

These two separate itineraries from Nice enable you to discover some of the Riviera's most spectacular scenery, its picturesque ports and finest gardens.

Around Nice in Two Days

Day One

Morning
Drive the **❶ Corniche Inférieure** (➤ 64–65) from Nice via Villefranche-sur-Mer to St-Jean-Cap Ferrat to visit the beautiful rose-pink **❸ Villa Ephrussi de Rothschild** (below, ➤ 70–71), with its sumptuous period interiors, impressive art collection and beautiful gardens.

Lunch
The elegant coffee shop at Villa Ephrussi is ideal for lunch or some light refreshment. The *gâteaux* are especially delicious.

Afternoon
Walkers will enjoy the shaded coastal path around the cape. The numerous coves are ideal for a lazy afternoon spent swimming and sunbathing. Or join locals promenading in the port of St-Jean-Cap Ferrat, where there are pleasant waterfront bars, cafés and restaurants.

Evening
Return to Villefranche-sur-Mer (➤ 64–65) for a meal at one of the waterside eateries beside the yacht harbour. Try La Mère Germaine (➤ 81) for exceptional seafood.

Day Two

Morning

Take the dramatic **1 Moyenne Corniche** (► 66) route and zigzag your way to the teetering village of **2 Èze** (► 68–69), breathtakingly perched on the cliff edge high above the Riviera. Leave your car and explore the narrow, stepped alleys and flower-filled, cobbled pathways, full of tiny craft shops and boutiques hidden in caves within the rocks. Visit the exotic garden (right) with its cacti and vivid tropical flowers, and the perfume factories at the foot of the hill.

Lunch

Considering its tiny size, Èze has more than its fair share of fine restaurants – perfect for a long, lazy lunch. Splash out on a lavish meal at La Bergerie (► 79) or La Chèvre d'Or (► 79). For budget travellers, Le Cactus (► 79) serves cheap, tasty crêpes in a tiny, vaulted restaurant in the old gateway.

Afternoon

Continue eastwards by car onto the scenic **1 Grande Corniche** (► 66). Admire the dazzling coastal views over Monaco from La Turbie, then proceed to the beautiful seaside town of **4 Menton** (left, ► 72–73), France's warmest resort. If you enjoy driving you may wish to follow a lengthy, winding detour at La Turbie (along the D53 and D22), to visit the tiny "twin" hilltop villages of **6 Peille** (► 74–75) and **7 Peillon** (► 75–76). The scenery along this stretch is truly wild and spectacular.

On arrival in Menton explore the delightful Old Town, with its medieval houses painted in ice-cream shades, or relax in the fragrant gardens of Palais Carnolès (Europe's largest citrus fruit garden). Art aficionados should not miss the Musée des Beaux-Arts, Musée Jean Cocteau and the Salle des Mariages (► 72–73).

Evening

Try tasty Mentonnaise cuisine at Au Pistou (► 80).

The Corniches

Three famous cliff roads, the Corniche Inférieure, the Moyenne Corniche and the Grande Corniche, traverse one of the most scenic stretches of the Riviera from Nice to Menton via Monaco.

The roads each zigzag their way along vertiginous ledges at three different heights. The lowest route, Corniche Inférieure (also known as the Lower or Basse Corniche) follows the coastal contours through all the seaside resorts, and is best avoided in the high season. The steep Moyenne Corniche at the middle level is the most dramatic. It was on this cliff-hanging route, with its hair-raising bends, sudden tunnels and astounding views, that Princess Grace of Monaco met her untimely death in 1982. Today the road is frequently used for filming car commercials and movie car chases. The highest road, the Grande Corniche, was originally constructed by Napoléon and is by far the best choice for picnickers and lovers of plants and wildlife.

Corniche Inférieure (N98)
Villefranche-sur-Mer
This small fishing village, with boats bobbing about in the harbour, has changed little since it was founded in the 14th century as a customs-free port (hence its name). Considering its proximity to Nice and Monte-Carlo, Villefranche remains surprisingly unspoiled. Its beautiful deep bay is fringed with warm-hued houses, atmospheric waterfront bars, cafés and restaurants.

A maze of steep stairways and cavernous passageways climb from the harbour through the Old Town. Dark and eerie **rue Obscure**, a narrow, vaulted 13th-century street, has sheltered the inhabitants of Villefranche from bombardments throughout history right up to World War II.

In a sturdy 16th-century **citadel** on the waterfront is the Mairie (town hall) and two *musées* with work by local artists and some by Miró and Picasso.

The 14th-century **Chapelle St-Pierre** on the quay, once used to store fishing nets, was decorated in 1957 with frescoes by Villefranche's most famous resident – poet, playwright and film director Jean Cocteau. His luminous paintings depict St Peter living among the local fisherwomen and gypsies.

Cap Ferrat

Cap Ferrat, like Cap d'Antibes and Cap Martin, has long been a favourite haunt of the world's rich and famous. Considered the most desirable address in the Riviera, the Cap is smothered in huge, impenetrable villas hidden amid sumptuous, subtropical gardens. Among the properties here is the lavish **Villa Ephrussi de Rothschild** (➤ 70–71).

Left: Fishing boats anchored at Villefranche-sur-Mer

Below: The marina, St-Jean-Cap Ferrat

Despite its wealth and exclusivity, Cap Ferrat is quite open to visitors and has a tourist office in the peninsula's small main town, St-Jean-Cap Ferrat, an approachable, sleepy place with a few restaurants and cafés along the port. Away from the harbour, the streets and houses are far less grand than the mansions elsewhere on the peninsula. Walking paths link much of the Cap and the tourist office will be happy to point you in the direction of the little harbour or the trails that are marked out around the 14km (9-mile) coastline, with wonderful sea views.

Beaulieu-sur-Mer

True to its name, Beaulieu is a "beautiful place", and is also one of the warmest resorts on the Riviera, sheltered by a natural amphitheatre of hills. It had its heyday in the late 19th century when many celebrities stayed here, including the then Prince of Wales, Empress Sissi of Austria, Piotr Ilyich Tchaikovsky and Gustav Eiffel. This prosperous little town has a glamorous casino built in the 1920s, an elegant Edwardian Rotonde (today a local history museum), *belle-époque* villas and a palm-lined promenade on the sheltered Baie des Fourmis.

The town's most curious attraction is the extraordinary **Villa Grecque Kérylos**, sitting on the tip of the northern headland. This seaside villa was built in 1908 by archaeologist Théodore Reinach, and is a perfect reproduction of a Greek villa from the second century BC. No expense was spared in the villa's lavish interior of marble, ivory and bronze. Reinach lived here for almost 20 years, eating, dressing and behaving as an Athenian citizen.

From Beaulieu-sur-mer the Corniche Inférieure continues up the coast through Monaco (► 83–104), and ends at Roquebrune-Cap Martin (► below).

Moyenne Corniche (N7)
Èze
Èze, the most strikingly situated and best-preserved Provençal **hilltop village**, stands high on a rocky pinnacle ten minutes' drive from Nice and Monaco, and has spectacular views over the entire Riviera as far as Corsica. From the top of the Jardin Exotique at Èze (► 68–69), there is a view of all three corniches.

Grande Corniche (D2564)
La Turbie
The teetering village of La Turbie sits on a ridge in the hills above Monaco. The monument for which this village is famous, the **Trophée des Alpes**, is situated at the loftiest point of the old Roman highway (the Via Julia), 480m (1,575 feet) above sea level. This enormous monument, originally 50m (165 feet) high and 38m (125 feet) wide, was built in 6 BC to commemorate Augustus' conquest of the Alpine tribes. It was used as a fortress in the Middle Ages, largely dismantled under the orders of Louis XIV in 1705, and further destroyed in the 19th century when its stonework was quarried to build a nearby church. However, enough of the monument survived to enable its partial restoration in later years. The present structure stands 35m (115 feet) high and has a long inscription on its base listing the conquered local tribes.

The gardens surrounding the trophy have fantastic panoramic views and a small museum documenting the trophy's restoration. The nearby baroque **Église St-Michel-Archange** contains works attributed to the schools of Veronese, Raphaël, Bréa, Ribera and Murillo.

Roquebrune-Cap Martin
Roquebrune-Cap Martin is divided into two areas: old Roquebrune, an attractive medieval hilltop village, and the smart coastal resort of Cap Martin.

Old Roquebrune is a fascinating tangle of ancient flower-filled lanes, stairways and vaulted passages, which cluster around its **castle**, the oldest feudal château remaining in France and the sole example of Carolingian style. Built in the 10th century to ward off Saracen attack, it was later remodelled by the Grimaldis, and restored in 1911 by Lord Ingram, one of the first wave of wealthy tourists drawn to stylish Cap Martin.

Other visitors to **Cap Martin** included Queen

A 10th-century Carolingian castle over-looks the rooftops of Roquebrune-Cap Martin

Below:
The Trophée des Alpes

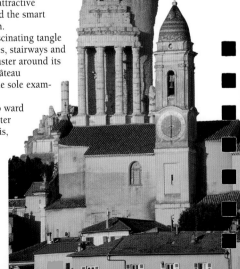

Victoria, Winston Churchill, Coco Chanel and architect Le Corbusier, who
drowned off the cape in 1965 and lies buried in Roquebrune cemetery. A
coastal path in his honour circles the cape, past sumptuous villas shrouded in
dense foliage (► 160–161).

➕ 181 D3
Villefranche-sur-Mer Tourist Office
✉ Jardin Francois-Binon ☎ 04 93 01 73 68; www.villefranche-sur-mer.com

Chapelle St-Pierre
✉ Quai Courbet, Port de Villefranche ☎ 04 93 76 90 70 🕓 Tue–Sun 10–12, 4–8, summer;
Tue–Sun 10–12, 2–6, winter; Tue–Sun 10–12, 3–7, spring. Closed mid-Nov to mid-Dec
💰 Inexpensive

Beaulieu-sur-Mer Tourist Office
✉ Place Georges-Clemenceau ☎ 04 93 01 02 21; www.ot-beaulieu-sur-mer.fr 🕓 Mon–Sat
9–12:30, 2–7, Sun 9–12:30, Jul–Aug; Mon–Fri 9–12:15, 2–6, Sat 9–12:15, 2–5, Sep–Jun

Villa Grecque Kérylos
✉ Beaulieu-sur-Mer ☎ 04 93 01 01 44; www.culturespaces.com 🕓 Daily 10–6, Feb–Oct;
Mon–Fri 2–6, Sat–Sun 10–6, Nov–Jan 💰 Moderate, entry includes audioguide

La Turbie Tourist Office
✉ Place Detras ☎ 04 93 41 21 15; www.ville-la-turbie.fr

Trophée des Alpes
✉ Avenue Albert 1er ☎ 04 93 41 20 84 🕓 Tue–Sun 9:30–1, 2–6, mid-May to mid-Sep; 10–1,
2–5, mid-Sep to mid-May 💰 Moderate

THE CORNICHES: INSIDE INFO

Top tips Coming from Villefranche-sur-Mer to St-Jean-Cap-Ferrat, a **shaded
coastal path** winds around Cap Ferrat past countless enticing inlets (ideal for a
refreshing dip) towards St-Jean, where you can have lunch by the harbour.
• The top two corniches are notoriously accident prone, so if you are in a hurry
it is better to take the **A8** *autoroute*, which carves its way through the mountains behind the three coast roads from Nice as far as the Italian border.

❷ Èze

Without doubt one of the region's most strikingly situated and best-preserved hilltop villages, Èze affords truly breathtaking views.

The town is often referred to as the Nid d'Aigle (Eagle's Nest) because of its remarkable location, sitting atop a 430m (1,375-foot) spike of rock beside the Moyenne Corniche, halfway between Nice and Monaco, where the mountains meet the coast. The village is exceptionally picturesque, with narrow medieval lanes and steps, and several vantage points looking straight down onto the sparkling sea below.

The settlement records of Èze date back as far as the 11th century, although the site has been occupied since the Bronze Age. The village was fortified in the 14th century and belonged to the Counts of Savoy for hundreds of years. In 1792, following the creation of the Alpes-Maritimes region, Èze became part of the principality of Monaco. It was only after the plebiscite of 1860, when locals voted in the village chapel for annexation to France, that peace finally came to Èze.

On entering through the only gateway in the **ancient ramparts**, you will be struck by the tall, golden houses and the labyrinth of tiny vaulted passages with cobbled alleys and stairways. These climb steeply up to the ruins of a once massive **Saracen fortress**, destroyed by the French at the beginning of the 18th century, giving dazzling views out to sea. The ruins are surrounded by an exotic garden (**Jardin Exotique**), bristling with more than 400 kinds of magnificent cacti, succulents and rare palms.

Be sure to take time to explore the flower-filled passage-ways within the medieval village, where there are deluxe château-hotels, fine restaurants and little shops hidden in caves within the rock – tiny treasure troves of antiques, ceramics, pewter and olive wood.

Below left: The hilltop village of Èze

Below: Visitors exploring the village's narrow passageways

At the foot of the hill two Grassois perfume factories, **Galimard** and **Fragonard**, contain interesting museums in which the secrets of perfume production are explained. Near by, the **chemin de Nietzsche** (a narrow path once frequented by the German philosopher, see Inside Info below) zigzags steeply down to the beach and the former fishing village of Èze-Bord-de-Mer, a more modern town and popular coastal resort.

TAKING A BREAK

There are some lovely places to eat in Èze, but most of them are quite expensive. In the old village, **Le Nid d'Aigle** or **Le Cactus** (➤ 79) are good options. There are also cafés and restaurants close to the tourist office on **place du Général de Gaulle**.

✚ 181 D3
Tourist Office
✉ Place du Général de Gaulle
☎ 04 93 41 26 00;
www.eze-riviera.com
🕐 Mon–Sat 9–7, Sun 2–7, May–Sep;
Mon–Sat 9–6:30, Sun 9:30–1, 2–6:30, Oct–Apr

Jardin Exotique
☎ 04 93 41 10 30 💲 Inexpensive
🕐 Daily 9–8, Jul–Aug; 9–12, 2–7, Sep–Jun

ÈZE: INSIDE INFO

Top tips The **summit of the Jardin Exotique**, 429m (1,408 feet) above the sea, is a wonderful vantage point, and has a viewpoint indicator marking out places of interest that can be seen from the top of the garden.
• The **café terrace** of the Château Èza has one of the best views in the village.
• The **Fragonard** perfume factory just past the village on Moyenne Corniche has a shop selling a large range of perfumes. More Fragonard products and home-wares can be found at Fragonard Maison, on avenue du Jardin Exotique at the entrance to the village.
• Vehicles cannot enter the old village. There is a large **parking area** at the foot of the village.
• For a better understanding of how remote and inaccessible Èze was before the invention of the car, come here on foot. A precipitous **path up from the shore** is named after the 19th-century philosopher Friedrich Nietzsche who, living by the sea, often took this strenuous walk up to the medieval village.

3 Villa Ephrussi de Rothschild

This rose-pink *belle-époque* palace, surrounded by immaculate formal gardens and wonderful sea views, was constructed by the flamboyant Baroness Béatrice Ephrussi de Rothschild in 1912 as a place to hold banquets, entertain guests and house her extensive art collection.

Beatrice de Rothschild (1864–1934), wife of wealthy banker Maurice Ephrussi, was a woman of seemingly unlimited means who had a passion for travel and fine art. She created her dream villa here in the glorious style of the great palaces of the Italian Renaissance, and set it in immaculate gardens. The villa took a series of 40 architects five years to build, some of the architects lasting only a few hours before their dismissal. Located on exclusive Cap Ferrat, with sea views on all sides, the villa claims one of the most beautiful outlooks on the Riviera.

The Baroness died in 1934, leaving the villa to France's Académie des Beaux-Arts. Visitors can now wander around the beautiful gardens and the ground floor of the villa, although you have to take a guided tour to see the collections on the first floor.

The extravagant pink villa and gardens Ephrussi de Rothschild, St-Jean-Cap Ferrat

VILLA EPHRUSSI DE ROTHSCHILD: INSIDE INFO

Top tips On the first floor is the **Salon des Singes** (Monkey Room), with monkey friezes on the walls and porcelain monkeys on display, reflecting the Baroness's particular fondness for monkeys. Entrance to this room and the rest of the first floor will cost an additional fee.

• Watch at least the first part of the 18-minute film, which evokes the splendour of daily life on the Riviera during the *belle époque*, and then goes on to retrace the history of the house and the collection.

Getting there Via **public transport**, the villa is 800m (875 yards) from Beaulieu-sur-Mer station.

The **interior of the villa** is lavishly decorated with rare furniture (including some pieces that once belonged to Marie Antoinette), set off by rich carpets, tapestries and an eclectic collection of rare *objets d'art*, and one of the world's most beautiful collections of Vincennes and Sèvres porcelain. There are around 5,000 works of art in the collection here, ranging from French period furniture and tapestries to Renaissance religious art, fine 18th-century porcelain, and art from the Far East, including a display of pink jade and rare Chinese chests. Despite being filled with priceless works of art, the villa has retained the atmosphere of an occupied residence.

The **gardens** are divided into nine distinct areas, following Spanish, Florentine, Stone, Japanese, Exotic, Rose, Provençal, French and Sèvres (porcelain) themes. The main (French) garden is landscaped to resemble a ship's deck with a Temple of Love on the bow. The Baroness even decreed that her gardeners dress as sailors while tending the gardens.

TAKING A BREAK

The villa has an elegant **tea room** with wonderful views of the Bay of Villefranche from its large windows. Open from lunch until closing time, it serves a range of salads and pastries.

Villa Ephrussi de Rothschild
181 D3 St-Jean-Cap Ferrat 04 93 01 33 09; www.culturespaces.com
Daily 10–6, Feb–Oct (10–7, Jul–Aug); Mon–Fri 2–6, Sat–Sun and school hols 10–6, Nov–Jan
Expensive

The villa's entrance foyer

④ Menton

Lying only 1.5km (1 mile) from the Italian border, it comes as no surprise that Menton is France's most Italianate resort, a lovely jumble of tall, pale ochre houses at the foot of a sheltering mountain backdrop. This long-established resort town is so close to the border that Italians sometimes visit on foot.

Until the mid-19th century, when the Riviera became a fashionable and wealthy winter resort, Menton was a little-known fishing port belonging to the Grimaldis of Monaco. In 1860 it was annexed by Napoléon III. Its warm climate made it a popular winter resort with the Russian and English aristocracy, including Queen Victoria who visited here in 1882. *Fin de siècle* hotels resembling palaces started to spring up throughout the town and exotic Edwardian gardens were planted, some of which are still beautifully maintained today. After World War I, Menton lost out to its more glamorous neighbours – Nice, Cannes, St-Tropez and Monaco – although the faded elegance of the *belle époque* is still apparent.

By contrast, the **Old Town**, dating mainly from the 17th century, is a hotchpotch of ancient pastel-coloured houses dissected by terracotta-paved steps, alleys and tiny squares. The Italianate air of many of the buildings here provides an insight into the period before Menton became French. Climbing the narrow rue Longue towards the place de la Concepcion, you will find two magnificent baroque churches with finely ornamented façades: **St-Michel** and the **Chapelle des Penitents Blancs**. Between them is the **parvis St-Michel**, a mosaic square of black and white cobbles depicting the Grimaldi coat of arms. This square provides a delightful setting for the summer Chamber Music Festival (► 82).

At the top of the Old Town is a fascinating **cemetery** with sweeping sea views, once described by writer Guy de Maupassant as "the most aristocratic in Europe". Other notable sights include the **Palais Carnolès**, the 18th-century summer residence of the Princes of Monaco, now home to Menton's Musée des Beaux-Arts; and the **Musée Jean Cocteau**, dedicated to the town's most famous son. Cocteau (1889–1963) also decorated the remarkable **Salle des Mariages** (registry office) in the Hôtel de Ville, reflecting romantic and spiritual images of matrimony.

Menton is France's warmest town, with an annual 300 days of sun. The town is bursting with semitropical gardens created by wealthy Edwardian horticulturalists. Most of the parks and gardens are in the prosperous Garavan district, in the foothills behind the town near the Italian border. The best are

MENTON: INSIDE INFO

Top tips The **Fête du Citron** (Lemon Festival) starts on Shrove Tuesday and lasts for ten days.

• A **chamber music festival** is held in August in the parvis St-Michel (▶ 82).

• Take a stroll through the **local market** (Marché Municipal), at Halles Municipales just behind the quai de Monléon, for an authentic experience of food shopping in France (daily 5 am–1 pm).

• The Service du Patrimoine, based at 5 rue Ciappetta (Mon–Fri 8:30–12, 2–5 tel: 04 92 10 33 66), runs **guided tours** of Menton and its gardens.

the **Jardin Botanique**, the ancient olive grove of **Parc du Pian** and the Valencian **Jardin Fontana Rosa**, dedicated to writers by Spanish author Blasso Ibáñez. These gardens catch the sun even in winter, and enabled aristocratic gardeners to cultivate exotic plants from around the world (▶ 12–14).

Menton is also the "lemon capital of the world"; its surrounding slopes are covered in **citrus groves**. The garden around the Palais Carnolès claims to be the largest citrus fruit garden in Europe. The Biovès garden in the town centre, bordered with palms and lemon trees, is the venue of Menton's **Fête du Citron** (Lemon Festival) in February, when it is covered with spectacular displays and floats made entirely out of citrus fruits.

Top: The town's coat of arms

Above: The baroque church of St-Michel in Menton's Old Town

TAKING A BREAK

Le Lido (▶ 80) is casual, with fresh seafood and salads.

➕ 181 E4

Tourist Office
✉ 8 avenue Boyer ☎ 04 92 41 76 76; www.villedementon.com 🕐 Daily 9–6, Jun–Sep; Mon–Sat 8:30–12:30, 2–6, Sun 9–12:30, Oct–May

Musée Jean Cocteau
✉ Quai Napoléon III ☎ 04 93 57 72 30 🕐 Wed–Mon 10–12, 2–6 💰 Inexpensive

Salle des Mariages
✉ Hôtel de Ville, place Ardoïno ☎ 04 92 10 50 00 🕐 Mon–Fri 8:30–12:30 (last visit 11:30), 2–5 💰 Inexpensive; under 18 free

At Your Leisure

5 Gorbio

This medieval hilltop village, 10km (6 miles) northwest of Menton, provides welcome relief from souvenir shops along the main tourist trail. Strolling around the **central square** is not a bad way to spend an afternoon. There you will find a 300-year-old elm tree, and the grand castle of the Alziari counts, the baroque Église St-Barthélémy and the 15th-century Chapelle des Pénitents Blancs. There are also several other interesting churches and chapels to be seen in or near the village.

The best time to visit Gorbio is during the Fête Dieu (Corpus Christi) in May and June, when the enchanting **Procession dai Limaça** takes place. This night-time procession takes its name from the snail

The terraced houses of Peille, above the Faquin ravine

shells (*limaça* in Provençal) which are filled with olive oil and lit to create little flickering lamps that illuminate the village during the procession. A traditional pagan ritual, the procession gives thanks for the winter's olive harvest and wards off any demons that might damage the next crop. The snail is a pagan symbol of renewal, and the shell-lamps are fixed onto walls, doorways, windowsills and pavements, lighting up the village with a spectacular glow.

🔁 181 D4
Tourist Office
✉ Mairie: 30 rue Garibaldi
☎ 04 92 10 66 50

6 Peille

Just a short distance inland and set in wild, underpopulated countryside, Peille is a perfect retreat from the touristic frenzy of the coast. It is

reached by steep, narrow roads and stands on a ridge 20km (12.5 miles) inland from Monaco. Historically, Peille's remote and inaccessible location was not only an excellent defence strategy, but it allowed the village to develop independently, to the point where it had its own Provençal dialect, *Pelhasc*.

The village also had unusual ideas on religion. During the Middle Ages, it was excommunicated several times rather than pay the bishop's tithes. The **Chapelle des Pénitents Noirs** was converted into a communal oil press and its splendid domed Chapelle de St-Sébastien into the Hôtel de Ville (Town Hall).

Peille has plenty of character. Along the cobbled alleys and passageways you will find old buildings with fine doorways, and fountains and other Gothic and Renaissance stonework. Inside the **Église Ste-Marie** is a painting of the village in medieval times, showing the now-ruined feudal castle of the Counts of Provence in its former glory (ask at the Mairie for the key). The church also has a 16th-century polyptych of the Rosary by Honoré Bertone of the Nice School.

➕ 181 D4
Tourist Office
✉ Mairie: Place Carnot
☎ 04 93 91 71 71

🔼 Peillon

Peille's twin and neighbouring village, Peillon is one of the Riviera's most beautiful hilltop villages, nestled among the lofty, rocky peaks high above the Peillon valley and cleverly camouflaged against the landscape. From high up, these medieval *villages perchés* (perched villages) had a distinct advantage over any invaders, as the villagers could watch over the hinterland as well as the coast. Today the village's natural defences keep it from major tourist development, and as a result, although much restored, the village remains remarkably unspoiled and uncommercialised.

Pellion's huddle of cobbled alleys, steps and arches lead up to a charming little **church** at the summit. But the main attraction here is the

---

For Kids

• **Zoo du Cap Ferrat** has more than 300 animals, including crocodiles, monkeys and tigers. You can get really close to the tigers, protected by a Plexiglas wall. A snack bar and playground are available on the site, at 117 boulevard Général-de-Gaulle, St-Jean-Cap Ferrat (tel: 04 93 76 07 60: www.zoocapferrat.com, open daily 9:30–7, Apr–Oct; 9:30–5:30, Nov–Mar; expensive, under 3 free).

• **Koaland** in Menton is an amusement park for kids, with all the usual rides, as well as a small train and mini-golf (avenue de la Madone, tel: 04 92 10 00 40, open 10–12, 4–midnight, summer; 10–12, 2–7, winter).

• Many small villages hold **festivals** throughout the year that are repositories for traditional ways of life, such as Peille's **Wheat and Lavender Festival** in August, Coaraze's **Medieval Festival** in August, and **Winter Solstice Fireworks** in September. The festivals are often colourful and great fun for children. Check with local tourist offices for more details.

A quiet cobbled lane in Coaraze

Chapelle des Pénitents Blancs just outside the village, with 15th-century frescoes by Giovanni Canavesio depicting the Passion of Christ. Phone the Mairie in advance to arrange a visit. Beyond the chapel, a **footpath walk** to Peille takes about two hours along what was once a Roman road.

✚ 181 D4
Tourist Office
✉ Mairie: 672 avenue de l'Hôtel de Ville
☎ 04 93 79 91 04

8 Coaraze

This tiny and picturesque village is perched on a peak in the hills behind Nice. The village owes its name to a local legend which claims the people of Coaraze captured the devil and, in order to escape, he had to cut off his tail. In the local dialect, *coa* means "cut" and *raza* "tail".

The village is also reputed to be a sunny place, and is sometimes called the **Village du Soleil** (Village of the Sun). This inspired Jean Cocteau and other artists in the 1960s to decorate the town with large, colourful ceramic **sun dials** which can be seen throughout the village. Cocteau's is on the town hall.

Like other medieval hilltop villages, Coaraze has a maze of cobbled stairways, lanes, vaulted passageways, fountains and sunny squares. It has also become something of a chic hideaway, with fashionable Niçois purchasing second homes here.

On the outskirts of the village is the **Chapelle Bleue**, renamed after the artist Ponce de Léon redecorated the interior with bright blue murals and vivid green stained-glass windows in 1965. The chapel was formerly known by the more sombre name, Chapelle Notre-Dame des Sept Douleurs (Our Lady of the Seven Sorrows). The small road beside the Bar Tabac Les Arts leads to the chapel, which can be reached either by car or on foot (20 minutes return).

✚ 180 C4
Tourist Office
✉ 7 place Sainte-Cathérine
☎ 04 93 79 37 47
🕐 Tue–Sat 10–12, 3–5

Where to... Stay

Prices
Expect to pay per double room, per night
€ under €80   €€ €80–€150   €€€ over €150

BEAULIEU-SUR-MER

La Réserve €€€

One of the most exclusive seafront hotels of the Riviera, with an elegant and formal atmosphere. Hôtel La Réserve in Beaulieu-sur-Mer reached the height of its fame in 1887 when millionaire playboy James Gordon Bennet, owner of the *New York Herald*, was cast out from American society following a scandal, and moved here to run the Paris edition of his paper from the hotel during the 1880s and 1890s.
⊞ 181 D3 ⊠ 5 boulevard Maréchal-Leclerc ☎ 04 93 01 00 01;
www.reservebeaulieu.com

ÈZE

Château Èza €€€

The view from this château is breathtaking, making the hundreds of steps you must climb to reach the top worthwhile. The former home of the prince of Sweden, this stunning hotel consists of several medieval houses that have been linked together to form a luxury eyrie. The perched restaurant terrace is incredible (▶79).
⊞ 181 D3 ⊠ Rue de la Pise
☎ 04 93 41 12 24;
www.chateaueza.com
Ⓢ Closed Nov to mid-Dec, restaurant closed Tue in low season

MENTON

Hôtel Aiglon €€

This stylish three-star hotel close to the sea is set in a lovely garden, and has an elegant interior with a marble staircase and fine furniture. There is also an outdoor heated pool, solarium and children's playground. The restaurant, Le Riaumont, serves traditional Provençal cuisine, and you can dine on the poolside terrace.
⊞ 181 E4 ⊠ 7 avenue de la Madone
☎ 04 93 57 55 55;
www.hotelaiglon.net

Des Ambassadeurs €€€

Menton's top hotel boasts all the mod cons you would expect and is situated in a prime location in the centre of town, close to the Biovès gardens.
⊞ 181 E4 ⊠ 3 rue Partouneaux
☎ 04 93 28 75 75;
www.ambassadeurs-menton.com

Claridge's €

Just a couple of kilometres from Monaco and close to beaches, this two-star hotel is good value. The rooms are small and simply decorated, but quite comfortable. There is a bar and lounge, and a pleasant terrace looking out onto the street, but at this distance from Monaco your evening could be best spent exploring the principality.
⊞ 181 E4 ⊠ 39 avenue de Verdun
☎ 04 93 35 72 53;
www.claridges-menton.com

PEILLON

Auberge de la Madone €€

This typical *auberge* has been lovingly decorated in traditional Provençal style. The rooms are filled with quality antiques, and outside there is a terrace with a wonderful view over the surrounding countryside, the perfect place to enjoy the establishment's regional cuisine.

✚ 181 D4 ☒ 2 place au Village
☎ 04 93 79 91 17;
www.chateauxhotels.com/madone
Ⓒ Closed Jan, mid-Oct to mid-Dec

ROQUEBRUNE

Vista Palace €€€

Don't be put off by this ugly modern building, perched on a cliff 300m (985 feet) above sea level on the Grande Corniche and overlooking Monaco, for inside you will find the ultimate in luxury.

✚ 181 D4 ☒ D2564/Grande Corniche
☎ 04 92 10 40 00;
www.vistapalace.com

ROQUEBRUNE-CAP MARTIN

Les Deux Frères €€

This hotel, boasting wonderful views of the Mediterranean and Monaco, has ten lovely rooms which are themed and stylish. The Marine room has blue-and-white striped bed linen, the Medieval room a wrought-iron bench, and the Moroccan room a leopard skin. Meals are served in the restaurant, on the terrace overlooking the sea, or by the fireplace in winter.

✚ 181 E3 ☒ Le Village
☎ 04 93 28 99 00;
www.lesdeuxfreres.com

ST-JEAN-CAP FERRAT

Hôtel Brise Marine €€

This Italian-style villa built in 1878 is today a welcoming three-star hotel. The villa's ochre façade and blue shutters overlook the sea, and there are excellent views from the garden, terraces and from some of the elegant bedrooms. No restaurant on site, but several in town (▶ 80).

✚ 181 D3 ☒ 58 avenue Jean Mermoz
☎ 04 93 76 04 36;
www.hotel-brisemarine.com
Ⓒ Closed Nov–Jan

Clair Logis €€

This simple villa hotel is in a quiet street at the heart of the wooded peninsula. A good choice for those looking for the elegance of the Cap without the prices. No restaurant.

✚ 181 D3 ☒ 12 avenue Centrale
☎ 04 93 76 51 81;
www.hotel-clair-logis.fr
Ⓒ Closed Nov–Jan

Hôtel Royal Riviera €€€

An extravagant hotel with sumptuous rooms, its own helipad, magnificent gardens and popular poolside lunchtime barbecues.

✚ 181 D3 ☒ 3 avenue Jean Monnet
☎ 04 93 76 31 00;
www.royal-riviera.com

LA TURBIE

Hostellerie Jérôme €€

This luxurious old Provençal house has rooms with views of either the village or the sea. The food at the *hostellerie* is excellent, the restaurant serving everything from breakfast (€12.50) to an exceptional *dégustation* menu (€90).

✚ 181 D3 ☒ 20 rue du Comte de Cessole
☎ 04 92 41 51 51;
www.hostelleriejerome.com

VILLEFRANCHE-SUR-MER

Hôtel Welcome €€€

Originally a 17th-century convent, this restored building today has a distinctly modern feel. All the rooms are bright and have balconies with views over the bay. The artist Jean Cocteau stayed here at the time when he was working on the frescoes of the Chapelle St-Pierre.

✚ 181 D3 ☒ 1 quai Amiral Courbet
☎ 04 93 76 27 62;
www.welcomehotel.com
Ⓒ Closed 20 Nov–22 Dec

Where to...
Eat and Drink

Prices
Expect to pay for a three-course meal for one, excluding drinks and service
€ under €25   €€ €25–€60   €€€ over €60

BEAULIEU-SUR-MER

Le Capitole €€
Quality Provençal dishes are on the menu here, and the *cassoulet* served up by the Toulousan chef is a prime example of the hearty fare that is his speciality. The satisfying and unpretentious dishes are accompanied by a good list of local wines at very reasonable prices. You'll find parking across the street.

✚ 181 D3 ☒ 26 boulevard Général Leclerc ☎ 04 93 01 17 33
🕒 Closed Sun dinner–Mon, first week Jul and mid-Nov to 7 Dec

ÈZE

La Bergerie €€
Traditional dishes with a good choice of Côtes de Provence wines. Dine in winter by the welcoming open fire, and in summer on the shady terrace overlooking the sea.

✚ 181 D3 ☒ N7 ☎ 04 93 41 03 67
🕒 Dinner only weekdays; closed Wed

Le Cactus €
Take a break from sightseeing at this affordable little café, with a lunchtime menu that includes salads, crêpes, ice cream and restorative cups of tea.

✚ 181 D3 ☒ La Placette, entrée Vieux Village ☎ 04 93 41 19 02
🕒 9–9 Mar–Oct; Sat–Sun and school hols in winter

Château Èza €€
For a special meal, this ten-room château has a restaurant that serves superb food as well as having panoramic views looking down onto the sea some 400m (1,300 feet) below. The menu is contemporary and gourmet, featuring fresh seafood, quality vegetarian options and enticing desserts. A good selection of wines is available.

✚ 181 D3 ☒ Rue de la Pise
☎ 04 93 41 12 24;
www.chateaueza.com 🕒 Closed Nov to mid-Dec, Tue in low season

La Chèvre d'Or €€€
A wonderful view of the sea and coastline as well as cosmopolitan cuisine such as raw bass prepared sushi-style, tagine of chicken with lemon grass, or fillets of bream *à la plancha* can be found in this extravagant and well-renowned restaurant in the luxury Château de la Chèvre d'Or hotel.

✚ 181 D3 ☒ Moyenne Corniche, rue du Barri ☎ 04 92 10 66 66
www.chevredor.com
🕒 Daily 12–2, 7–11

Le Nid d'Aigle €
This "Eagle's Nest" restaurant serves up Provencal classics in an informal setting just across from the Jardin Exotique. A great place to try the local specialities at a good price.

✚ 181 D3 ☒ Rue du Château
☎ 04 93 41 19 08
🕒 Closed Jan–Feb and Wed

GORBIO

Les Terrasses €
Provençal cuisine and local pasta dishes are on the menu at this friendly restaurant in lofty Gorbio.

✚ 181 D4 ☒ 88 place de la République ☎ 04 93 35 95 78
🕒 Closed dinner Oct–May

MENTON

Au Pistou €

Regional and Mentonnaise specialities beside the old fishing harbour. Try the bouillabaisse here to see how it should be done.

➕ 181 E4 ✉ 9 quai Gordon Bennett
☎ 04 93 57 45 89 ⓢ Closed Mon

Don Cicco €

Italian cuisine less than a kilometre from the Italian border.

➕ 181 E4 ✉ 11 rue St-Michel
☎ 04 93 57 92 92 ⓢ Closed Wed

Le Lido €

A lively brasserie specialising in seafood dishes. There are freshly shucked oysters and enormous seafood platters, as well as pasta, paella and salads.

➕ 181 E4 ✉ 24 rue Saint Michel
☎ 04 93 28 48 71 ⓢ Daily

L'Olivo €€

This cosy restaurant at the foot of the Old Town serves giant pizzas from an open oven, along with mouthwatering *moules frites* or beef carpaccio *à discretion*.

➕ 181 E4 ✉ 21 place du Cap
☎ 04 93 35 45 65 ⓢ Close Thu
Apr–Oct closed Thu, 2 weeks Nov,
2 weeks Jan

PEILLON

Auberge de la Madone €€€

This family-run restaurant has a menu featuring Niçois classics full of flavour, with lashings of olive oil, truffles, goat's cheese, olives and mountain cheeses. There are garden-fresh vegetables, pasta, game birds and veal, all accompanied by an excellent wine list. The food is matched by the wonderful view from the terrace where dinner is served.

➕ 181 E4 ✉ 2 place au Village
☎ 04 93 79 91 17;
www.chateauxhotels.com/madone
ⓢ Closed Jan, mid-Oct to mid-Dec

ROQUEBRUNE

Le Grand Inquisiteur €€

These cave-like, vaulted dining rooms were once used to shelter livestock. Today they make the perfect setting for a candle-lit dinner *à deux*.

➕ 181 D4 ✉ Rue du Château
☎ 04 93 35 05 37 ⓢ Closed Mon,
and Tue lunch

La Grotte €

"The Cave" is a popular troglodyte restaurant at the entrance to the village, with tables spilling out into the square, and a good *plat du jour* or pizza at a reasonable price.

➕ 181 D4 ✉ Place des Deux-Frères
☎ 04 93 35 00 04 ⓢ Closed Wed;
Oct–Mar closed Tue dinner

ST-JEAN-CAP FERRAT

Capitaine Cook €€

Just outside St-Jean, this seafood restaurant serves a range of quality shellfish. The terrace is perfect for summertime dining.

➕ 181 D3 ✉ 11 avenue Jean Mermoz
☎ 04 93 76 02 66
ⓢ Closed Wed, and Thu lunch

Le Provençal €€€

The classy cuisine here features a lot of seafood, varying in price from moderate to very expensive, if you feel like something special.

➕ 181 D3 ✉ Place Clemenceau
☎ 04 93 76 03 97
ⓢ Closed Mon–Tue

LA TURBIE

Hostellerie Jérôme €€

The restaurant attached to this lovely old house serves meals showcasing regional produce. A stylish establishment with delicious food.

➕ 181 D3 ✉ 20 rue du Comte de
Cessole ☎ 04 92 41 51 51;
www.hostelleriejerome.com
ⓢ Closed Mon–Tue lunch Jul–Aug;
Mon–Tue Sep–Jun

VILLEFRANCHE-SUR-MER

Le Joïa €€

Exotic influences permeate both the food and décor here. Sit among the buddhas and Moroccan lamps and enjoy the fusion of Asian and French cuisine.

⊞ 181 D3 ⊠ 18 rue du Poilu ☎ 04 93 76 62 40 ⓒ Daily 7 pm–12.30 am

La Mère Germaine €€€

One of the most popular waterfront seafood restaurants in Villefranche-sur-Mer. Menus change daily, depending on the catch.

⊞ 181 D3 ⊠ 7 quai Amiral Courbet ☎ 04 93 01 71 39 ⓒ Closed mid-Nov to 25 Dec

Michel's €€

Lovingly prepared seafood, shellfish and local specialities in the pedestrian zone (parking opposite). Sit out on the sunny terrace overlooking the bay.

⊞ 181 D3 ⊠ place Amélie Pollonnais ☎ 04 93 76 73 24 ⓒ Closed Tue

Where to...
Shop

MARKETS

Many of the small villages along the Corniche roads hold daily or weekly markets.

Along the Corniche Inférieure, **Beaulieu-sur-Mer** has a daily fruit and vegetable market (place du Marché). At the same location there are clothes and household goods for sale on Saturdays. An antiques market is also held on the third Sunday of month.

Villefranche-sur-Mer holds a flea market (Jardin François Binon and avenue Amélie Pollonnais) each Sunday, and a Provençal market (Jardin François Binon and promenade de l'Octroi) every Saturday morning.

Of the Grande Corniche villages, **Roquebrune** has a daily Provençal

market (place du Marché), and in mid-September holds an annual flea market. **La Turbie** has a general market every Thursday morning.

Menton has a daily food market (les Halles), with fresh meat, fruit, vegetables and cheese; a clothes market every Saturday morning (Vieux Port) and a flea market each Friday (place aux Herbes).

FOOD

Buy tins of organic *foie gras* and pâté from **Comtesse du Barry** (36 rue Partouneaux, Menton, tel: 04 93 35 35 05). Also has outlets in Cannes and Nice.

Stock up on Italian goodies without crossing the border at **DOC D'Italia** (5 rue Piéta, Menton), where you'll find everything from *panettone* to *pecorino*.

SPECIALITY

The 100-year-old **Coutellerie E Garnero** (8 rue St-Michel, Menton,

tel: 04 93 57 03 60) specialises in the unlikely combination of knives and umbrellas, and is well worth a visit as it is surely one of the most old-fashioned, eccentric shops on the Riviera.

l'Herminette Ezasque (1 rue Principale, Èze, tel: 04 93 41 13 59, open summer daily 10–7, winter 10–6), situated within the walls of Èze's old gateway, is bursting with *santons* (traditional clay figurines) and gifts and sculptures made from olive wood.

PROVENÇAL GOODS

Les Images de Provence (21 rue St-Michel, Menton, tel: 04 93 57 09 98, open daily 9–7) designs and prints its own beautiful Provençal fabrics, which it sells by the metre or transformed into finished items, from tablecloths, napkins and bed linens to other soft furnishings.

Where to...
Be Entertained

FESTIVALS AROUND NICE

In **February**, Menton holds the Fête du Citron, a 15-day festival celebrating the area's main crop: lemons (▶ 20). The highlight is a parade of floats decorated with thousands of lemons. There are also static displays in the Jardin Biovès.

In **March**, Villefranche-sur-Mer hosts a *bataille des fleurs* – a battle of the flowers, or, less dramatically, flower competition – and you'll find others celebrated throughout the area.

April brings various religious festivals with the coming of Easter, such as the Procession of the Dead Christ (Maundy Thursday/Good Friday) in Roquebrune-Cap Martin.

May Day (Fête du Travail) on **1 May** is a public holiday in France,

with festivals taking place throughout the country. Also in May, Menton holds a parade of vintage cars, and a festival of Franco-Italian street theatre.

June is an excellent time to visit Gorbio and experience the Procession dai Limaca, where villagers celebrate the previous winter's olive harvest with a magical night-time procession (▶ 22). Check with the tourist office for exact dates, as the procession sometimes takes place in May. June is Gardens Month in Menton, with private and public gardens in the town open to visitors. Throughout France, the Fête de la Musique is celebrated with outdoor concerts.

July and **August** are packed with various festivals. Throughout France, there are numerous arts and

music festivals. In **July**, a series of musical evenings is held at Monastère de l'Annonciade in Menton, and there are music festivals and Latin dance performances in the gardens. In Roquebrune-Cap Martin, a Medieval Festival takes place at the start of the month. The Fête de St-Pierre (second Sunday in July) is celebrated in Cap d'Antibes, Villefranche-sur-Mer and Nice. Throughout the country, Bastille Day celebrations including fireworks, parties and *batailles des fleurs* are held on **14 July**.

During the Menton Music Festival in **August**, there are open-air chamber music concerts (all month). Menton also holds open-air theatrical evenings, and a Karting Grand Prix. Roquebrune has a Passion Procession (**5 August**), and in Peille a Fête des Blés et de la Lavande (wheat and lavender festival) is held.

The **first Sunday of September** is the Festin des Baguettes in Peille, and Menton holds plant and garden

shows during the Mediterranean Days of the Garden.

Many celebrations take place during **December**. Christmas markets and lights spring up around towns. Look out for nativity displays with *santons* (traditional clay figurines) of everyday people as well as the holy family.

OTHER ENTERTAINMENT

The **Théâtre Français Palermo** (Palais de l'Europe, avenue Boyer, tel: 04 92 41 76 50) shows French plays, operettas and recitals.

Formal attire is required to visit the **Casino de Menton**, with its slot machines, games rooms, two bars, restaurant and club Le Brummell (2 avenue Félix Fauré, tel: 04 93 35 78 38; open 10 am–3 am (until 4 am Fri–Sat).

Golf Club de Monte-Carlo (route du Mont Agel, La Turbie, tel: 04 93 41 09 11, open Mon 8–5, Tue–Sun 8–6), has 18 holes and views to the coast and Italian Alps.

Monaco

Getting Your Bearings

Rich, chic and exclusive, Monaco is a magnet for the world's
jetsetters, attracted by the lack of taxes and the world's highest incomes. Renowned for its princesses and excesses, it
also boasts the world's most celebrated casino – a symbol of
all that is dazzling, opulent and glamorous in Monte-Carlo.

Monaco's real crowd-puller is the Grand Prix, which takes place annually in
May, when thousands of spectators flank the narrow twisting pavements of
Monte-Carlo, wild in flag-waving suspense for a day of ear-splitting noise and
heart-stopping speed right through the centre of town.

   Even though the Grand Prix is over in a day,
Monégasques live life in the fast lane all year
round in their tiny principality – a spot-
lessly clean, pint-sized strip of
sky-scraper-clad land
squeezed between the
sea and the
mountains.

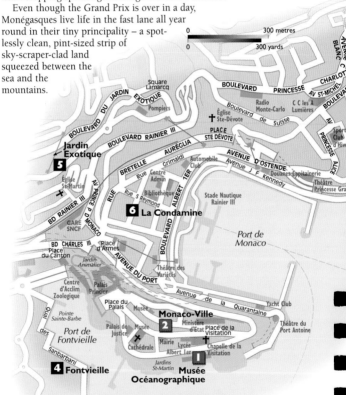

Monaco is the second smallest sovereign state in the world, after the Vatican.
Only 6,000 of its 30,000 residents are actually locals. The remainder are all
prepared to pay extortionate real-estate prices just to be part of Monaco's
über-rich community of millionaires, gamblers, "offshore" bankers and
royalty. Citizenship here is the most sought after in the world. Out of count-

less applications, only 4,000 have been accepted in the last 15 years, including Karl Lagerfeld, Anthony Burgess, Steffi Graf, Alain Prost, Claudia Schiffer and Luciano Pavarotti. After all, this is the home of the rich and famous, the world's most sophisticated holiday playground.

★ Don't Miss

- ❶ Musée Océanographique ➤ 88
- ❷ Monaco-Ville ➤ 90
- ❸ Casino de Monte-Carlo ➤ 93

At Your Leisure

- ❹ Fontvieille ➤ 96
- ❺ Jardin Exotique ➤ 96
- ❻ La Condamine ➤ 97
- ❼ Musée National ➤ 97
- ❽ Larvotto ➤ 97

Page 83:
Monte-Carlo

Right: The
Palais Princier

Below: Monte-
Carlo's casino

Finding your way round Monaco can prove difficult, but this itinerary should help you to discover the various facets of this tiny principality, from the historic heart of Monaco-Ville to the museum quarter of fashionable La Condamine, and the high-rise district of Monte-Carlo – a startling contrast with its dazzling designer boutiques, bars, restaurants and glitzy casino.

Monaco in a Day

Morning
Spend the morning exploring **2 Monaco-Ville** (➤ 90–92), with its ancient narrow streets and pastel-coloured houses perched on The Rock – a sheer-sided finger of land extending 800m (875 yards) into the sea. At its heart, the lavish neo-Romanesque cathedral (➤ 92), funded by casino profits, contains precious 16th-century retables by Niçois artist Louis Bréa and the tomb of the much-mourned Princess Grace. In summer, when Prince Albert II is away, guided tours of the Palais Princier (Prince's Palace, ➤ 90–91) take you through the priceless treasures of the State Apartments and the small Musée Napoléon. When he is in residence, you must content yourselves with the Changing of the Guard (daily at 11:55 am). The elevated position of Monaco-Ville affords visitors bird's-eye views of the port quarter, **6 La Condamine** (➤ 97), a busy commercial district wrapped around one of the Riviera's most prestigious moorings. Many of the luxury yachts moor stern-to, to give onlookers a glimpse of the high life.

Lunch
Tuck into some traditional Monégasque cuisine at Le Castelroc (➤ 100), opposite the Prince's Palace.

Afternoon
Allow a couple of hours to visit Monaco's must-see sight, the **1 Musée Océanographique** (top right, ➤ 88–89) – the finest aquarium and museum

of marine science in the world. Formerly under the direction of underwater explorer Jacques Cousteau, it offers a dazzling collection of marine life, nautical instruments, the world's first submarine and a 20m (65.5-foot) whale skeleton. Then head to the chic **4 Fontvieille** district (➤ 96), which contains specialist attractions to please all the family: the late Prince Rainier's private collection of classic cars; the Naval Museum with 180 models of famous ships; the Museum of Stamps and Coins, documenting Monaco's unique postal history; a sculpture trail and the fragrant Princess Grace Rose Garden.

Evening

Fontvieille is considered the "Chelsea of Monaco" and there's nowhere better to celebrity-spot than on the cool terrace of the Columbus brasserie (➤ 98), owned by Formula One driver David Coulthard.

Later in the evening, even if you are not a gambler, it is worth visiting the ornate **3 Casino de Monte-Carlo** (below, ➤ 93–95) to try your luck at breaking the bank. Then, if you have any money left, rub shoulders with the rich and famous at Le Point Rouge (11 rue du Portier, Monte-Carlo) or Jimmy'z (➤ 103), arguably the chicest disco on the Côte d'Azur.

◻ Musée Océanographique

Perched on a sheer cliff high above the Mediterranean, this museum of marine science, with its spectacular aquarium, is the finest of its kind, and a highlight of Monaco.

The prestigious museum was founded in 1910 by Prince Albert I, who was a keen oceanographer, as an institute for scientific research and to house the many marine specimens he collected on his voyages. Financed by profits from the casino, it took 11 years and 100,000 tonnes of white stone from La Turbie (➤ 66) to build. The resulting structure, with its staggering 85m (279-foot) façade that plunges straight into the sea, is a masterpiece of monumental architecture.

The museum is built over several floors, and its main drawcard is the **aquarium** in the basement, which exhibits thousands of rare fish with beautifully lit displays of living corals from all over the world. The largest fish are behind a thick glass panel to the left of the entrance, connected to the part of the reef exposed to the open sea. Several species of sharks, giant turtles and large groupers can be seen here.

The facade of the Musée Oceanographic, built into the cliff face of The Rock

Opposite: A tank of clown fish in the museum's aquarium

MUSÉE OCÉANOGRAPHIQUE: INSIDE INFO

Top tips An **English-language guide** to the museum is available for €8, but the aquarium also has information panels in several languages, including English. The displays on the first floor are mostly in French.

• On the second floor of the museum is a **terrace with panoramic views** stretching over the principality, mountains and out to sea. An information panel points out landmarks and places of interest in the area.

Other tanks contain a wonderful array of sea life, including delicate jellyfish, Caribbean moray eels and their friend the small cleaning shrimp, sinister black lantern-eye fish (aptly nicknamed "demons of the night") and many cunningly camouflaged marine chameleons, such as the wide-eyed flounder.

The first floor contains some exceptional **collections** of nautical instruments and marine flora and fauna, including the skeleton of a 20m (65.5-foot) whale complete with its impressive baleens, for filtering krill. Also on this floor is the **laboratory** installed in Prince Albert's last boat, *Hirondelle II*. Displays demonstrate natural oceanographic phenomena such as waves, tides, currents and salinity; and the world's first submarine – powered by pedals, it was built in 1774 and used against English ships during the American War of Independence.

The ground level has **models** of all the magnificent ships built for the sovereign's voyages, and a **cinema** where films made by marine explorer Jacques Cousteau, who directed the research centre here until 1988, are regularly screened.

TAKING A BREAK

The **café** on the second floor of the museum is open for most of the year. Close by, in the old quarter, try **Da Sergio** (place de la Mairie, tel: 04 91 16 53 64) for cheap pizzas and an espresso.

Musée Océanographique

✚ 182 B1 ✉ Avenue St-Martin ☎ 377 93 15 36 00; www.oceano.mc ⏰ Daily 9:30–7:30, Jul– Aug; 9:30–7, Apr–Jun, Sep; 10–6, Oct–Mar 💷 Expensive, under 6 free

2 Monaco-Ville

Monaco is today made up of several districts, although it started out, like many other Provençal hilltop villages, on top of a rock. The original town was Monaco-Ville, consisting of the palace and the Old Town. They cling on to The Rock (Le Rocher), which juts 800m (875 yards) out into the Mediterranean with a sheer drop of 300m (984 feet) into the sea.

Palais Princier

The Prince's Palace stands solidly at the western end of The Rock. The current palace was constructed over the bones of an original stronghold, built in the 13th century by the Genoese. Disguised as a Franciscan monk, François Grimaldi penetrated this stronghold and took control of Monaco in 1297. The current prince, Albert II, is his direct descendent, continuing the dynasty of the oldest ruling family in Europe.

The Renaissance-style façade of the Prince's Palace, home to the royal Grimaldi family

Monaco-Ville, perched on The Rock above the Mediterranean

The elegant palace seen today dates from the 17th century. Standing guard in front of the palace is the immaculately preened Prince's Guard, armed with rifles to protect the princely seat from anyone with any more smart monk-disguise ideas. The **Changing of the Guard** takes place every morning at 11:55 sharp. When the Prince is in residence, the royal colours are flown from the tower.

From June to October visitors can take **audio-guided tours** through the palace. The tour covers the Court of Honour, the Hercules Gallery (decorated with 17th-century frescoes), the Throne Room, and the plush State Apartments filled with priceless treasures. The small **Musée Napoléon** in the south wing of the palace contains a collection of Napoléon Bonaparte's personal items, including some of his socks and one of his hats.

François Grimaldi

Monaco was founded in 1215 as a colony of Genoa. The Genoese built a fortress atop the strategically important Rock, but it was seized in 1297 by François Grimaldi who, disguised as a monk in need of shelter, was admitted into the fortress together with his men, also in disguise. Once inside, they killed the guards and took control of the garrison. Despite seizing power in 1297, there was a 300-year struggle for The Rock, during which time Monaco was captured and recaptured by several parties, before the Grimaldis gained permanent possession and established themselves as princes of Monaco in the 17th century. Above the entrance to the palace is the Grimaldi family crest with its two sword-bearing monks. A statue of François Grimaldi, dressed as a monk with a sword hidden beneath his cloak, also stands in front of the palace.

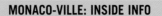

MONACO-VILLE: INSIDE INFO

Top tips Monaco-Ville is closed to visitors' vehicles, but can be reached by a long, steep **walkway** from place d'Armes, or by **elevator** from parking des Pêcheurs on the seafront at the bottom of The Rock. There are several **free** public lifts and escalators in Monaco, all of which are marked on a free map available at the tourist office.

• If you're in town in summer, look out for the **open-air cinema** showing original -language films every night on Europe's largest screen at the Terraces du Parking-des-Pecheurs (end June to early September, tel: 377 95 25 86 60).

• Unless you are into motor racing, don't come to Monaco during the **Grand Prix** in May, when thousands of visitors cram into the principality and many roads are closed.

Old Quarter

A large proportion of Monaco-Ville is taken up by the palace and its surrounding gardens and plaza. The rest of The Rock is covered by the Old Town, which often draws toy-town comparisons. It's an immaculately kept labyrinth of cool, cobbled streets, with lovely fountain-filled squares and fine Italianate façades, although, inevitably, the shops around the royal palace sell the usual tacky souvenirs.

In rue Colonel Bellando de Castro, at the heart of the Old Town, is Monaco's neo-Romanesque **Cathédrale**, where Rainer III is buried next to the much-loved Princess Grace (1929–82), whose grave is often covered in flowers. The stone used to construct the cathedral was taken from La Turbie. It's not an especially attractive cathedral, but along with the tombs of Princess Grace and Rainer III, it houses a Louis Bréa altarpiece and the tombs of the other Grimaldi princes.

Other things to see in the Old Town include the often-overlooked **Musée de la Chapelle de la Visitation**, housing religious art by Ribera, Rubens and other Italian baroque artists; **St-Martin Gardens**, offering stunning sea views; and the outstanding Musée Océanographique (▶ 88–89).

Top: Changing of the guard

Above: The formidable fortifications of the palace

Opposite: Monte-Carlo's casino and gardens

🔲 182 B1
Palais Princier
🔲 182 A2 ✉ Place du Palais ☎ 377 93 25 18 31; www.palais.mc
🕐 Daily 9:30–6, Jun–Sep; 10–5, Oct. Closed Nov–May
🎫 Entry by guided tour only, moderate 🚌 1, 2

Tourist Office
🔲 183 D4 ✉ 2a boulevard des Moulins ☎ 377 92 166 166;
www.monaco-tourisme.com 🕐 Mon–Sat 9–7, Sun 10–12

③ Casino de Monte-Carlo

No visit to Monaco would be complete without visiting the world's most famous casino, with a façade so grand it borders on the ridiculous. The casino was for many years the chief source of income for the principality, and today symbolises the opulence and glamour of Monte-Carlo.

The Grimaldi princes of Monaco once ruled a much larger stretch of coast and used the tax levied on Menton's olives and lemons as their main source of income. The high taxes provoked a revolt in 1848, with Menton and Roquebrune claiming their independence from the principality and causing the Grimaldis to lose 80 per cent of their land. As a result, Monaco was brought down to its present size, and Prince Charles III was pushed into financial crisis. In 1878 the Prince (after whom Monte-Carlo is named) opened the Casino de Monte-Carlo to save himself from bankruptcy. The scheme put 95 per cent of the casino's takings into the royal

coffers, and was so successful that, five years after its opening, the Prince abolished taxation altogether, a situation still enjoyed in Monaco today. Yet gone are the days when the Monégasques could live entirely off the folly of others. Revenue from the casino has declined, so that now it is worth much more as a tourist attraction.

The splendid building was designed by Charles Garnier, architect of the Paris Opéra. Known in its heyday as the "Cathedral of Hell", its lavish *belle-époque* interior is a riot of pink, green and gold, with marble floors, bronze sculptures, onyx columns and highly ornate ceilings, lit by crystal chandeliers. To the left of the casino is the **Café de Paris** and the casino's **Salons Américains** gaming room. You must be 18 to enter this clattering room stuffed with poker and slot machines, but there is no admission charge. You can stroll around the casino gardens, admire the array of lavish cars

The grand façade of the casino is lit up at night

parked outside the entrance and view the ostentatious entrance hall of the casino proper without paying, but you will be charged a fee to enter into the more serious gaming rooms inside.

Since the casino's opening, bronzed, bejewelled gamblers have come here from all over the world to try their luck at the gaming tables. Ten euros will gain you entry into the **Salons Européens**, a mini-Vegas beneath gilded rococo ceilings where you'll find roulette, craps and blackjack tables. A further €10 and suitable attire is required to enter the exclusive **Salons Privés**, where the stakes are higher and décor even more extravagant. Here, high-rolling James Bond types place inordinate sums on the roulette and *chemin de fer* tables. Few tourists enter this part of the casino; cameras are not allowed and business is serious as the croupiers silently slide chips to poker-faced players. If you enter this far into the casino, don't miss the **Pink Salon Bar**, famed both for its ceiling depicting female nudes smoking cigars, and the fact that Charles Deville Wells turned $400 into $40,000 in a three-day gambling spree that took place in this room in 1891, inspiring the song "The Man Who Broke the Bank at Monte-Carlo".

The casino building also houses the ornate **Salle Garnier opera house**, which takes its name from the famed architect. The casino is flanked on one side by the swanky **Café de Paris**, and on the other by the **Hôtel de Paris**, home of decadent dining room Louis XV (➤ 100). Around the casino, a golden circle of designer fashion boutiques and jewellers make great shopping should you wish to blow your winnings.

TAKING A BREAK

Take in the atmosphere with a drink on the terrace of the **Café de Paris** (➤ 103).

Casino de Monte-Carlo
🏠 183 D3 ✉ Place du Casino ☎ 377 92 16 20 00; www.casino-monte-carlo.com

Tourist Office
🏠 183 D4 ✉ 2A boulevard des Moulins ☎ 377 92 16 61 16 🕐 Mon–Sat 9–7, Sun 10–12. In summer, additional tourist information kiosks are set up at the railway station and main sites

---

CASINO DE MONTE-CARLO: INSIDE INFO

Top tips You must be **18** to enter the casino, and have suitable identification, such as a **passport**.
• The casino follows a **strict dress code**, and if you intend to enter the casino proper, it is a good idea for men to wear a jacket and tie. Shorts and T-shirts are frowned upon, and a jacket and tie are required to enter the private rooms in the evening. Uniforms of any kind are not allowed.
• Monégasque citizens and members of the clergy are **not allowed to gamble**.
• Credit cards are **not** accepted.
• Just around the corner, **Sun Casino** has slot machines open from 11 am, table games from 5 pm, and free entry (Fairmont Monte-Carlo, tel: 377 92 16 21 23; www.casino-monte-carlo.com).

At Your Leisure

4 Fontvieille

This zone of modern residential and commercial development, built on reclaimed land below The Rock of Monaco-Ville, has a yacht harbour, sports stadium, shops, numerous museums, and a zoo (**Jardin Animalier**) where animals from the tropics are brought to acclimatise to the European environment.

Stroll along the **sculpture trail**, a path lined with modern sculptures that winds its way up from the place du Campanile St-Nicholas towards the **Roseraie Princesse Grace**. This garden is dedicated to the former Hollywood actress and wife of Prince Rainer III, who died in a car accident on the Moyenne Corniche in 1982. The garden, in avenue des Papalins, is a peaceful oasis, fragrant with the scent of 4,000 rose bushes.

The museums in Fontvieille include the **Musée des Timbres et des Monnaies**, a stamp and coin gallery; the **Musée Naval,** with hundreds of models of famous ships; and the **Collection des Voitures Anciennes**, a collection of gleaming, historic motor vehicles.

➕ 182 A1
Jardin Animalier
✉ Terrasses de Fontvieille
☎ 377 95 25 18 31 ◷ Daily 9–12, 2–7, Jun–Sep; 10–12, 2–6, Mar–May; 10–12, 2–5, Oct–Feb 💷 Inexpensive

Musée des Timbres et des Monnaies
✉ Terrasses de Fontvieille ☎ 377 95 15 41 50 ◷ Daily 10–6, Jul–Sep; Daily 10–5, Oct–Jun 💷 Inexpensive

Musée Naval
✉ Terrasses de Fontvieille
☎ 377 92 05 28 48;
www.musee-naval.mc ◷ Daily 10–6
💷 Inexpensive 🚌 5, 6

Collection des Voitures
✉ Terrasses de Fontvieille
☎ 377 92 05 28 56; www.palais.mc
◷ Daily 10–6. Closed 25 Dec
💷 Moderate 🚌 5, 6

5 Jardin Exotique

In a lofty location above Fontvieille, just off the Moyenne Corniche (N7), lies one of Monaco's finest attractions, the Jardin Exotique. It contains several thousand cacti

Jardin Exotique, Monaco

For Kids

• Fontvieille has several attractions for kids, including a **zoo** and various hobby museums along the Terrasses de Fontvieille (➤ above).
• Children will love the dolls and moving automaton at the **Musée National** (➤ oppsite).
• The aquarium in the **Musée Océanographique** (➤ 88–89) is fascinating for kids
• The **Monte-Carlo International Circus Festival** is held annually at the end of January (➤ 104).
• There is a **diving pool** on quai Albert 1er at Port Hercule, a great place to cool off in summer; in winter, it is converted into an **ice-skating rink**.

and succulents of vivid colours and amazing shapes, some nearly 10m (30 feet) high.

The ticket price includes a tour of the **Grottes de l'Observatoire**, caves which were inhabited in the Palaeolithic era. Also included is entrance to the **Musée d'Anthropologie Préhistorique**, with a display of prehistoric bones and some early human artefacts.

➕ 182 off A3 ✉ 62 boulevard du Jardin-Exotique ☎ 377 95 15 29 80 🕐 Daily 9–7, mid-May to mid-Sep; 9–6 or nightfall, mid-Sep to mid-May 💵 Moderate 🚌 2

❻ La Condamine

In medieval times La Condamine referred to cultivable land at the foot of a village or a castle. Today this area, at the foot of the royal palace, is a busy shopping area wrapped around the port of Monaco, and the starting point of the Formula 1 Grand Prix. **Rue Grimaldi** is the main shopping street, where there are everyday food stores. Monaco's food market has been taking place in **place d'Armes** daily since 1880. This area also has the **railway station**, some reasonably priced hotels and bars where the old locals still speak Monégasque. Strolling along the harbour you'll find some casual restaurants, and views of the extravagant yachts moored in Monaco port.

➕ 182 B2 🚌 1, 2, 4, 5, 6 🚢 Daily excursions around The Rock at 11, 2:30 and 4, Jun to mid-Sep, from quai des États-Unis, Port d'Hercule, tel: 377 92 16 15 15

❼ Musée National

Somewhat unconventionally, Monaco has devoted its national museum entirely to dolls. Along with the casino and opera house, Charles Garnier designed the impressive villa surrounded by a rose garden, which houses the extensive collection.

Most of the dolls on display are from the 19th century, although there are also some modern dolls, and some dating back to the 18th century, complete with period costumes and miniature furnishings. The automata (moving dolls) are perhaps the most interesting in the collection, with the delicate workings open to view. They are demonstrated several times a day.

➕ 183 F4 ✉ 17 avenue Princesse-Grace ☎ 377 93 30 91 26 🕐 Daily 10–6:30, Easter–Sep; 10–12:15, 2:30–6:30, Oct–Easter 💵 Moderate

❽ Larvotto

What Monaco lacks naturally, it creates artificially. Rainer III was responsible for extending Monaco by a fifth of its size, reclaiming land to create Fontvieille, and constructing man-made beaches and swimming facilities here at Larvotto, close to Beausoleil on the other side of the French border. Larvotto is also home to **Le Sporting Club**, an exclusive 6ha (15-acre) seafront area.

Near Larvotto beach, in stark contrast to the glitz of Monte-Carlo, is the peaceful **Jardin Japonais**, an authentic Shinto garden with bubbling ponds, waterfalls and a wooden tea house (open daily 9–sunset). The **Grimaldi Forum** is a large convention centre where temporary exhibitions are held. On the top floor of the forum is the sophisticated bar/restaurant, Zebra Square (▶ 101).

➕ 183 F4 **Le Sporting Club** ✉ Avenue Princesse-Grace ☎ 377 92 16 36 36

Where to... Stay

Prices
Expect to pay per double room, per night

€ under €80 €€ €80–€150 €€€ over €150

Hôtel Alexandra €€

Centrally located and relatively good value in comparison with other hotels in this exclusive area, the Hôtel Alexandra is less than 500m (550 yards) away from all the main attractions of Monte-Carlo, in addition to being only ten minutes' walk from the beach. From the outside, the hotel flaunts its *belle-époque* features, while its interior is modern, with comfortable air-conditioned and sound-proofed rooms.

🚇 182 D4 ☒ 35 boulevard
Princesse-Charlotte, Monte-Carlo
☎ 377 93 50 63 13;
www.monte-carlo.mc/alexandra

Hôtel Balmoral €€

This venerable hotel opened in 1896 and has been run by the same family ever since. It's known for its wonderful views over the sea, and also has a restaurant and bar.

🚇 182 C3 ☒ 12 avenue de la Costa,
Monte-Carlo ☎ 377 93 50 62 37;
www.hotel-balmoral.mc

Columbus €€€

While the rest of Monaco is trying to capture the glory of its *belle-époque* heyday, this chic designer hotel steps away from the 21st century, offering all the luxury and none of the fuss. Neutral tones and contemporary design give this hotel a simple and relaxed feel. It also has a stylish modern brasserie.

🚇 182 off A1 ☒ 23 avenue des
Papalins, Fontvieille ☎ 377 92 05 90
00; www.columbushotels.com

Hôtel Diana €

On the border of Monaco and Beausoleil, just a few minutes' walk from the casino, is this budget hotel with a large parking station right next door. Some of the rooms have a good view over Monaco and down to the sea, and there is a lively daily fruit and vegetable market just behind on rue du Marché.

🚇 183 E4 ☒ 17 boulevard de
Général Leclerc, Beausoleil
☎ 04 93 78 47 58;
www.monte-carlo.mc/hotel-diana-
beausoleil/

Hôtel de France €€

Hôtel de France is one of the few affordable hotels in the principality. Located near the train station in La Condamine, this small and brightly coloured little hotel is cheerful and welcoming, with comfortable rooms, some of which have balconies.

🚇 182 A2 ☒ 6 rue de La Turbie,
Monte-Carlo ☎ 377 93 30 24 64;
www.monte-carlo.mc/france

Helvetia €

This affordable, two-star hotel is clean and friendly, and close to the port. It has two entrances and is accessible from rue Grimaldi and rue de La Turbie.

🚇 182 A3 ☒ 1 bis rue Grimaldi,
Monte-Carlo ☎ 377 93 30 21 71;
www.monte-carlo.mc/helvetia

Hôtel Hermitage €€€

You need a princely sum to stay at this luxury *belle-époque* palace in the heart of Monte-Carlo, overlooking the Mediterranean. It features a spectacular Winter Garden where you can breakfast under a stained-glass dome designed by Gustav

Where to...
Eat and Drink

Eiffel. Its lavish pink and gold restaurant, Le Vistamar, has panoramic views and serves fabulous seafood. There is direct access to Les Thermes Marins de Monaco Spa and Health Resort, and a helicopter shuttle service between Monaco and Nice airports.

➕ 183 D3 ⌖ Square Beaumarchais, Monte-Carlo ☎ 377 98 06 25 25; www.montecarloresort.com

Hôtel de Paris €€€
Monte-Carlo's first and most famous hotel, full of showy *belle-époque* features, marble colonnades and crystal chandeliers. The Hôtel de Paris opened in 1865 to provide the kind of accommodation fit for visiting tsars, royalty and aristocrats, and today guests staying at Monte-Carlo's most prestigious address still enjoy an extreme level of luxury and exclusivity. It houses three restaurants, including the gastronomically élite Louis XV (➤ 100), and offers direct access to the fashionable Thermes Marins spa

resort, as well as every other possible luxury.

➕ 183 D3 ⌖ Place du Casino, Monte-Carlo ☎ 377 98 06 25 25; www.montecarloresort.com

Port Palace €€€
A stylish, modern hotel overlooking the port and The Rock. The focus here is general wellbeing: a "wellness centre" offers beauty treatments in addition to fitness rooms, a yoga studio, sauna and hammam.

➕ 183 D3 ⌖ 7 avenue JF Kennedy ☎ 377 97 97 90 00; www.portpalace.com

Hôtel Le Versailles €
Conveniently situated between the station and The Rock, and a few minutes' away from Monte-Carlo, this two-star hotel has reasonably priced rooms with all the basics, as well as a decent restaurant.

➕ 182 A3 ⌖ 4–6 avenue Prince-Pierre, La Condamine ☎ 377 93 50 79 34; www.monte-carlo.mc/versailles

Dining in Monaco can be a truly glamorous affair, but eating economically is not out of the question. Being so close to the Italian border, baguette and pizza are good-quality, inexpensive options.

Le Bambi €
Give your wallet a rest at this friendly eatery in La Condamine, one of several in the area that serves good-value Italian food. The dish of the day is particularly economical.

➕ 182 B3 ⌖ 11 rue Princesse-Antoinette, La Condamine ☎ 377 93 303 506 ⏰ Sun–Fri 11–3, 6–11

Bar et Boeuf €€€
Alain Ducasse's seasonal restaurant, open only for the summer, focuses its meals around *bar* (sea bass) and *boeuf* (beef). Although the creations are unmistakably Gallic, this rather Zen-like approach to ingredients is reflected in the minimalist interior of the restaurant. Designed by Philippe Starke, this stylish venue, with wonderful views out to sea, is the place to see and be seen.

➕ 183 E3 ⌖ Avenue Princesse-Grace, Larvotto ☎ 377 98 06 71 71; www.alain-ducasse.com ⏰ Mid-May to late Sep dinner only

Quai des Artistes €

A contemporary Parisian-style brasserie on the port with a reasonably priced menu and a good-sized terrace on which to enjoy your meal.

➕ 182 B2 ✉ 4 quai Antoine 1er, La Condamine ☎ 377 97 97 97 77; www.quaidesartistes.com ⏱ Closed 24 Dec, 31 Dec

La Rose des Vents €€

Having its own private beach, you could theoretically step straight out of the sea to your table, although the waiters may not appreciate you walking sand over their polished floor. On a sunny day, have a long lunch at one of the tables outside beneath the shade of a parasol. The menu offers seafood, salads and a combination of traditional Monégasque and Italian dishes.

➕ 183 off F4 ✉ Plage du Larvotto ☎ 377 97 70 46 96; www.larosedesventsmonaco.com ⏱ Daily 12–3:30, 7:30–10:30

88 64; www.alain-ducasse.com ⏱ Thu–Mon 12–2, 7:30–9:30; Wed dinner, Jul–Aug; closed Dec, 1st 2 weeks Mar

La Maison du Caviar €€

This simple yet smart restaurant serves copious quantities of caviar, blinis, salmon and vodka – redolent of the days of the Tsar.

➕ 183 D4 ✉ 1 avenue St-Charles, Monte-Carlo ☎ 377 93 30 80 06 ⏱ Closed Sat lunch, Sun and Aug

Polpetta €€

Hidden away from the clamour of central Monte-Carlo, this Italian restaurant nonetheless attracts jet-setters and celebrities for a taste of *la dolce vita*. A rustic trattoria serving up wonderful antipasto, home-made pasta, seafood risotto and veal. There's also an extensive list of quality Italian wines.

➕ 182 C3 ✉ 6 avenue de Roqueville ☎ 377 93 50 67 84 ⏱ Closed Tue, and Sat lunch

Le Castelroc €€

A crowded and popular lunch spot opposite the royal palace that has been run by the same family for more than 50 years. Exceptional Monégasque cuisine including some wonderful seafood, such as *stocafi* (stockfish) cooked with garlic, wine, tomatoes and olives.

➕ 181 A1 ✉ Place du Palais, Monaco-Ville ☎ 377 93 30 36 68 ⏱ Closed Sat and Jan

La Cigale di Mare €

This lively and down-to-earth seafood restaurant is popular with locals, and is relatively easy on the pocket.

➕ 182 B3 ✉ 4 rue Baron de Ste-Suzanne ☎ 377 97 77 14 64 ⏱ Closed Sat–Sun and Aug

Joël Robuchon Monte-Carlo €€€

Big-name chef Joël Robuchon's simple food philosophy, that food should taste like what it is, is quite

refreshing in this land of excess, and his restaurant here presents dishes with no more than three flavours on one plate, allowing you to fully enjoy the taste of every ingredient. This seemingly simple theory works well within the restaurant's elegant, but not overly excessive, surroundings.

➕ 183 D4 ✉ 4 avenue de la Madone, Monte-Carlo ☎ 377 93 15 15 15 ⏱ Daily breakfast, lunch and dinner

Louis XV €€€

A gastronomic shrine run by celebrated chef Alain Ducasse with a very highly regarded three Michelin stars. Set within the majestic Hôtel de Paris, dining here is the height of hedonistic luxury. The (hugely expensive) Mediterranean-inspired menu changes seasonally, with food served in a dining room that transports you to 17th-century Versailles. Book well ahead.

➕ 183 D3 ✉ Hôtel de Paris, place du Casino, Monte-Carlo ☎ 377 98 06

Stars'N'Bars €

For families looking for somewhere less formal to take the kids, this popular, American-style bar-restaurant has burgers, wedges and Tex-Mex food, with games to keep kids occupied. Sporting memorabilia lines the walls, and there's an excellent view over the port from the terrace. There's also an internet café, and a disco in the evenings.

🖪 182 C2 ⊠ 6 quai Antoine Ier, La Condamine ☎ 377 97 97 95 95; www.starsnbars.com ⏴ Daily; closed Mon in winter. Food served 11:30 am–midnight

Il Terrazzino €

This tiny, family-run Italian restaurant is very popular with the Italian locals, and is a linguistically confusing, place to eat – the staff may greet you in Italian, but you can order in English or French. The atmosphere is unpretentious, the food is delicious and the portions are generous. The menu includes irresistible antipasti, Neapolitan-

style risotto, calzone, home-made pasta and enticing desserts.

🖪 183 D4 ⊠ 2 rue des Iris ☎ 377 93 50 24 27 ⏴ Closed Sun

Le Texan €

Rub shoulders with celebrities and sports stars over fajitas, enchiladas, burritos and cheap beers at this lively Tex-Mex bar-cum-restaurant. For dessert, there's American-style treats including chocolate brownies and apple pie on the menu.

🖪 182 B3 ⊠ 4 rue Suffren-Reymond, La Condamine ☎ 377 93 30 34 54 ⏴ Daily

Zebra Square €€

This chic Mediterranean restaurant has a sunny terrace that is the perfect place to rub shoulders with the beautiful people. True to its name, the décor, menu and crockery all have zebra stripes.

🖪 183 F4 ⊠ Grimaldi Forum, 10 avenue Princesse-Grace, Larvotto ☎ 377 99 99 25 50 ⏴ Daily 12–3, 8–midnight; closed Feb

Where to...
Shop

For a full guide to the shops and restaurants of Monaco, pick up the *Monaco Shopping Guide* available at the tourist office (2a boulevard des Moulins, tel: 377 92 16 61 16, www.monaco-tourisme.com).

FASHION AND JEWELLERY

Monaco has a reputation for high fashion, jewellery and boutique shopping, and if this is what you are looking for, you won't be disappointed by the strip of designer shops known as the "golden circle" around the Casino and Hôtel de Paris. Along **avenue de Monte-Carlo**, big names Gucci, Valentino, Hermès, Lalique and Prada strut their stuff. On the other side of the Hôtel de Paris, **avenue des Beaux-Arts** sparkles with Cartier, Céline,

Bulgari, Louis Vuitton, Yves Saint Laurent, Piaget and Dior.

Inside the **Hôtel Hermitage** on place Beaumarchais is an array of elegant shops, including the exclusive Italian label Prada, and Salvatore Ferragamo, a label made famous by its trademark Italian shoes, but also encompassing a full range of couture for men and women.

Along **boulevard des Moulins** there are more jewellery stores, including the rebellious **Bijoux Cassio** (10 boulevard des Moulins, tel: 377 93 25 55 10) which specializes in imitation jewellery, reproducing big-name designs in gold-plated silver for a fraction of the price. In the same street, mothers who adore Dior can dress their darlings in designer children's clothing from **Baby Dior** (31 boulevard des Moulins, tel: 377 93 25 71 12).

Boutiques also stretch along the **avenue Princesse-Grace**, and on the boulevard des Moulins towards

Larvotto. For designer labels at discounted prices, look in **Stock Griffe** (5 bis, avenue St-Michel, tel: 377 93 50 86 06).

The **Centre Commercial le Métropole** in the heart of Monte-Carlo (17 avenue des Spélugues, open Mon–Sat 10–7:30) has it all under one roof, keeping shoppers in an extravagant mood by flaunting *belle-époque* décor such as marble alleys and Bohemian glass chandeliers. You can find just about anything here – it has three levels of shopping with 80 boutiques specialising in fashion, beauty, household goods and leisure equipment.

SPECIALITY

Also within the Centre Commercial le Métropole is the big French store **FNAC**, selling books (some in English), CDs and electronic goodies. You can order tickets for theatre, opera and concert performances here (Centre Commercial le Métropole, tel: 377 93 10 81 81).

Manufacture de Monaco (Centre Commercial le Métropole, tel: 377 93 50 64 63) is a small, exclusive shop which supplies Monaco's royal family with traditional Monégasque porcelain, silverware, crystal and table linen.

In **La Condamine** you'll find shops at the more affordable end of the scale. **Marie Dentelle** (10 rue Princesse-Caroline, tel: 377 93 30 43 40) is an Aladdin's cave of feminine gift ideas, brightly coloured local pottery, and beautiful bed-linen, including quilts made in traditional Provençal material.

The more affordable **rue Grimaldi** in La Condamine is the shopping street for real Monégasques, as well as Formula 1 enthusiasts. A plethora of sporting paraphernalia designed by Porsche and Ferrari can be found at **Boutique Formule 1** (15 rue Grimaldi, tel: 377 93 15 92 44) and, just up the street, you can get your official Automobile Club de Monaco T-shirt from l@ **Boutique** (46 rue Grimaldi, tel: 377 97 70 45 35).

If you're feeling inspired after a visit to Monaco's remarkable Musée Océanographique, **Monaquatic-Aquariophile** in Monte-Carlo (5 rue de la Colle, tel: 377 97 77 81 41) is the place for all your aquarium needs.

FOOD AND DRINK

Les Caves du Grand Échanson (7 rue de la Colle, tel: 377 92 05 61 01) supply exclusive wines and spirits for the royal family.

L'Oenothèque (Sporting Club d'Hiver, 2 avenue Princesse-Alice, tel: 377 93 25 82 66) is an old wood-panelled store which stocks fine cognacs, armagnacs and French wines from 1928 to 2003.

For more ordinary shopping, the bakeries and flowershops along **rue Princesse-Caroline** in La Condamine are refreshingly modest. The **Fontvieille Centre Commercial** is a large mall and supermarket where Monégasques do their everyday shopping.

MARKETS

For a real taste of Monaco, the daily vegetable, flower and fruit market takes place at the **place des Armes,** in La Condamine, where there are both indoor and outdoor markets from 9–12. The place des Armes is an attractive spot, with cafés and an old fountain. At the Port de Fontvieille on Saturdays there is a flea market at Espace Fontvieille, from 9–5.

There is also a daily fruit and vegetable market in nearby **rue du Marché**, Beausoleil, just a few minutes' walk from the casino. In the same street, the bakery **Moulin de Païou** (tel: 04 93 78 48) sells wonderful fresh croissants and pastries.

Where to...
Be Entertained

Visit the tourist office to pick up an in-depth guide to the nightlife and entertainment in Monaco, with up-to-date listings for what's on and when.

The **Café de Paris** (place du Casino, tel: 377 92 16 20 20; www.casino-monte-carlo.com, open from 10 am), famed brasserie of the Hôtel de Paris, has an outdoor terrace in a prime position for people-watching. It's popular with those looking to experience the high life, and its glamorous reputation seems enough to compensate for the expense. English king Edward VII was a frequent visitor here, and the delicious flambéed dessert *crêpe suzette* was created here, named after one of his companions. As well as serving food, the café has a gaming room with slot-machines to rival those in the casino.

A night out in Monaco would not be complete without a visit to **Casino de Monte-Carlo** (place du Casino, tel: 377 92 16 20 00; www.casino-monte-carlo.com, open noon–dawn). This fabulous *belle-époque* gambling temple, is a famous haunt of the rich and famous. Dress to impress – and men are required to wear jacket and tie to enter the private rooms in the evening. You must be over 18, and bring your passport to enter (▶ 93–95).

In order to party with the jet set, head to **Jimmy'z** (Le Sporting Club, avenue Princesse-Grace, tel: 377 92 16 22 77, open May–Oct daily 11 pm–5 am; Nov–Apr Wed–Sun 11:30 pm–5 am). You'll have to pass the highly selective entry process, so dress as if you're famous, look beautiful and be prepared to pay an extortionate amount of money for your drinks. It's a half-indoors, half-outdoors affair, with a Cuban cigar room, a glass-tiled dance floor, and a Japanese garden.

The **Living Room** (7 avenue des Spélugues, tel: 377 93 50 80 31, open Mon–Sat 11 pm–6 am) is a hip club in the centre of Monte-Carlo, with a mix of dance music and live music. Beware the fashion police on the doors, and expect the drinks to be pricey.

Down-to-earth **McCarthy's** (7 rue du Portier, tel: 377 93 25 87 67; www.monte-carlo.mc/mccarthys, open daily 6 pm–5 am) is a friendly Irish pub attracting a lively crowd, particularly in summer, when the terrace provides a prime position to soak up the sun. There's Guinness on tap, good bar food, live music at weekends and a big screen to catch the big games.

The terrace of **Zebra Square** (10 avenue Princesse-Grace, tel: 377 99 99 25 50) on the top floor of the Grimaldi forum, with panoramic views over the yacht-filled harbour, is one of the best places in Monaco to enjoy an evening cocktail. This hip restaurant-bar serves good food, but is also perfect for a glamorous pre-dinner drink or a tipple in the small hours. The low lighting, relaxed lounge atmosphere and terrace with a view make it a good night spot.

Le Sporting (Galerie du Sporting d'Hiver, place du Casino, tel: 377 93 25 36 81; www.cinemasporting.com, open daily 2–9) in the centre of Monte-Carlo is Monaco's main cinema complex, and screening some films in their original language.

MUSIC

Salle Garnier, Monaco's opera house (Opéra de Monte-Carlo, place du Casino, tel: 377 92 16 22 99; www.opera.mc) has played host to many great artists over the years, and stages new productions annually, with orchestral music performed by the Philharmonic Orchestra of Monte-Carlo.

La Salle des Étoiles (Le Sporting, avenue Princesse-Grace, tel: 377 98 06 36 36; www.sportingmontecarlo.com, open Jun–early Sep only from 8 pm) is a concert hall in a majestic setting that welcomes big international stars to its stage. Enjoy cocktails on the terrace before a show, and bear in mind that the dress code requires men to wear a dinner jacket.

HEALTH AND BEAUTY

While many of the beaches in Monaco charge a fee, a swim at **Plage du Larvotto** (avenue Princesse-Grace) is free, and it's patrolled by lifeguards during the high season.

The **Country Club de Monte-Carlo** (155 avenue Princesse-Grace, Roquebrune, tel: 04 93 41 72 00; www.mccc.mc, open daily 8 am–8:30 pm) is the site of the ATP Masters Tennis Championship, with 23 clay courts and two hard courts, all of which are open year-round and have wonderful views over the Mediterranean. There's also a pool, a fitness centre equipped with physiotherapists, a sauna and a Jacuzzi. Day passes can be purchased by non-members.

Float away at the Thermes Marins de Monte-Carlo (2 avenue Monte-Carlo, tel: 377 98 06 69 00; www.montecarlospa.com, open daily 8–8). This blissful spa over-looking the sea is renowned for thalassotherapy. It has a complex of pools, heated sea-baths and hammams (turkish baths), as well as classic spa treatments, solariums, massages with essential oils, and the latest in marine therapy.

FESTIVALS AND EVENTS

Ste Dévote, patron saint of Monaco, was martyred in Corsica, and her body was placed in a boat bound for Africa. Legend has it that a dove that flew out of her mouth led the boat towards Monaco. On the site where the boat ran aground, the Église Ste-Devote stands today. Her feast day is celebrated on **27 January** with a national holiday. Mass is celebrated in Monégasque, and in the evening there is a procession and symbolic boat-burning in front of the church.

Also held in the last week of **January** is the Monte-Carlo Rally: a three-day event testing the driving skills of competitors as they race along the icy roads outside Monaco. For information, contact the Automobile Club de Monaco (23 boulevard Albert Ier, tel: 377 93 15 26 00; www.acm.mc).

The circus comes to town at the end of **January**/start of **February** each year for the Festival International du Cirque (espace Fontvieille, avenue des Ligures, tel: 377 92 05 23 45; www.montecarlofestivals.com). Circus performers strut their stuff, with the best acts invited to perform again on the closing night.

In **April** you'll find some of the world's top tennis players in Monaco for the ATP masters tennis championship (Country Club de Monte-Carlo, 155 avenue Princesse-Grace, Roquebrune, tel: 04 93 41 30 15; www.mccc.mc).

Monte-Carlo's most famous event takes place in **May**, when the Grand Prix transforms the principality into a race track (Automobile Club de Monaco, 23 boulevard Albert Ier, tel: 377 93 15 26 00; www.acm.mc).

Throughout **August**, an International Fireworks Festival takes place in Monaco.

In and Around Cannes

Getting Your Bearings

There's no denying Cannes is one of the world's most sophisticated resorts – the "Queen of the coast" and "Pearl of the Riviera" – with its grand *belle-époque* hotels, designer boutiques and palm-lined promenade framing a voluptuous sandy bay. Little wonder this elegant town is twinned with Beverly Hills. Best known for the glitz and glamour of its annual International Film Festival, behind its glamorous façade the Old Town, Le Suquet, oozes character, with its maze of medieval buildings and ancient fishing harbour.

Cannes takes centre stage amid several chic, somewhat over-developed resorts and millionaires' yacht-havens, including Antibes and Juan-les-Pins. They provide a stark contrast to the wild, deserted Corniche de l'Esterel, with its ragged shoreline of startlingly red cliffs and craggy inlets, and the tiny, unspoiled Îles de Lérins, with their scenic walks and lovely coves for bathing.

Just inland from this dramatic and varied coastline lies the authentic soul of the region: market towns and ancient honey-coloured villages hidden in a wild, beautiful landscape of lavender fields, vineyards and olive groves, fragrant with the perfumes of Provence and illuminated by a crisp and brilliant light which has drawn artists to the south coast for centuries.

The area has long attracted a rich assortment of artists, actors, chefs, writers and royalty to its shores. As the cradle of Impressionism, it boasts a remarkable legacy of art collections, including those of Musée Picasso, Fondation Maeght and Musée Renoir. It is also a popular area for traditional Provençal crafts – notably hand-blown glass in Biot and perfume-making in Grasse.

VAR

E80 A8

N7

Fréjus

St-Raphaël

Page 105:
A modern sculpture in Cannes represents the town's annual film festival

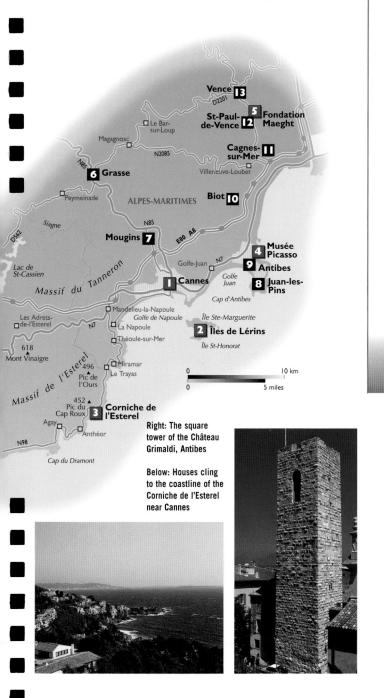

Vence **13**

St-Paul-
de-Vence **12** **5** Fondation
Maeght

Le Bar-
sur-Loup

Magagnosc

N2085

Cagnes-
sur-Mer **11**

N85

6 Grasse

Villeneuve-Loubet

Peymeinade

ALPES-MARITIMES

Biot **10**

Siagne

N85

Mougins **7**

E80 A8

Lac de
St-Cassien

Golfe-Juan

N7

4 Musée
Picasso

9 Antibes

Massif du Tanneron

I Cannes

Golfe
Juan

8 Juan-les-
Pins

Cap d'Antibes

Mandelieu-la-Napoule

Les Adrets-
de-l'Esterel

N7

Golfe de Napoule

La Napoule

Île Ste-Marguerite

2 Îles de Lérins

Théoule-sur-Mer

Île St-Honorat

618
Mont Vinaigre

Massif de l'Esterel

496
Pic de
l'Ours

Miramar

Le Trayas

0 _____ 10 km

0 _____ 5 miles

452
Pic du
Cap Roux

3 Corniche de
l'Esterel

Agay

Anthéor

N98

Cap du Dramont

Right: The square
tower of the Château
Grimaldi, Antibes

Below: Houses cling
to the coastline of the
Corniche de l'Esterel
near Cannes

From star-struck Cannes and dazzling art collections to beautiful country walks, a simple picnic and some island-hopping, this itinerary embraces the region's most varied and impressive sights, and includes a handful of top-notch restaurants for the ultimate Mediterranean gourmet experience.

In and Around Cannes in Two Days

Day One

Morning
Potter round **1 Cannes** (right, ► 110–112). Admire the luxury hotels and private beaches of the Croisette and the Palais des Festivals (venue of the Film Festival) and search out your favourite celebrity's handprint in the paving stones of the allée des Stars. Then explore the old Roman hilltop town to the west, known as Le Suquet (► 111–112), with its castle containing the Musée de la Castre (► 112). There are plenty of tempting bars and cafés for refreshments, too.

Lunch
Enjoy a fish lunch overlooking the Old Port at Au Poisson Grillé (► 129–130), or treat yourself to a lavish picnic from Cannes' Marché de Forville (► 131) to eat on the unspoiled Îles de Lerins. And be sure to visit Ceneri (► 130–131) for your cheeses!

Afternoon
It is a short boat-ride to the **2 Îles de Lérins** (► 113–114) from Cannes harbour. Visit the austere fort on Île Ste-Marguerite (left), where the Man in the Iron Mask was imprisoned, and the monastery-fortress on Île St-Honorat. Both islands offer fantastic walks and bathing opportunities.

Evening

Return to Cannes for a once-in-a-lifetime meal at the exemplary two-Michelin-starred La Palme d'Or (➤ 129).

Day Two

Morning

Visit the modern art collection at **5 Fondation Maeght** (left, ➤ 120), on the outskirts of St-Paul-de-Vence, then explore this delightful hill-top village, with its steep, cobbled alleys, art galleries and chic boutiques.

Lunch

Café de la Place in St-Paul-de-Vence (➤ 130) makes an ideal lunch venue. Enjoy some hearty regional cuisine on the terrace overlooking locals playing pétanque.

Afternoon

Nature lovers should head to the **3 Corniche d'Esterel** (right, ➤ 115–117) to swim in the secret coves and tiny deserted bays, and to walk amid the blood-red porphyry mountains of the Massif de l'Esterel – while art aficionados should visit the **4 Musée Picasso** (➤ 118–119) in the fashionable resort of Antibes. Here the celebrated Spanish artist once had his studio in a seaside fortress. He left his entire output of that period on permanent loan to the castle museum, and today it forms one of the finest collections of his work in the world.

Evening

Head into the *arrière pays* (hinterland) for dinner in one of the villages. **7 Mougins** (➤ 121–122), known as a culinary centre *par excellence*, boasts some of the region's finest restaurants including Alain Llorca's Le Moulin de Mougins (➤ 129) and Le Mas Candille (boulevard Rebuffel, tel: 04 92 28 43 43). For a more affordable option, consider the Auberge du Jarrier (➤ 128–129) in Biot.

❶ Cannes

Classy Cannes brings to mind movies and film stars, expensive boutiques, palatial hotels and paparazzi. After all, it is one of the world's most chic resorts and, within France, second only to Paris for shopping and major international cultural and business events. This is largely thanks to the world-famous Cannes International Film Festival, which is held here every May, turning the town into Hollywood-on-Sea.

With so much glitz and glamour, it is easy to forget Cannes' humble origins as a simple fishing village, named after the canes and reeds of the surrounding marshes – since transformed into luxury yacht havens. Cannes was first put on the map in 1834 by retired British Chancellor Lord Brougham, who was forced to stop in Cannes en route to Nice because of an outbreak of cholera. Enchanted by its warm climate and quaint setting, he abandoned his former plans, built a villa here and stayed for 34 winters, singing the praises of Cannes to his most distinguished compatriots. Soon gentry and royalty followed his example by the hundreds. Grand hotels began to spring up along the waterfront and by the end of the century Cannes had become the "aristocracy's winter lounge".

In the 1920s, a popular rhyme claimed "Menton's dowdy, Monte's brass, Nice is rowdy, Cannes is class", but it was not until the 1930s that Cannes became a summer resort, made fashionable by visiting Americans, including Harpo Marx and Scott and Zelda Fitzgerald, who used to frequent the gaming tables of Casino Croisette. By the 1950s, mass summer

Allée des Stars, in front of the Palais des Festivals

tourism had taken off, and it has been the life-blood of Cannes ever since.

While Cannes lacks the great museums, galleries and monuments of other large resorts or towns, there is always plenty to do, with its casinos, fairs, sandy beaches, boat trips to the Îles de Lérins (► 113–114) and shopping. Luxury boutiques flank the waterfront and the **rue d'Antibes**.

Boulevard de la Croisette

Modern Cannes is built round the fabulous boulevard de la Croisette, which competes with the promenade des Anglais in Nice (► 44–45) as the region's most elegant seaside promenade. Like the promenade des Anglais, La Croisette is lined with palms and grand *belle-époque* hotels on one side, and with a sparkling bay on the other. The hotels at the eastern end of the promenade are attractions in their own right. The famous twin cupolas of the **Hôtel Carlton**, opened in 1912, were modelled on the prized assets of the courtesan and femme fatale La Belle Otero, who was associated with such powerful men as the British King Edward VII and Russian tsars Peter and Nicholas. Otero was reputedly such a heart-breaker that six men committed suicide after their affairs with her ended.

Other glamorous hotels along La Croisette include the **Majestic**, the **Noga-Hilton** and the white art deco master-piece, the **Martinez** (► 126–127). The main hotels have their own beaches, each with bars, restaurants and immaculate rows of coloured parasols and plush mattresses. The private beaches aren't always reserved exclusively for hotel guests, but if you're tempted to sit on a deckchair, keep in mind you'll be charged about €35 for the pleasure. There's a public beach at the western end of La Croisette, and also along Cannes' other seafront boulevard, **du Midi**. La Croisette has been a focus for the paparazzi since Brigitte Bardot graced the beaches here in 1953, and those same beaches are packed in summer with sunbathers making the most of the soft sand.

The famous film festival is centred around the unsightly **Palais des Festivals**, on the waterfront at the western end of the boulevard de la Croisette, near the flower market. Along the **allée des Stars**, in front of the Palais des Festivals, you can see where film stars have had their handprints immortalized in the paving stones. Today the most likely places to spot celebrities at festival time are the Hôtel Carlton or Hôtel Martinez.

Le Suquet

The boulevard de la Croisette comes to an end at the Palais des Festivals, where the Old Town begins. Originally the Roman hilltop town of Canois Castrum, this area, situated on a small hill to the west of modern Cannes, is today known as **Le Suquet**. This was Cannes' original fishing village and, appropriately, shares its name with the Provençal word for a kind of fish soup. Unlike much of Cannes, Le Suquet has managed to preserve

Visitors flock to Cannes' sandy beaches in summer

the air of warmth and intimacy of bygone days. Its lively lanes of fishermen's cottages have been transformed into cosy restaurants, and the district is crowned by an imposing **castle** and watch tower affording sweeping coastal views.

Cannes' castle was constructed by the monks of Lérins in the 11th and 12th centuries, together with a small chapel, and today houses the **Musée de la Castre**, containing archaeological and ethnographical collections from all over the world. The austere church in the centre of the Old Town, **Notre-Dame d'Espérance**, was built in 1648 when the chapel became too small.

The Old Town (Le Suquet) and harbour

At the foot of the hill, in the Vieux Port (Old Port), bobbing fishing craft are juxtaposed with millionaires' yachts. Stroll along the spacious waterside esplanade, **La Pantiéro**, or head over to the tree-shaded **square Lord Brougham**, where you'll often see the locals playing a game of pétanque. The **allée de la Liberté**, shaded by palm trees, has a vibrant morning flower market. From here, narrow shopping streets lead down to the daily covered market, **Marché Forville**, where you'll find mouthwatering displays of regional produce.

TAKING A BREAK

La Piazza, close to the port, serves good Italian food (► 129).

✛ 180 B2
Cannes Tourist Offices
✉ Palais des Festivals et des Congrès, 1 boulevard de la Croisette
☎ 04 92 99 84 22; www.cannes.com
🕐 Daily 9–8, Jul–Aug; 9–7 Sep–Jun

✉ Gare SNCF, rue Jean-Jaurès
☎ 04 93 99 19 77 🕐 Mon–Sat 9–7

CANNES: INSIDE INFO

Top tips Book a long way ahead for any kind of **accommodation** in Cannes at any time of year.
• During the **film festival** in May, hotel prices skyrocket and the town is packed. Unless you want to star-gaze, this is not the best time to come.

2 Îles de Lérins

The charming Lérins islands, a short ferry ride from Cannes, are a perfect refuge from the crowded Riviera resorts, where you can enjoy a quiet stroll along the shore, a picnic and a swim in the unspoiled coves and bays.

The tiny, car-free Îles de Lérins lie just 20 minutes by ferry from Cannes. They are named after two saints – St Honorat, who founded a monastery on the smaller of the two islands at the end of the fourth century, and his sister St Marguerite, who set up a nunnery on the other island – and were once the most powerful ecclesiastical centres in the south of France.

The fort on Île Ste-Marguerite, where the Man in the Iron Mask was imprisoned

Ferries frequently run to **Île Ste-Marguerite**, the largest of the islands. There are peaceful paths and picnic areas under pine trees, coves and bays in which to swim, and simple fish restaurants by the quay. The island's main attraction is the **Fort Royal**, which contains the **Musée de la Mer** (Maritime Museum), made up of old prison cells. The fort was used as a prison from 1685 until the early 20th century, its most illustrious occupant being the shadowy Man in the Iron Mask. You can see the stark cell in which he was incarcerated from 1687 to 1698, as well as murals painted by the imprisoned artist Jean Le Gac. The first floor holds Ligurian, Greek and Roman artefacts excavated on the island, alongside objects recovered from ships sunk off its shores.

The smaller, farther **Île St-Honorat** is owned by Cistercian monks who arrived here in the fifth century, building the

Ancienne Monastère Fortifiée, which dominates the island's south. The ruins of this abbey are open to visitors daily. The monks have since built a new home for themselves, and today an active group of 25 Cistercians maintain a simple and austere life in the 19th-century Abbaye Notre Dame de Lérins. The monks produce wine, lavender, oranges, honey and a sweet liqueur, made from aromatic Provençal plants that can be purchased in the souvenir shop.

Both islands offer pleasant **walking trails**. One of the most enjoyable is a shaded route round Île St-Honorat, past the **seven chapels** scattered across the island, of which **Chapelle de la Trinité** and **Chapelle Ste-Croix** are particularly interesting.

TAKING A BREAK

There are several **cafés and restaurants** on Ste-Marguerite at the port where the ferry arrives. There are also designated **picnic areas** on the island.

✚ 180 B2
Tourist Office
✉ Palais des Festivals et des Congrès, 1 boulevard de la Croisette, Cannes ☎ 04 92 99 84 22; www.cannes.com 🕐 Daily 9–8, Jul–Aug; 9–7 Sep–Jun

Île Ste-Marguerite
Musée de la Mer
✉ Fort de l'Île Ste-Marguerite ☎ 04 93 43 18 17 💰 Inexpensive, free on 1st Sun of month
🕐 Closed Mon

Île St-Honorat
Abbaye Notre Dame de Lérins
☎ 04 92 99 54 00; www.abbayedelerins.com 🕐 Church open all year

Ancienne Monastère Fortifiée
🕐 Daily 10:30–4. Guided visits Mon–Fri 10:30–12:30, 2:30–4:45, Sun 2:30–4:45, Jul to mid-Sep
💰 Guided tour: inexpensive; mid-Sep to Jun entry free

Chapelle de la Trinité
🕐 Guided visits Mon–Fri 10:30–12:30, 2:30–4:45, Sun 2:30–4:45, Jul–Sep 💰 Free

ÎLES DE LÉRINS: INSIDE INFO

Top tips Mass is said at the Abbaye Notre Dame de Lérins, Île St-Honorat, on weekdays at 11:25 am, and on Sundays at 9:50 am.
• It is **forbidden to ride bicycles** on the islands. Dogs are welcome but must be kept on a leash.

Getting there
Île Ste-Marguerite: Compagnie Maritime departs from quai Laubeuf, Cannes (tel: 04 92 98 70 30; www.trans-cote-azur.com, Apr–Oct on the hour 9–12, 2–4; Nov–Mar on the hour 10–12, 2–3, expensive). Journey takes 15 minutes. Service also departs for Ste-Marguerite from quai Lunel, Port de Nice (tel: 04 92 00 42 30).
Île St-Honorat: Société Planaria departs from quai des Îles (next to quai Laubeuf), Cannes (tel: 04 92 98 71 38, May–Sep on the hour 8–12, 2–3, and 4:30, 5:30 pm; Oct–Apr on the hour 8–12, 2–3, and 4:30 pm, expensive). Journey takes 20 minutes.

3 Corniche de l'Esterel

Edging a wild massif of blood-red porphyry mountains, the picturesque Esterel coast road from St-Raphaël to Théoule-sur-Mer passes some of the Riviera's most spectacular scenery.

The Corniche de l'Esterel, also known as the Corniche d'Or (Golden Coast Road) or N98, was carved into the impressive seafront cliffs over a century ago. The Touring Club de France was involved in its development, and the route is perennially popular with cyclists. Just as dramatic by car, bus or train, the tortuous road offers stunning views of wild red mountains and a sparkling blue sea, and is punctuated by viewpoints overlooking inviting beaches, sheltered yacht harbours, jagged inlets and deserted coves. The Massif de l'Esterel provides a perfect backdrop, with its harsh, rugged mountains of brilliant red volcanic rock jutting out into the sea.

The red rocks of the Pic du Cap Roux provide spectacular scenery along the corniche

The wild, rocky coastline of the Corniche de l'Esterel

Travelling from east to west, start at **Théoule-sur-Mer**, a small seaside resort at the rim of the Parc Forestier de la Pointe de l'Aiguille, an extensive coastal park offering a variety of scenic walking trails. There are plenty of hiking possibilities into the Massif de l'Esterel from the coast road. A quick climb along the Pointe de l'Esquillon at **Miramar** is rewarded by spectacular views of Cap Roux farther along the coast.

Le Trayas is at the highest point of the corniche. Just beyond, a strenuous inland trail climbs the Pic du Cap Roux. The road continues to twist and turn westwards via **Anthéor**, **Agay** and **Le Dramont** to **St-Raphaël**, the Esterel's main resort, beautifully situated around a deep horseshoe bay that is considered one of the best anchorages on this stretch of coast. Napoléon put St-Raphaël on the map when he landed here on his return from Egypt in 1799. It developed into a fashionable seaside resort in the 19th century. Sadly, many of the *belle-époque* hotels were destroyed during World War II, but it still remains popular with families, mainly because of its large sandy beach.

To avoid the crowds in summer when the Corniche de l'Esterel can be packed, take the N7 from **Fréjus** to **Cannes**, which follows the path of the Roman Via Aurelia through extensive cork forests past Mont Vinaigre (614m/2,015 feet), the highest peak in the Esterel. A short path leads to its summit, from where there is an overview of the wilderness that for centuries was a popular haunt of brigands and a refuge for hermits and escaped galley slaves from Toulon.

TAKING A BREAK
Kick off (or finish) your trip along the coast at **Le Marco Polo** (▶ 130), right on the beach at Théoule-sur-Mer.

🔶 180 A1
Tourist Offices
Théoule-sur-Mer
✉ 1 Corniche d'Or ☎ 04 93 49 28 28; www.theoule-sur-mer.org

St-Raphaël
✉ Place de la Gare ☎ 04 94 19 52 52; www.saint-raphael.com

CORNICHE DE L'ESTEREL: INSIDE INFO

Top tip There are various places along the Corniche de l'Esterel to pull over and enjoy the view. Look out for **Calanque de Petit Caneret**, where there is a wonderful view of the rocky red pinnacles.

Getting there Local **trains** run hourly from Cannes to St-Raphaël, stopping at Agay and Théoule-sur-Mer. Check timetables for details.
• The **Rafaël bus** (tel: 04 94 83 87 63) No 8 runs hourly from St-Raphaël to Le Trayas, with eight services a day meeting a connecting bus from Le Trayas to Cannes. See the Cannes or St-Raphaël tourist office for more details.

4 Musée Picasso

The striking fortress of Château Grimaldi in Antibes, used by Picasso as a studio in 1946, today houses one of the world's finest collections of his works.

The Grimaldi family ruled for centuries from this beautiful 13th- to 16th-century castle, constructed following the design of an ancient Roman fort. In 1928, the city of Antibes bought the castle to house its Museum of Art, History and Archaeology. When Pablo Picasso (1881–1973) returned to his beloved Mediterranean in 1946, after spending the war years in Paris, he had nowhere suitable to work, so the Mayor of Antibes lent him a room in Château Grimaldi.

The collection includes ceramics, paintings and other works by Picasso, covering a wide range of themes and periods, but focuses on the works he created here in 1946. Much of the artist's work from this period reflects his joyous post-war mood. His work here took on a new dimension, reflecting the *joie de vivre* of the Mediterranean, bathed in sunny colours and incandescent light. A combination of his bold

Musée Picasso, housed in the Château Grimaldi, Antibes

new techniques and the mythological themes that had begun to fascinate him led Picasso to create such masterpieces as *Ulysée et les Sirènes* (1947), *Nu Couché au Lit Bleu* (1946) and his famous *La Joie de Vivre* (1946).

Although Picasso spent only three months working here, it was one of his most prolific phases. In gratitude, he donated the complete works of this period to the castle museum, together with a lively collection of tapestries, sculptures and more than 150 ceramics designed at nearby Vallauris.

La Joie de Vivre
(1946)

In addition to Picasso's works, there are also black-and-white photographic portraits of the artist and a collection of works by other artists representative of main trends of the 20th century. Stone and bronze sculptures by Germaine Richier, Miró and Pagès are displayed outdoors among cacti and flowers, with wonderful views of the sparkling sea.

TAKING A BREAK

Nearby are **cafés** around the port and a **food market** at cours Massena (➤ 131). On Cap d'Antibes is **Le Bacon** (➤ 128).

➕ 180 C2
Musée Picasso Antibes
✉ Château Grimaldi, place Mariéjol ☎ 04 92 90 54 20; www.antibes-juanlespins.com 🕐 Building closed for restoration work, due to re-open late 2007. Contact tourist office for information 💷 Moderate, under 18 free

Tourist Information
✉ 11 place de Gaulle, Antibes ☎ 04 92 90 53 00; www.antibes-juanlespins.com 🕐 Daily 9–7, Jul–Aug; Mon–Fri 9–12, 1:30–5:30, Sat 9–12, 2–6, Sep–Jun

---

MUSÉE PICASSO: INSIDE INFO

Top tip If you are staying in Antibes for a few days, a combined ticket covers entrance to the **Musée Picasso**, as well as the other museums in town: the **Archaeological Museum** in the 17th-century Bastion St- André; the **Peynet Museum**, housing the work of Raymond Peynet and also holding exhibitions of humorous cartoons and illustrations; the **Napoleonic Museum**; **Tower Museum**; and **Fort Carré**. It's valid for seven consecutive days and costs €10. Ask about it at the tourist office, or in the museums.

5 Fondation Maeght

Hidden in a woodland above St-Paul-de-Vence, this is one of the most important collections of modern art in Europe.

The Maeght Foundation was established by Marguerite and Aimé Maeght, successful art dealers and close friends of many artists, including Matisse, Miró, Braque, Bonnard and Chagall. Their private collection formed the basis of the museum. Intended to function as a living creative space, the foundation provided accommodation for artists and aimed to be the ideal environment in which to display contemporary art.

The building blends artfully into the wooded surroundings. It respects the curves of the landscape and is full of natural light.

The permanent collection contains works by nearly every major artist of the past 50 years, focusing on Bonnard, Chagall, Giacometti, Léger, Kandinsky and Miró. Behind the museum, Miró's **Labyrinthe** is a multi-level maze of mosaics, sculptures, fountains, trees and ceramics by the Spanish surrealist. Also in the grounds are **cour Giacometti**, a courtyard peopled with Giacometti figures; and a tiny, sombre **chapel** housing Braque's stained-glass window, *White Bird on a Mauve Background* (1962), created in memory of the Maeghts' son who died in childhood.

Fondation Maeght, St-Paul-de-Vence

TAKING A BREAK

There is a **café** at the foundation (open April to November) and several others in St-Paul-de-Vence (➤ 130).

Fondation Maeght
✚ 180 C3 ✉ Route de Pass-Prest, St-Paul-de-Vence ☎ 04 93 32 81 63; www.fondation-maeght.com ⏱ Daily 10–7, Jul–Sep; 10–12:30, 2:30–6, Oct–Jun
💶 Expensive, under 10 free

At Your Leisure

6 Grasse

Lavender fields are one of the most memorable sights of Provence, and the flowers they produce are a key ingredient in the modern perfume industry. **Molinard**, **Galimard** and **Fragonard** are the great perfumeries located in Grasse, the perfume capital of the world, which supplies perfumes to all the biggest names, including Chanel and Dior. All three offer factory tours. Roses and jasmine, flowers essential to the industry, are celebrated with their own **festivals** in May and August.

The **cathedral**, on place

The bell tower of the Cathédrale Notre-Dame-du-Puy towers over the red rooftops of Grasse's Old Town

Godeau, is worth a quick look inside for the three early paintings by Rubens, dating from 1601.

➕ 180 A3
Tourist Office
✉ Palais des Congrès, 22 cours Honoré Cresp ☎ 04 93 36 66 66; www.grasse-riviera.com 🕐 Mon–Sat 9–7, Sun 9–1, 2–6, Jul–Sep; Mon–Sat 9–12:30, 2–6, Oct–Jun

7 Mougins

Outwardly, Mougins seems a typical Provençal hilltop village, but inside its medieval ramparts you will find one of the Côte d'Azur's smartest villages, whose past residents have included Jacques Brel, Yves St Laurent, Catherine Deneuve and Picasso – who spent the last 12 years of his life here. Numerous celluloid portraits of him can be seen in the **Musée de la Photographie**.

Mougin's main attraction, however, is the sheer number of renowned restaurants. People come from all around to dine at **La Ferme**

de Mougins, **Le Mas Candille** or, for
a real treat, **Le Moulin de Mougins**
(► 129–130), which is considered to
be one of the world's most prestigious gourmet temples.

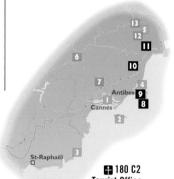

➕ 180 B2
Tourist Office
✉ 15 avenue Charles Mallet
☎ 04 93 75 87 67

Musée de la Photographie
✉ Porte Sarrazine
☎ 04 93 75 85 67 🕔 Daily 10–8,
Jul–Aug; Mon–Fri 10–6, Sat–Sun 11–6,
rest of year. Closed Nov 💰 Inexpensive

🎱 Juan-les-Pins

Juan-les-Pins and Antibes merge
together at the head of the Cap
d'Antibes peninsula. Known for the
annual **jazz festival** held here every
July since the 1960s, the resort has
a lively nightlife throughout the
year, attracting a young crowd to its
sandy shores.

Queen Victoria's son, the Duke of
Albany, established a resort here in
the 1880s, but it remained obscure
until the 1920s, when Nice restaura-
teur Monsieur Baudoin went into
partnership with American railway
tycoon Frank Jay Gould to launch
the Riviera's first summer resort, at a
time when holidaying in summer
was something of a novelty. Success
followed, helped by the scandal of
being the first beach where women
wore modern-style swimsuits, and
Juan developed a racy, hedonistic air.
The town gained its named from a
large pine forest that once stood
behind the coast.

➕ 180 C2
Tourist Office
✉ 51 boulevard
Guillaumont ☎ 04 92 90 53
05; www.antibes-juanlespins.com
🕔 Mon–Fri 9–12, 2–6, Sat 9–12,
Jul–Aug; Mon–Fri 9–12:30, 1:30–6,
Sep–Jun

🎱 Antibes

Antibes is the biggest city in the area,
but is less showy than either Nice or
neighbouring Cannes. Nonetheless,
it still manages to attract its share of
luxury yachts. The most appealing
parts of the town are in the old quarter, where Italianate buildings are
crowded into the remains of a 17th-
century defensive wall designed by
the great military engineer Vauban.

Antibes' main attraction is the
Musée Picasso (► 118–119), where
artworks, mostly dating from the
time Picasso spent here in 1946, are
housed in a fortress that was once
owned by the Grimaldis of Monaco.

Catching the sun, Antibes

Locally made goods, Biot

➕ 180 C2
Tourist Office
✉ 11 place de Gaulle
☎ 04 92 90 53 00 🕐 Daily 9–7,
Jul–Aug; Mon–Fri 9–12:30, 1:30–6,
Sat 9–noon, 2–6, Sep–Jun

🔟 Biot

This pretty hilltop village is set in a
typical Provençal landscape of
cypresses, olives and pines. It
encompasses a mass of steep,
cobbled lanes fanning out from the
arcaded main square, which is lined
by quaint sand-coloured houses and
dotted with cafés and antiques shops.

Some of the streets are decorated
with huge earthenware jars, ablaze
with geraniums and tropical plants;
for centuries, Biot has been a prosperous pottery centre. It is also
known for its gold and silverwork,
ceramics, olive-wood carvings and
thriving glassworks. The craftsmen's
wares can be admired in the **Musée
d'Histoire Locale et de Céramique
Biotoise**. At the **Verrerie de Biot**
(➤ 131) visitors can watch glass-
blowers demonstrating the manufacture of their unique *verre bullé*
(bubble glass).

Twenty minutes' stroll from the
village is the **Musée national
Fernand Léger**, with a brilliantly
coloured mosaic façade and huge
stained-glass windows. The cubist
painter Léger bought a villa here in
1955, intending to make Biot his
home, but sadly died 15 days later.
His widow founded the museum in
1959. It contains nearly 400 of his
works, and was the first major
museum in France to be dedicated
entirely to one artist.

➕ 180 B3
Tourist Office
✉ 46 rue St Sébastien
☎ 04 93 65 78 00

**Musée d'Histoire Locale et de
Céramique Biotoise**
✉ Place de la Chapelle ☎ 04 93 65
54 54 🕐 Wed–Sun 10–6 (summer),
2–6 (winter) 💷 Inexpensive

Musée national Fernand Léger
✉ Chemin du Val de Pôme
☎ 04 92 91 50 30;
www.musee-fernandleger.fr
🕐 Wed–Mon 10:30–6, Jul–Sep;
Wed–Mon 10–12:30, 2–5:30, Oct–Jun
💷 Inexpensive, free under 18; free
first Sun of month

🔢 Cagnes-sur-Mer

Cagnes is divided into three: the
main beach area and old fishing
quarter of **Cros-de-Cagnes**, with its
traditional boats called *pointus* and a
glut of excellent fish restaurants;
Cagnes-Ville, a busy commercial
centre with a smart racecourse
(France's second largest) right beside
the sea; and **Haut-de-Cagnes**. This

inviting hilltop village, with its brightly coloured houses smothered in bougainvillaea, mimosa and geraniums, is encircled by medieval ramparts and crowned by a 14th-century castle, built as a pirate lookout by Admiral Rainier Grimaldi. The castle contains the **Château-Musée**, which houses several permanent exhibitions, including the Olive Tree Museum and the Museum of Modern Mediterranean Art, with works by Chagall, Matisse and Pierre Auguste Renoir (1841–1919), Cagnes' most famous artist.

Renoir spent his last 12 years just outside Cagnes at Domaine des Collettes, as arthritis forced him to leave Paris for a warmer climate. His villa is now the **Musée Renoir**, where his palette and wheelchair have been preserved, along with several of his paintings, drawings, sculptures and bronzes.

A narrow lane in St-Paul-de-Vence

✚ 180 C3
Tourist Office
✉ 6 boulevard Maréchal Juin
☎ 04 93 20 61 64

Château-Musée de Cagnes
✉ Place Grimaldi, Haut-de-Cagnes
☎ 04 92 02 47 30 ⏰ Wed–Mon 10–12,
2–5 (May–Sep to 6 pm) 💶 Moderate

Musée Renoir
✉ 19 chemin des Collettes
☎ 04 93 20 61 07 ⏰ Wed–Mon 10–12,
2–6, May–Sep; 10–12, 2–5, Oct,
Dec–Apr. Closed Tue and Nov
💶 Moderate

🔢 St-Paul-de-Vence

This large picture-postcard hilltop village, draped gently over a hill close to Cagnes, was appointed a "Royal Town" by King François in the 16th century, and the wealth of the village is still apparent.

In the 1920s, St-Paul-de-Vence was discovered by a group of young, impoverished artists – Signac, Bonnard, Modigliani and Soutine – who stayed at the modest Auberge de la Colombe d'Or, paying for their lodgings with their paintings. Word of the *auberge* spread and soon other artists and young intellectuals arrived. Today the exclusive **Hôtel La Colombe d'Or** boasts an impressive past guest list including Braque, Camus, Derain, Maeterlinck, Matisse, Kipling, Picasso and Utrillo and, as a result, one of the finest private collections of modern art in France.

The village is still an artists' colony, although perhaps better described as a tourist honeypot, with coach-loads flocking to the **Fondation Maeght** (➤ 120) and to the smart shops and galleries which line its steep, cobbled streets. Despite the crowds, it remains one of Provence's most exquisite villages, especially at night when the narrow alleys are lit with tiny lanterns.

180 C3
Tourist Office
✉ 2 rue Grande ☎ 04 93 32 86 95;
www.saint-pauldevence.com

13 Vence

Once the Roman forum of Vintium, this delightful village became a bishopric in the Middle Ages. Its tenth-century **cathedral** is the smallest in France, and has an interior rich in treasures, with Roman tombstones embedded in the walls and a remarkable Chagall mosaic.
Artists and writers – including Gide, Valéry, Dufy and D H Lawrence – have long been attracted to the town, just 10km (6 miles) from the crowded coast. In 1941, Henri Matisse moved here, but soon fell seriously ill. Dominican sisters nursed him back to health, and in gratitude he built and decorated the beautiful **Chapelle du Rosaire** for them. The interior is compelling in its simplicity, with powerful black line-drawings of the Stations of the Cross on white *faïence*, coloured only by pools of yellow, blue and green light from the enormous stained-glass windows. Matisse worked on this masterpiece well into his 80s, considering it his "ultimate goal, the culmination of an intense, sincere and difficult endeavour".

If you're passing through Vence by car, there's free parking near the swimming pool (*piscine*).

180 B3
Tourist Office
✉ Place du Grand-Jardin
☎ 04 93 58 06 38; www.ville-vence.fr
🕐 Mon–Sat 9–6; also Sun 10–6, Jul–Aug

Chapelle du Rosaire
✉ Avenue Henri Matisse
☎ 04 93 58 03 26 🕐 Mon, Wed, Sat 2–5:30; Tue, Thu 10–11:30, 2–5:30; Sun service at 10, Fri 2–5:30 school hols only. Closed mid-Nov to late Dec
💰 Inexpensive

For Kids

- **Mougins:** At Buggy Cross, three tracks offer racing on quad bikes, karts or mini-motorcycles, and there are even vehicles for over-4s (by the Automobile Museum, tel: 04 93 69 02 74, open Wed and Sat–Sun).
- **Mougins Musée de l'Automobile:** Older children in particular enjoy visiting the unique, radiator-shaped car museum and viewing footage of classic races (772 chemin de Font-de-Currault, just off the A8, exit Les Hautes Bréguires, tel: 04 93 69 27 80, open daily 10–6).
- **Antibes:** Antibes Land is an amusement park with a big wheel, roller-coaster and even bungee-jumping (N7, tel: 04 93 33 68 03; www.azurpark.com, open Apr–Oct daily).
- **Marineland:** Performing sea lions, killer whales, dolphins and close underwater encounters with sharks (safely, from within a transparent tunnel). Children love the Jungle des Papillons with exotic butterflies, huge hairy spiders and other creepy-crawlies. Younger children enjoy the pony rides, face-painting and stroking the animals at La Petite Ferme Provençale. Water slides and crazy golf are also on site (N7, tel: 04 93 33 82 72, open Feb–Dec daily 10–6, Wed and Sat–Sun until 8, Jul–Aug 10 am–midnight).

Where to... Stay

Prices
Expect to pay per double room, per night
€ under €80   €€ €80–€150   €€€ over €150

ANTIBES

Auberge Provençale €
A traditional-style hotel with friendly service and five comfortable bedrooms, overlooking the main square of the Old Town.
⊞ 180 C2 ⊠ 61 place Nationale
☎ 04 93 34 13 24;
www.aubergeprovencale.com

Hotel du Cap Eden Roc €€€
This swanky and incredibly expensive hotel (a room here will set you back anywhere from €400 to €1,000) on the Cap Antibes is the height of luxury, generally patronised by celebrities and their entourages. Non-guests can use the bar and, for a fee, ride the cable car from the hotel to the private beach.
⊞ 180 C2 ⊠ Boulevard Kennedy
☎ 04 93 61 39 01;
www.edenroc-hotel.fr

Le Relais du Postillon €
This comfortable old hotel in the heart of Old Antibes has 16 peaceful rooms, and is within walking distance of the Musée Picasso. The restaurant serves gourmet meals. Sit out on the garden patio in summer, or by the cosy fireplace in winter. A public car park is situated near by.
⊞ 180 C2 ⊠ 8 rue Championnet
☎ 04 93 34 20 77;
www.relaisdupostillon.com

BIOT

Galerie des Arcades €–€€
A 15th-century hotel in a splendid arcaded square, with a restaurant covered in artworks and specialising in local Provençal cuisine.
⊞ 180 B3 ⊠ 14 place des Arcades
☎ 04 93 65 01 04

CANNES

Carlton Intercontinental Hotel €€€
Legendary hotel with 338 rooms, including 36 über-luxurious suites. Stay in the Sean Connery suite for the kind of class and luxury befitting the likes of James Bond. The Carlton has everything from restaurants and bars to fitness centres and ballrooms, and is surrounded by some of Cannes' most upmarket boutiques.
⊞ 180 B2 ⊠ 58 La Croisette
☎ 04 93 06 40 06;
www.cannes.intercontinental.com

Chalet de l'Isère €
Just a ten-minute walk from the Palais des Festivals, this two-star hotel is good value. Bedrooms are simple, clean and comfortable. Breakfast can be served in the pretty garden.
⊞ 180 B2 ⊠ 42 avenue de Grasse
☎ 04 93 38 50 80;
http://hotelchaletisere.monsite.wanadoo.fr

Hôtel l'Esterel €
This modern hotel is just across from the train station. The simple rooms lacks character, but are affordable, comfortable and clean, and there are wonderful views over Cannes from the breakfast room on the top floor.
⊞ 180 B2 ⊠ 15 rue du 24 Août
☎ 04 93 38 82 82;
www.hotellesterel.com

Martinez €€€
The deluxe Martinez contains Cannes' top restaurant, La Palme

d'Or (▶ 129), and is an excellent place for star-spotting during the film festival. Features include a stylish art deco interior, luxurious Givenchy spa and a private beach.

☐ 180 B2 ⊠ 73 La Croisette
☎ 04 92 98 73 00;
www.hotel-martinez.com

Hôtel Molière €€

A centrally located hotel with a grand façade, immaculately kept gardens, and comfortable rooms decorated in Provençal colours, most with balconies. It's close to boulevard de la Croissette and the beaches. Book well in advance, especially if you're planning to be here at festival time.

☐ 180 B2 ⊠ 5–7 rue Molière ☎ 04 93 38 16 16; www.hotel-moliere.com

Villa de l'Olivier €€–€€€

A family-run hotel in Cannes' ancient Le Suquet district, near the beach and Vieux Port, with 24 rooms, swimming pool and garden with views overlooking Cannes.

☐ 180 B2 ⊠ 5 rue des Tambourinaires ☎ 04 93 39 53 28; www.hoteloliver.com

Bastide St-Antoine €€€

This luxurious Relais et Châteaux hotel, set in the grounds of an olive grove, is a truly special place to stay. It has 11 spacious rooms, and a well-renowned restaurant where the creations by chef Jacques Chibois are sublime.

☐ 180 A3 ⊠ 48 avenue Henri-Dunant ☎ 04 93 70 94 94; www.jacques-chibois.com

Hôtel des Parfums €€

Facilities include a swimming pool and Jacuzzi. The hotel has a special 90-minute film, "Introduction to Perfume", which guests are invited to watch prior to visiting the perfume factories.

☐ 180 A3 ⊠ Boulevard Eugène-Charabot ☎ 04 92 42 35 35; www.hoteldesparfums.com

Le Manoir de l'Étang €€€

An intimate, 19th-century manor house, set in 5ha (12 acres) of parkland, with pool and solarium, a classy restaurant and five golf courses near by. Dine on the restaurant's quality local cuisine by the pool in summer.

☐ 180 B2 ⊠ 66 allée du Manoir, route d'Antibes ☎ 04 92 28 36 00; www.manoir-de-letang.com
🕒 Closed Nov to mid-Mar

Les Muscadins €€€

Pablo Picasso once stayed at this former guesthouse, now a four-star boutique hotel owned by Hôtel Le Mas Candille. Les Muscadins has the look of a quaint old Provençal house, but is far from rustic inside. Guests have access to all the facilities of the five-star luxury spa hotel, Le Mas Candille.

☐ 180 B2 ⊠ 18 boulevard Courteline ☎ 04 92 28 43 43; www.hotel-mougins-muscadins.com

La Colombe d'Or €€€

Once a modest 1920s café where Braque, Matisse, Picasso and Léger used to pay for their drinks with canvases. Now a deluxe hotel. Book in advance.

☐ 180 C3 ⊠ Place du Général de Gaulle ☎ 04 93 32 80 02;
www.la-colombe-dor.com
🕒 Closed Nov–24 Dec

La Grande Bastide €€–€€€

An 18th-century country house with ten charming Provençal-style rooms and views of St-Paul. Excellent value. No restaurant.

☐ 180 C3 ⊠ Route de la Colle ☎ 04 93 32 50 30;
www.la-grande-bastide.com

Hostellerie Les Remparts €

The most affordable accommodation in the village. Nine charming rooms and a restaurant on site.

☐ 180 C3 ⊠ 72 rue Grande ☎ 04 93 32 09 88

Where to...
Eat and Drink

Prices

Expect to pay for a three-course meal for one, excluding drinks and service

€ under €25   €€ €25–€60   €€€ over €60

ANTIBES

Le Bacon €€€

There's no bacon on the menu here; this is one of the coast's best fish restaurants with exceptional views over old Antibes and an unforgettable bouillabaisse: a fish soup that originated in Provence, made with fish cooked in a rich stock and served with croûtons smeared with *rouille* (garlicky mayonnaise).

180 C2 ⊠ Boulevard Bacon, Cap d'Antibes ☎ 04 93 61 50 02; www.restaurantdebacon.com
🕐 Closed Mon, Tue lunch (except Jul–Aug) and Nov–Jan

Le Brûlot €

An unpretentious and cosy Provençal restaurant with a rustic interior and an antique wood oven, of which it makes good use. Traditional cuisine such as *socca*, grilled steak in Provençal herbs and scampi flambéed with pastis.

180 C2 ⊠ 3 rue Frédéric Isnard ☎ 04 93 34 17 76; www.brulot.com
🕐 Mon–Sat; closed Aug

BIOT

Auberge du Jarrier €€

This friendly restaurant in an old jar factory serves imaginative local

---

Le St-Paul €€€

This romantic old Relais et Châteaux hotel offers four-star accommodation at the heart of the village, and has spectacular views over the valley or the village.

180 C3 ⊠ 86 rue Grande ☎ 04 93 32 65 25; www.lesaintpaul.com

ST-RAPHAËL

Le Jardin des Arènes €

A quirky little hotel with stained-glass windows in the stairway, a lovely garden and clean, comfortable rooms. It is centrally located and offers the best value in town.

179 F4 ⊠ 31 avenue du Général Leclerc ☎ 04 94 95 06 34
🕐 Closed Jan

LE TRAYAS

Le Trayas Hostel €

A youth hostel in a 1930s villa with dormitory rooms for four or eight people and fantastic panoramic views of the sea and coastline. It's a

---

2km (1.3-mile) uphill walk from La Trayas station or the "Auberge" bus stop. An additional fee is charged for non-members of Hostelling International or the French hostelling association FUAJ.

180 A2 ⊠ 9 avenue de la Veronese ☎ 04 93 75 40 23; www.fuaj.org 🕐 Apr–Sep

VENCE

Château St-Martin €€€

Attractive villas built around a ruined Templar fortress with a swimming pool and sporting facilities for riding, fishing and tennis.

180 B3 ⊠ Avenue des Templiers ☎ 04 93 58 02 02; www.chateau-st-martin.com 🕐 Mid-Mar to mid-Oct

Le Relais Cantemerle €€–€€€

A tranquil oasis in the heart of the Vençoise hills, with duplex rooms, a pool and an excellent restaurant.

180 B3 ⊠ 258 Chemin Cantemerle ☎ 04 93 58 08 18; www.relais-cantemerle.com

cuisine, and has a terrace on which to enjoy a Provencal feast.

180 B3 ⊠ 30 passage de la Bourgade ☎ 04 93 65 11 68 Closed Tue–Wed

CANNES

Caffe Roma €
A lively Italian bar-restaurant across from the Palais des Festivals serving specialities such as ravioli stuffed with cheese and spinach, and veal with lemon sauce and pine nuts. Leave room for their home-made tiramisu. Eat in the dining room, or outside on the sunny terrace.

180 B2 ⊠ 1 square Mérimée ☎ 04 93 38 05 04; www.cafferoma.fr Daily 7 am–1 am

Chez Astoux €€
A popular bistro with large shellfish platters, freshly shucked oysters and a wide range of fruits de mer to enjoy. The covered terrace is a good spot to eat, but a take-away service is also available.

180 B2 ⊠ 27 rue Félix Fauré ☎ 04 93 39 21 87; www.astouxbrun.com Daily 8 am–midnight

La Palme d'Or €€€
Join the stars at Cannes' most prestigious restaurant to experience the latest culinary creations of prize-winning chef Christian Willer.

180 B2 ⊠ Hôtel Martinez ☎ 04 92 98 74 14 Closed Sun–Mon in low season

La Piazza €
Home-made pasta, pizzas, meat and fish dishes in a big, buzzing restaurant near the Old Port. Not to be confused with La Pizza (similar name, inferior pizzas) on the quai.

180 B2 ⊠ 9 place Cornut-Gentille ☎ 04 92 98 60 80; www.restaurant-lapiazza.com Daily 12–2:30, 7–11:30

Au Poisson Grillé €€
This restaurant by the Old Port has specialised in grilled fish dishes for over 50 years, and has a reasonably priced three-course menu.

180 B2 ⊠ 8 quai St Pierre ☎ 04 93 39 44 68; www.poisson-grille.com Daily 12–4, 7–11

La Tarterie €
Delicious sweet and savoury tarts to eat in or take away – perfect for a picnic on the Corniche de l'Esterel.

180 B2 ⊠ 33 rue Bivouac Napoléon ☎ 04 93 39 67 43 Daily

GRASSE

La Bastide St-Antoine €€€
Jacques Chibois, one of the Riviera's top chefs, serves up delectable Provençal cuisine in this 18th-century town house surrounded by olive groves, just outside Grasse. Book well ahead. If you're on a budget, the lunch menu is excellent value.

180 A3 ⊠ 48 avenue Henri-Dunant ☎ 04 93 70 94 94; www.jacques-chibois.com Daily 12–1:30, 8–9:30

MIRAMAR

La Marine €€
Serving possibly the best sardines on the Corniche de l'Esterel, on a breezy terrace overhanging the Mediterranean.

180 A2 ⊠ La Figuerette ☎ 04 93 75 49 30 Closed Wed and low season

MOUGINS

Le Moulin de Mougins €€€
This bastion of Provençal cuisine, in a 16th-century former olive mill, is headed up by chef Alain Llorca. The menu changes seasonally, and the wine cellar boasts more than 5,000 vintages. Cooking classes available.

180 B2 ⊠ Quartier Notre-Dame-de-Vie ☎ 04 93 75 78 24; www.moulin-mougins.com Tue–Sun 12–2:30, 7:30–9:30

Les Muscadins €€€
Upmarket restaurant attached to the hotel of the same name (▶ 127)

and serving delicious regional cuisine with an Italian influence.

➕ 180 B2 ☒ 19 boulevard Courteline ☎ 04 92 28 30 90; www.les-muscadins.com ⏰ Closed Tue–Wed, and Dec–Feb

ST-PAUL-DE-VENCE

Café de la Place €–€€

Simple bistro fare at the entrance to the village, overlooking a lively pétanque pitch in the leafy square.

➕ 180 C3 ☒ Place Général de Gaulle ☎ 04 93 32 80 03 ⏰ Closed Nov–23 Dec

Chez Andreas €

A cheerful café-bar on the village ramparts, ideal for a light lunch or a glass of wine as the sun goes down. There is a small outdoor seating area with views over the valley.

➕ 180 C3 ☒ Rempart Ouest ☎ 04 93 32 98 32 ⏰ Daily noon–10 pm

Malabar €

Tibetan prayer flags and smiling Indian gods adorn this friendly, modern café. The menu is full of tasty and affordable options.

➕ 180 C3 ☒ 7 Rempart Ouest ☎ 04 93 32 60 14 ⏰ Daily 12–3, 7–9

Le Mas d'Artigny €€€

Set in beautiful parkland and part of an exquisite Relais et Château hotel, this gourmet restaurant serves exceptional fish dishes.

➕ 180 C3 ☒ Route de la Colle ☎ 04 93 32 84 54; www.mas-artigny.com ⏰ Daily

THÉOULE-SUR-MER

Le Marco Polo €–€€

The fish couldn't come any fresher than at this restaurant on the sandy beach at Théoule-sur-Mer.

➕ 180 A2 ☒ 47 avenue de Lérins ☎ 04 93 49 96 59 ⏰ Daily 12–2:30, 7:30–10:30

Where to…
Shop

FASHION AND SCENT

Cannes is well known for its boutique shopping. A shopping festival takes place here each January, with fashion shows in the Palais des Festivals. The main shopping streets are **rue de Antibes** and **boulevard de la Croisette**, where – between the Majestic and Carlton hotels – you'll find the likes of Chanel, Lacroix, Gucci, Bulgari, Louis Vuitton, Salvatore Ferragamo, Hermes, Dior, Dolce and Gabbana, Fendi, Yves Saint Laurent, Valentino and Cartier, to name but a few.

If designer is not your style, **Bleu comme là-bas** (38 rue Grande, St-Paul-de-Vence, tel: 04 93 32 04 17) is a wacky, bright orange jewellery shop owned by a young, imagina-

tive designer. Affordable and fun. This region is well known for its sweet scents. One of the two major perfume factories in Grasse, **Parfumerie Fragonard** (20 boulevard Fragonard, tel: 04 93 36 44 65) has some of the finest perfumes from Provence for sale.

L'Occitane (14 rue Maréchal Joffre, Cannes, tel: 04 93 68 20 32) has all-natural fragrances, soaps and skincare products embracing the scents, colours and traditions of Provence. **Herbier à Provence** (7 Monté de la Castre, St-Paul-de-Vence, tel: 04 93 32 91 51) has locally made soaps, herbs, perfumes and bath products.

FOOD AND DRINK

No one does cheese like the French, and **Ceneri** (22 rue Meynadier, Cannes, tel: 04 93 39 63 68) confirms this fact. This is one of France's leading cheese stores, with over 300 varieties, from huge rounds of runny Brie to tiny *boutons de culotte* (trouser-button) goat's cheese. In St-Paul-de-Vence, find wine to accompany your cheese at **La Petite Cave de Saint-Paul** (7 rue de l'Étoile, tel: 04 93 32 59 54), an authentic 14th-century cellar containing a choice selection of Provençal wines, including those produced in the surrounding vineyards. Also in St-Paul, **Les Huiles de Monde** (68 rue Grande, tel: 04 93 32 58 35) has quality olive oil and a range of other olive products. **La Cave Gourmande** (64 rue Grande) is a sweet shop with pick-and-mix marshmallows, caramels and lollipops.

The regional sweet speciality is nougat. Stock up at St-Raphaël's **Nougat Cochet** (98 boulevard Félix Martin, tel: 04 94 95 01 67).

ARTS, CRAFTS AND BOOKS

All kinds of artworks of varying quality are available in the area. In Biot, **Galerie Daniele Vogt** (27 impasse des Arcades, tel: 04 93 65 50 13) has prints, etchings and original paintings for sale.

St-Paul-de-Vence is stuffed to the gills with art galleries. One of the better ones is **Galerie Pascal Retelet** (1 place Général de Gaulle), an exclusive gallery dealing in Arman, Appel, Bacon, Hartung, Chagall, Warhol and local contemporary artists.

Biot is famed for its pottery and **Poterie du Vieux Biot** (4 chemin Neuf, tel: 04 93 65 63 30) is a beautiful old shop that sells earthenware pots of every shape and size. Biot is also renowned for its glassware. The traditional bubble-flecked glassware from **Verrerie de Biot** (Chemin des Combes, tel: 04 93 65 03 00) makes an unusual souvenir or gift. Visitors can also watch the glass-blowers at work.

Heidi's English Bookshop (24 rue Aubernon, Antibes, tel: 04 93 34 74 11) is the biggest English bookshop on the Côte d'Azur, with a wide choice of new and used

books and a good range of French dictionaries and phrasebooks, as well as stationery and cards.

MARKETS

Antibes has a Provençal market in the cours Massena selling fruit, vegetables, flowers and other regional produce (Jun–Aug daily, Sep–May Tue–Sun). A flea market takes place every Thursday and Saturday at place Jacques Audiberti. There are also clothes markets in place Barnaud (open Tue and Sat) and parking de la Poste (open Thu am).

Biot has a fruit and vegetable market on Tuesday and Friday mornings.

Cagnes-sur-Mer has an attractive market in the Cité Marchande with a good range of fresh fruit, vegetables, meat, dairy produce and flowers (open Tue–Sun am). There's an additional food market in boulevard Kennedy (Fri am), and a general market with clothes

and bric-à-brac on Wednesday morning, opposite the bus station.

Cannes' Marché de Forville (rue du Marché de Forville, open Tue–Sun 7 am–1 pm) is a busy, partially covered market, with bright displays of fruit, vegetables, flowers and cheeses. Chefs from restaurants near by often buy their fresh produce here. An antiques market takes place here on Monday. Cannes also has a daily flower market at les Allées de la Liberté, and a Marché Brocante (flea market) at place de l'Étang on Friday from 3–7 pm.

Grasse has a general market in the place aux Aires (open Tue–Sun am), and an antiques market (1st and 3rd Fri of month) in cours H Cresp.

Vence's place du Grand Jardin is the town's main market place, where you'll find fresh fruit and vegetables, as well as clothes and general items for sale daily. There's also a flea market held here on Wednesdays.

Where to...
Be Entertained

NIGHTLIFE

In Cannes, **Cat Corner** (22 rue Macé, tel: 04 93 39 31 31, open daily 11:30 pm–5 am) is popular with the 20-something crowd that stays here till the wee hours.

The Cannes institution **Whisky à Gogo** attracts a young crowd, despite being one of the oldest discos in Europe (115 avenue de Lérins; tel: 04 93 43 20 63, open Wed–Sat, Jul; daily, Aug; Fri–Sat 11 pm–5 am, Sep–Jun).

Morrison's Irish Pub (10 rue Teisseire, tel: 04 92 98 16 17, open daily 7 pm–2 am) is just what you'd expect in an Irish pub: a cosy wooden interior, sport and news in English, and Guinness on tap. Live music on Wednesday and Thursday.

Gay-friendly **Zanzibar** (85 rue Félix-Fauré, tel: 04 93 39 30 75, open daily 6 pm–dawn) is situated near the Palais des Festivals. There's a maritime theme, with strapping sailors adorning the walls.

On the first floor of the Palais des Festivals, **Jimmy'z** (1 boulevard La Croisette, tel: 04 92 98 78 00), the Cannes version of the exclusive Monaco nightspot, has several dance floors for clubbers .

La Siesta (route du Bord-de-la-Mer, between Antibes and Biot, tel: 04 93 33 31 31, open mid-Jun to mid-Sep daily, rest of year Fri–Sat 11 pm–5 am) is one of the Côte d'Azur's most exotic nightclubs, with open-air dance floors, fountains, a swimming pool, restaurant and a wave-shaped casino.

At Cannes' **Casino Croisette** (1 esplanade Lucien Barrière, tel: 04 92 98 78 00, open 10 am–5 am) you can try your luck on a choice of 300 slot machines, or on roulette and blackjack if you pay to enter the games room. If you forgot your jacket, at **Casino de Cagnes-sur-Mer** (116 boulevard de la Plage, tel: 04 92 27 14 40, open 10 am–4 am) you can gamble on slot machines, poker and blackjack without having to worry about formal attire.

CINEMA

Cannes has very few film screenings in English. **Cinema Les Arcades** (77 rue Félix-Fauré, tel: 04 93 39 10 00) regularly screens films in their original language.

THEATRE AND MUSIC

Alexandre III (19 boulevard Alexandre, Cannes, tel: 04 93 94 33 44) stages a variety of plays, from the classics to modern works.

The 19th-century church, **Église Réformée de France** (9 rue Croix, Cannes, tel: 04 93 39 35 55) hosts choral, classical and chamber music concerts, and organ recitals.

During the Cannes Film Festival, the **Palais des Festivals et des Congrès** (1 boulevard La Croisette, tel: 04 93 39 01 01; www.cannes.fr) is abuzz with cinephiles. At other times it hosts international exhibitions, plays, ballet and concerts.

HEALTH AND BEAUTY

Thalazur Antibes (770 chemin Moyennes Bréguières, Antibes, tel: 04 92 91 82 00) offers thalassotherapy and swimming pools, a gym, hammam, sauna, Jacuzzi, solarium and nursery.

Spa Shiseido au Mas Candille (boulevard Clément-Rebuffel, Mougins, tel: 04 92 28 43 43, open 10–7) uses a combination of Eastern techniques such as shiatsu and qi (or chi), as well as Shiseido products in all its treatments.

In and Around St-Tropez

Getting Your Bearings

The former fishing village of St-Tropez is undoubtedly one of the smartest resorts on the Côte d'Azur, the Riviera's capital of "see-and-be-seen" and a veritable tourist honeypot. Despite the summer crowds, St-Tropez remains one of the most seductive resorts of southern France, exuding a carefree *joie de vivre*, with its picturesque pastel-shaded houses, tiny bistros and chic boutiques, all basking in the scorching Mediterranean sunshine, while millionaires' ostentatious yachts line the ancient port. For decades this hedonistic image has drawn artists, writers and celebrities. Its star-studded list of residents today includes Elton John, Jean-Paul Belmondo, Jean-Michel Jarre and the most famous Tropezienne of all – Brigitte Bardot.

The razzmatazz of heady St-Tropez is juxtaposed by the tranquillity and beauty of the *arrière pays* (hinterland). The St-Tropez peninsula has retained all the charm of the Provençal countryside beside the sea, splashed with wild flowers and swathed in vineyards. In their midst, the beautiful hilltop villages of Ramatuelle and Gassin afford magnificent views of the Gulf of St-Tropez and the distant Îles d'Hyères from their sloping streets. Farther inland is a region of wild, unexplored landscapes and slumbering villages where the pace of life is slow and locals play pétanque in the shade of plane trees or laze in cafés, offering visitors a chance to sample the true *douceur de vivre* of rural Provence.

★ Don't Miss

At Your Leisure

Page 133:
Vieux Port,
St-Tropez

Above:
St Tropez's
portside is
full of cafés,
shoppers and
sunseekers

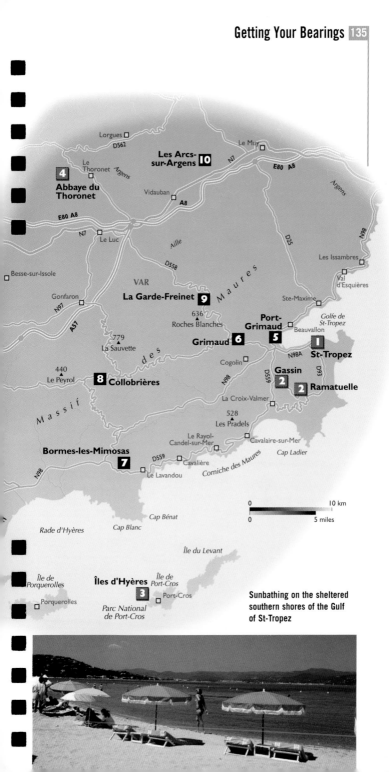

Lorgues
D562

Le Muy

Les Arcs-sur-Argens **10**

E80 A8

N7

Le Thoronet

4

Abbaye du Thoronet

Argens

Vidauban

A8

E80 A8

N7

Le Luc

Aille

Argens

D25

N98

Les Issambres

Val d'Esquières

Besse-sur-Issole

D558

VAR

La Garde-Freinet 9

Maures

Ste-Maxime

Gonfaron

N97

A57

636 ▲
Roches Blanches

779 ▲
La Sauvette

des

Grimaud 6

Port-Grimaud **5**

Golfe de St-Tropez

Beauvallon

1

St-Tropez

N98A

440 ▲
Le Peyrol

8 Collobrières

Massif

Cogolin

N98

D559

Gassin 2

2 Ramatuelle

D93

La Croix-Valmer

528 ▲
Les Pradels

Le Rayol-Candel-sur-Mer

Cavalaire-sur-Mer

Cap Ladier

Bormes-les-Mimosas

7

D559

Cavalière

Le Lavandou

Corniche des Maures

| 0 | 10 km |
| 0 | 5 miles |

Cap Bénat

Cap Blanc

Rade d'Hyères

Île du Levant

Île de Porquerolles

Îles d'Hyères

3

Île de Port-Cros

Porquerolles

Port-Cros

Parc National de Port-Cros

Sunbathing on the sheltered southern shores of the Gulf of St-Tropez

Enjoy a day in glamorous St-Tropez, then head into the
unspoiled hinterland to explore sleepy Provençal villages,
offshore islands and an ancient abbey.

In and Around St-Tropez in Three Days

Day One

Morning
Start your tour of **❶St-Tropez** (➤ 138–141) at the photogenic harbour
(above), which remains remarkably unchanged despite the razzmatazz of
this trend-setting resort. Sénéquier (➤ 156) is the perfect place for breakfast and people-watching. Wander the maze of cobblestoned back streets
at leisure, working up to La Citadelle (➤ 140–141) for its sweeping
coastal views, then taste some culinary delights in the morning Marché
Provençal (➤ 157, Tue and Sat) in place des Lices.

Lunch
Having whet your appetite, L'Eau à la Bouche (➤ 156) serves a light but
satisfying alfresco lunch.

Afternoon
Visit the Musée de l'Annonciade (➤ 141) with its magnificent post-
Impressionist canvases, painted by the first artistic visitors to St-Tropez –
Signac, Matisse, Bonnard, Utrillo and Dufy.

Spend the rest of the afternoon lazing (and celebrity-spotting) on
St- Tropez's fabled beaches in the Baie de Pampelonne (➤ 139–140).

Evening
Return to St-Tropez for dinner at La Citadelle (➤ 156) or, for that special
occasion, at legendary chef Alain Ducasse's Spoon Byblos (➤ 156). Then

party till dawn with the famous and fabulous at Les Caves du Roy or La Bodega de Papagayo (► 158).

Day Two

Morning
Explore the St-Tropez peninsula, its beautiful coastline and ancient villages. **2 Ramatuelle and Gassin** (right, ► 142–143) are especially attractive, with their steep streets, narrow alleyways and ice-cream-coloured houses tumbling down the hillsides.

Lunch
Le Micocoulier (place dei Barri, tel: 04 94 56 14 01) and Le Bello Visto (place dei Barri, tel: 04 94 56 17 30) in Gassin both offer appealing Provençal menus and breathtaking views.

Afternoon
Catch the ferry from Le Lavandou to visit the **3 Île de Port-Cros** (► 144–145), the wildest of the Îles d'Hyères. The island has palm-fringed shores, extensive nature trails and offshore snorkelling tours.

Evening
Return for a classic Provençal dinner at L'Escondudo (► 155) in the floral village of Bormes-les-Mimosas.

Day Three

Morning
Start the day at the **4 Abbaye du Thoronet** (left, ► 146–147), a beautiful 12th-century abbey in the heart of the unspoiled Vallée d'Argens.

Lunch
Head south along picturesque winding country lanes to **8 Collobrières** (► 151), at the heart of the surprisingly unfrequented Massif des Maures. Join the villagers for a simple, rustic lunch and local wine at La Petite Fontaine (► 155) in the main square.

Afternoon
The Massif des Maures is a fantastic place for rambling; its low hills are covered in dense forests of cork oaks, conifers and chestnut trees. Take time to explore and you will find the seemingly endless woodland is interrupted by the occasional sunny meadow or a splash of mimosa.

Evening
Drive to the ancient hilltop village of **6 Grimaud** (► 148), for dinner at Les Santons (► 155).

⓪ St-Tropez

With such a big and glamorous reputation, you might be surprised to find that St-Tropez is only a small town of about 5,500 people. Having reached the height of international fame in the 1950s and '60s with the rise of bikini-clad resident Brigitte Bardot, it continues to attract glitterati, millionaires and holidaymakers, all seduced by the luxury, relaxed atmosphere and natural beauty of this coastal village.

There's no doubt that life in St-Tropez can be extravagant, decadent and excessive. The French endearingly call it St-Trop, pronouncing the "p", but nonetheless evoking the double entendre: *trop* with a silent "p" is French for "too much". In summer, St-Tropez may well be too much for some, but if it's glamour you seek, it's the perfect place to rub shoulders with celebrities in the waterfront cafés, or get a close-up view of the yachts moored before the distinctive backdrop of pink and yellow pastel-coloured houses (reconstructed after being destroyed in World War II). But take time to discover another side of St-Tropez: explore the maze of narrow streets and peaceful squares of the Vieille Ville, or Old Town, where there is a village-like atmosphere and friendly markets and bistros.

Don't attempt to drive to St-Tropez in the high season. The traffic is terrible, with long waits on the roads into town, and no parking once you get there. Instead, use the large public parking areas at Port Grimaud and take the passenger ferry across the bay.

La Tarte Tropezienne, the pastry and coffee shop famous for its sweet custard brioche

Vieux Port

Despite large numbers of visitors and the huge luxury yachts moored here, the picturesque Old Port, lined with pastel-painted houses and cosy cafés, manages to maintain a village-like charm. However, the **waterfront** is still very much the place to pose, especially during summer. Try to arrive in style, preferably aboard an enormous yacht. But if you lack the finances for such a venture, there's no shame in wandering along the quayside, ogling the yachts and trying to catch a glimpse of their millionaire owners tucking into langoustines on deck, waited on by a white-frocked crew.

The quay curves along a sapphire-blue bay, punctuated at one end by the ruins of the town's old fortifications, **Tour Vieille, Tour Suffren** and **Tour de Portalet**, and the harbour breakwater, **Môle Jean-Réveille** – a good place to snap a photo of the whole port. Sitting behind Môle Jean-Réveille is the old fishermen's district, **La Ponche**, with **Tour Jarlier**, another fragment of the old fortifications, near by. At the other end of the quay is the **Musée l'Annonciade** (► 141).

Vieille Ville

The narrow streets of the Old Town

Left: St-Tropez's Old Port, overlooked by pastel-coloured buildings

Closed to traffic in summer, the Old Town is a cluster of narrow streets lined with small old houses and a handful of chic boutiques. The streets here are generally uncrowded, despite the large numbers of people sauntering along the nearby quay.

At the edge of the Old Town is the **place des Lices**, the town's main square and the real heart of St-Tropez, lined with ancient plane trees and Bohemian cafés such as **Le Café** (► 155). Visit on Tuesday or Saturday for the market, or at any time for a game of pétanque and a glass of pastis with the locals.

Beaches

The best beaches in St-Tropez are situated on the **Baie de Pampelonne**, a peninsula with over 6km (4 miles) of enticing golden sand, neatly divided into individual beaches. It was

St Torpes

St-Tropez is named after Tropez, or Torpes, a Roman centurion martyred under Nero in AD 68. His head was buried in Pisa, while his decapitated body was put in a boat and cast out to sea with a dog and cockerel, who were expected to consume his remains. St Torpes' link with St-Tropez was established when the boat washed up on the shore here, his body miraculously untouched. The town's most important festival – the **Bravade de St-Torpes** (16–18 May) – has been celebrated in his honour for more than 400 years. A gilt bust of St Torpes and a model of his boat can be seen in the 19th-century baroque church, **Église de St-Tropez**, with its distinctive pink-and-yellow bell tower.

along these sandy beaches that girls first dared to bathe topless in the 1960s. The beaches here are still a hot spot for the rich and beautiful, and are accompanied by pricey beach bars supplying music, drinks and beach chairs. The best way to get here in summer is to take the frequent minibus from the place des Lices.

A game of boules in the place des Lices

Above: The renowned Le Café

Within easy walking distance of St-Tropez, **Les Graniers**, on the Baie des Cenebiers just east of the citadel, is one of the most crowded beaches. On the other side of the Cap de St-Tropez, on the Baie de Pampelonne, trendy **Club 55** and **Voile Rouge** have replaced Tahiti Plage as the place to spot celebs. For privacy and seclusion, **plage de la Briande** is one of the best beaches in the region, situated halfway along the 19km (12-mile) coastal path that rounds the St-Tropez peninsula.

La Citadelle

The ruins of St-Tropez's 16th- and 17th-century defences sit on an oleander-covered hilltop to the east of town. The citadel is worth visiting for the view alone, which embraces the orange curved-tile roofs of the Old Town, the dark and distant Maures and Esterel hills, and the shimmering blue of the bay, flecked with sails. Keep an eye out for peacocks, those supermodels of the avian world; a number of them have decided to take up residence in the citadel grounds.

In the citadel keep is the **Musée Naval**, a maritime museum linked to the Musée de la Marine in the Palais de Chaillot in Paris. It displays models of ships, and focuses on the history of St-Tropez. There is also an interesting display about the 1944 Allied invasion that destroyed much of the town.

La Citadelle overlooks the town

Musée de l'Annonciade

In the late 19th and early 20th centuries, St-Tropez was an active centre for the artistic avant-garde, and this museum in a former 16th-century chapel showcases artworks from the period, with a particular focus on scenes of the local area. There are a hundred or so canvases here, encompassing turn-of-the-20th-century movements such as pointillism and fauvism. Be sure to seek out Paul Signac's *L'Orage* (1895), Camoin's *La Place des Lices* (1939), and works by Dufy, Dérain and Vuillard. There is also one painting by Matisse (*La Femme à la Fenêtre*, 1920), but enthusiasts of the artist are much better off visiting the Musée Matisse in Nice (➤ 40).

🔳 179 E3
Tourist Office
✉ Quai Jean-Jaurès ☎ 04 94 97 45 21; www.ot-saint-tropez.com 🕐 Daily 9:30–8, Jul–Aug; 9:30–12:30, 2–7, Apr–Jun, Sep; 9:30–12:30, 2–6, Oct–Mar. Closed Sun, Nov and Jan

La Citadelle
✉ Montée de la Citadelle ☎ 04 94 97 59 43 🕐 Daily 10–12:30, 1:30–6:30, Apr–Sep; 10–12:30, 1:30–5:30, Oct–Mar. Closed 1 Jan and selected hols 💷 Moderate, under 8 free

Musée de l'Annonciade
✉ Place Georges-Grammont ☎ 04 94 97 04 01 🕐 Wed–Mon 10–12, 3–7, Jun–Sep; 10–12, 2–6, Oct, Dec–May. Closed Tue, Nov and selected hols 💷 Moderate, under 12 free

---

ST-TROPEZ: INSIDE INFO

Top tips Pick up a *plan de la ville* (**town map**) at the tourist office. It has a detailed street plan of St-Tropez and a map of the surrounding areas, including a breakdown of the various beaches.

• Visit in mid-May or mid-June to catch one of the two colourful **bravades** festivals: the Bravade de St-Torpes in May, or the Bravade des Espagnols in June, which commemorates the involvement of the men of St-Tropez in the defeat of Spanish raiders farther along the coast in 1637.

• To get away from the **crowds**, visit the beautiful, unspoiled nearby villages of **Ramatuelle** and **Gassin** (➤ 142–143), situated on the St-Tropez peninsula.

• To gain a good overview of the town, including the main attractions as well as some quiet little corners, take the **walk** ➤ 162–163.

❷ Ramatuelle and Gassin

Just a short distance inland from St-Tropez lies a surprisingly uncrowded peninsula, scattered with wild flowers, home to the charming villages of Ramatuelle and Gassin, and surrounded by some of the region's best vineyards.

The hilltop village of **Ramatuelle** began as a stronghold of the Saracens, who called the village Rahmatu'llah, Arabic for "God's Gift". This impossibly pretty village is today, along with neighbouring Gassin, one of the most fashionable places in the region in which to own a *résidence secondaire*. Despite the influx of affluent second-home owners, Ramatuelle maintains its Provençal identity, and is a lovely place to visit, particularly during the two-week **Festival de Ramatuelle** held in August each year, when jazz musicians and thespians take to the stage. At other times of the year, the village is worth a visit just to delight in wandering along its old streets lined with houses that climb steadily up the hill; to explore its little artisan shops and art galleries; and admire its ·

Photogenic Ramatuelle on the St-Tropez peninsula is a typical Provençal hill-top village

Opposite: a cobbled lane in Ramatuelle

Romanesque church. Situated across from the tourist office, the church has a 17th-century doorway carved from green serpentine stone. The town is laid out concentrically and the **centre of the village** is through an arch to the left of the church.

From Ramatuelle, take the Moulins de Paillas road (D89) to Gassin. In between the two villages are what remains of five ancient windmills, the **Moulins de Paillas** (one of which has been restored). There are fantastic views from here out to sea towards the Îles d'Hyères, and across the surrounding countryside. The twin peaks of la Sauvette (779m/2,556 feet) and Notre-Dame-des-Anges (780m/2,560 feet), the highest points in the **Massif des Maures**, are clearly visible.

The medieval village of **Gassin** also has spectacular panoramas of the area, having been established as a lookout point during the time of the Saracen invasions. This colourful Provençal village is blessed with more than its fair share of smart boutiques and restaurants, thanks to its proximity to St-Tropez.

TAKING A BREAK

In Gassin, most of the restaurants are located in the **place dei Barri**, a paved square at the top of the village, where you can dine alfresco, enjoying the views that encompass everything from the mountains and vineyards, to nearby villages and the coast. Try Le Microcoulier or Le Bello Visto (➤ 137).

In the new village, Yann Bonneau's **Boulangerie-Patisserie** is good for a snack (corner of rue des Écoles and rue de Gallembert, tel: 04 94 56 03 01, open Thu–Tue 8–1, 4–7, closed Sun pm).

➕ 179 E2
Tourist Office
✉ Place de l'Ormeau, Ramatuelle
☎ 04 98 12 64 00;
www.ramatuelle-tourisme.com
🕐 Daily 9–1, 3–7:30, Jul–Aug;
Mon–Sat 9–1, 3–7, mid-season;
Mon–Fri 9–12:30, 2–6, low season

RAMATUELLE AND GASSIN: INSIDE INFO

Top tips This area is renowned for the excellent **Côtes du Provence** wines that are produced here. On the D61 between St-Tropez and Ramatuelle there are various châteaux where the wines can be tasted. Visit the Ramatuelle tourist office for more information about wineries to visit in the area.

• Try not to arrive **hungry** at a small village in search of a late lunch. Many restaurants, cafés and *pâtisseries* close at 1 or 2 pm and don't open again until the evening. This is particularly true during winter, when they may also be closed for months at a time.

3 Îles d'Hyères

The town of Hyères was a favourite holiday spot for the English aristocracy who wintered here in the 19th century. However, when summer became a more popular time to holiday than winter, the Îles d'Hyères off the coast came into their own, blessed as they are with beautiful beaches, azure seas and dense natural woodland. These quiet, car-free islands make an ideal daytrip away from the busy resorts.

Île de Porquerolles

The largest of the Îles d'Hyères, Porquerolles covers around 18sq km (7sq miles). A perfect day trip for walkers, cyclists and nature lovers, much of the island is a nature reserve, covered with woodland and peaceful walking paths. On the north coast of the island are beautiful sandy **beaches**, while on the south coast, some 40 minutes' walk away, jagged cliffs offer spectacular views over the sparkling sea. The island also has an impressive botanical garden bursting with olive, fig and peach trees (▶ 14).

The **main village** is on the north side of the island. In the **place d'Armes** you'll find (rather pricey) hotels and restaurants, as well as a large pétanque pitch. To the south of the village is **Fort Ste-Agathe**, which dates back to the 16th century and today functions as an exhibition space.

Île de Port-Cros

The wildest, most southerly of the islands is a protected national park, 10sq km (4sq miles) in area

Getting there

The Îles d'Hyères, can be accessed by ferry from Port St-Pierre in Hyères, or the harbour on the Giens peninsula.
• Île de Porquerolles can be reached from La Tour Fondue in Giens harbour in 20 minutes by ferry.
• In the high season, ferries from Giens continue from Porquerolles to Port-Cros island.
• Ferries from Port St-Pierre go to Port-Cros in one hour, and Le Levant in 90 minutes.
• All three islands can also be reached by a ferry from Le Lavandou, farther east.

ÎLES D'HYÈRES: INSIDE INFO

Top tips Check the time for the **last ferry** back before going to the islands.
• One of the **best beaches** on the islands is plage de la Palud, at Port-Cros.
• You can't use your car on the islands, so **park** at the ferry terminal at Giens or near Hyères harbour (moderate).
• **Nudity** is compulsory on du Levant's main nudist beach, plage Les Grottes.
• **You must not** drive a car, cycle (on Port Cros), camp, smoke, make a campfire, go fishing, drop litter or collect plants. Dogs are to be kept on a lead.

and covered with dense, unspoiled woodland. Marked **walking trails** pick through the woodland and its impressive flora. The *sentier botanique* (botanical path) is one of the shorter paths, but there are also more challenging trails of up to 10km (6 miles) to explore around the island.

The paths also extend into the sea; **snorkellers** can follow an underwater trail full of colourful marine life (free guided snorkelling tours leave from plage la Palud). Without a snorkel, you can view the marine life from the glass-bottomed **Aquascope** boat, which makes half-hour excursions.

Île du Levant

This tiny 8sq km (3sq miles) of rocky land is the most easterly of the three islands. The majority of the island is owned by the army and is strictly off limits to tourists, while the rest is a nudist colony known as Héliopolis. Large numbers of visitors come to the beaches here to work on their all-over tans in the summer, but there are also about 100 permanent residents, whose little chalets sit on the hills behind the harbour.

Opposite: Overlooking the old quarter of Hyères

The islands are surrounded by wildlife

Île de Porquerolles
➕ 178 B1 🚢 Daily from Giens, more frequent departures Jul–Aug
☎ 04 94 58 21 81; www.tlv-tvm.com
🎫 Moderate

Île de Port Cros and Île du Levant
➕ 178 D1 🚢 Daily from Port d'Hyères, reduced services in winter

☎ 04 94 57 44 07;
www.tlv-tvm.com;
www.portcrosparctional.fr;
www.iledulevant.com.fr
🎫 Moderate

Tourist Information Office
➕ 178 B2 ✉ 3 avenue Ambroise Thomas, Hyères ☎ 04 94 01 84 50; www.ot-hyeres.fr

4 Abbaye du Thoronet

It's worth wandering away from the coast to explore this abbey. Nestled deep in woodland in the Var region, Abbaye du Thoronet is one of the great sights of the Provençal interior.

Sitauted just off the D79 country road from Brignoles to Draguignan, Le Thoronet is the oldest of three 12th-century abbeys built in Provence by Cistercian monks – an order dedicated to a life of simplicity, austerity and manual labour. Their philosophy is reflected by the unadorned architecture of this lovely Romanesque abbey, and the woodland setting, which conveys a sense of serenity and peace.

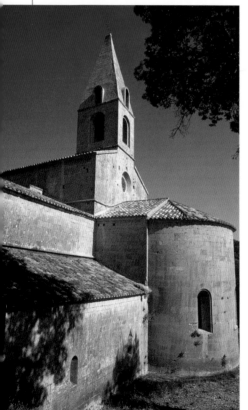

Rebelling against the corrupt riches of the Church, the Cistercians expressed their religious devotion through a rigorous, harshly simple and self-sufficient lifestyle. Based at Cîteaux in Burgundy, as their movement grew, the Cistercians founded three great abbeys in Provence: Le Thoronet, Silvacane and Sénanque. The monks shunned society, and chose to build their abbeys in isolated settings.

Building started on the Abbaye du Thoronet in 1160 and was completed in 1190, maintaining a Provençal Romanesque style despite the movement towards Gothic architecture at the time. Although the monks here strived towards a simple lifestyle, the monastery soon became extremely wealthy due to large donations. Over the years the abbey was gradually deserted, following poor harvests, a series of raids in the 14th century, and attacks during the Wars of Religion. During the French Revolution the building was seized and sold by the State, although in 1854 the government repurchased and restored this extraordinary building.

On entering the gatehouse, the beautifully proportioned **church**, with its square bell tower and rather low red-tile roof, is directly ahead. The church's interior is a sober and unembellished affair, but beside the church are the attractive **cloisters**, built over three levels to accommodate the uneven ground. In the middle of the cloisters is the **fountain house**, containing a fountain where the monks used to wash their hands before meals. Also near by is the less austere **chapter house**, where early Gothic influences can be seen in the architecture. A **dormitory**, where the monks slept, is on the top floor of the chapter house.

Opposite:
A stained-glass window inside the abbey

TAKING A BREAK

In nearby Le Thoronet are the **Hostellerie de l'Abbaye** (Chemin du Château tel: 04 94 73 88 81); and **Le Tournesol** (rue des Trois Ormeaux tel: 04 94 73 89 91, lunchtimes only).

Bottom left: The abbey church

The upper level of the cloisters

Abbaye du Thoronet
✚ 178 C4 ✉ Le Thoronet ☎ 04 94 60 43 90; www.monum.fr
🕐 Mon–Sat 10–6:30, Sun 10–12, 2–6:30, Apr–Sep; Mon–Sat 10–1, 2–5, Sun 10–12, 2–5, Oct–Mar. Closed Jan 1 and selected hols
💶 Moderate, under 18 free; free to all 1st Sun of month

ABBAYE DU THORONET: INSIDE INFO

Top tips Mass is sung here by the sisters of Bethlehem every Sunday at noon.
• **Medieval music** concerts are held in the abbey. Contact the Centre des Monuments Nationaux (tel: 04 94 60 43 90; www.monum.fr) for more information.

Getting there The abbey is 11km (7 miles) from **Carcès**. It lies off the D79, between the D13 and D84.

At Your Leisure

5 Port-Grimaud

Port-Grimaud is a modern mini-Venice of pastel-coloured villas on a series of islets, divided by canals and linked by shaded squares and neat bridges. Designed by architect François Spoerry in the 1960s, the village is today one of France's major tourist attractions and the ultimate property development; prices for the 2,500 canalside houses (all with private moorings) are absurdly high and many of the residents simply jet in for their summer holidays.

Port-Grimaud is an appealing place, with lively waterside cafés and scenic waterways, but it is closed off by high fences, has overpriced facilities, and drivers must leave their cars in an expensive parking area outside the resort. The port is best explored by water-taxi (*coche d'eau*), with boat tours leaving from the main square (**place du Marché**) every ten minutes. At the centre of the village, on its own islet, the pseudo-Romanesque church of **St-François-d'Assise** contains stained glass by Hungarian-born Victor Vasarély, and provides a sweeping view of the harbour from the top of its tower.

🞣 179 D3
Tourist Office
✉ Annexe Port Grimaud, Chemin Communal ☎ 04 94 55 43 83
🕐 Jul–Aug Mon–Sat 9–12:30, 3–7; Jun, Sep Mon–Sat 9–12:30, 2:30–6:15

6 Grimaud

Medieval Grimaud is one of Provence's most photogenic hilltop villages, and is well worth a visit. It is crowned by the ruins of a romantic

Pleasure boats moored in front of the pastel-coloured villas of Port-Grimaud

11th-century **château** which belonged to the Grimaldi family, after whom the village is named. From the château there are impressive vistas over Port-Grimaud and down to the gulf of St-Tropez.

Hidden amid flower-filled streets and shaded squares, you will find a beautiful Romanesque church (**Église St-Michel**) on the atmospheric rue des Templiers, a restored 12th-century mill and the **Hospice of the Knights Templars**.

🕂 179 D3
Tourist Office
✉ 1 boulevard des Aliziers ☎ 04 94 43 26 98; www.grimaud-provence.com
🕐 Jul–Aug Mon–Sat 9–12:30, 3–7; Apr–Jun, Sep Mon–Sat 9–12:30, 2:30–6:15; Oct–Mar Mon–Sat 9–12:30, 2:15–5:30

7 Bormes-les-Mimosas

Perched on a hilltop on the Massif des Maures, just inland from the coast, Bormes-les-Mimosas is a steep medieval village with ice-cream coloured houses, evocative lanes and passageways climbing up towards the ruins of a château on the hilltop.

During February, when the mimosa is in full bloom, the village celebrates with a sensational Corso Fleuri – an extravaganza of floral floats made from thousands of tiny yellow mimosa flowers. The village is perennially pretty and in summer bright bougainvillaea and geraniums replace the mimosa blooms.

Seek out the *circuit touristique* that starts at the Maisons des Associations on boulevard de la Republique. If you can't find the signs for the *circuit* (they are often stolen), pick up a map and information in English at the tourist office. The *circuit* explores Bormes' steep medieval stairways and alleys. Watch out for the charmingly named Venelle des Amoureux (Lovers' Lane), Draille des Bredouilles (Gossipers' Way) and, steepest of all, rue Roumpi-Cuou (Bone-Breaker road).

Along the route are the town's main sights, which include a fine 16th-century **chapel** dedicated to Bormes' patron saint, St François de Paule (who rescued the village from the plague in 1481); **Église St-Trophyme**, an 18th-century church built in Romanesque style and where the French president attends Mass in summer; and the ruined 13th- to 14th-century castle at the top of the hill, the **Château des Seigners de Fos**. The château is privately owned, but an area next to it is open to the public, with dazzling views across the bay of Le Lavandou and the Massif des Maures.

Gardening enthusiasts should keep an eye out for information plaques about many of the plants along the *circuit touristique*.

The **Musée d'Art et d'Histoire**, in 61 rue Carnot (open Tue–Sat 10–12, 2:30–5, Sun 10–12), holds temporary art exhibitions throughout the year, and also has an exhibition tracing the history of the village.

🕂 179 C2
Tourist Office
✉ 1 place Gambetta ☎ 04 94 01 38 38; www.bormeslesmimosas.com
🕐 Summer daily 9–12:30, 2:30–6:30; winter Mon–Sat 9–12:30, 2–6

8 Collobrières

In the centre of the Massif des Maures, this traditional little village, surrounded by a forest of chestnut trees, is well known for its nutty produce, particularly in the form of the sweet *marrons glacés* (candied chestnuts) made here. Collobrières holds an annual **festival** celebrating the humble chestnut at the end of October. Chestnuts proliferate at the **local market**, held every Sunday, and also on Thursdays in summer. Collobrières is also known for its cork, which grows in the forests near by.

The village has a 12th-century **bridge**, and a curiously arcaded street, **place Rouget de l'Isle**, that is worth exploring. Farther up the road (off the D14) is the beautiful **Chartreuse de la Verne**. This Carthusian monastery stands isolated among the dense Maures forest, 12km (7 miles) from Collobrières. Founded in 1170, it has been damaged and rebuilt many times. The complex encompasses cloisters, chapels and cells in a rambling formation, built from the local red schist stone, with doorways decorated in green serpentine. Originally inhabited by Carthusian monks, it has been home to a group of Sisters of Bethlehem nuns since the 1980s.

➕ 179 C3
Tourist Office
✉ Boulevard Charles Caminat
☎ 04 94 48 08 00 🕑 Tue–Sat 10–12, 2–6, Sep–Jun; Mon–Sat, Jul–Aug

A colourful, flower-filled path in the village of Bormes-les-Mimosas

Chartreuse de la Verne
🕑 Wed–Mon 11–6, mid-May to mid-Oct; Wed–Mon 11–5, mid-Oct to mid-May. Closed religious holidays

9 La Garde-Freinet

Encircled by groves of cork oaks, eucalyptus and chestnut, this village was France's major producer of cork in the 19th century. Much further back, lofty La Garde, perched 360m (1,180 feet) above sea level, was one of the last Saracen strongholds in Provence in the 10th century. Today it is known as the "capital" of the Massif des Maures. Alleys, fountains and courtyards make it a wonderful place to wander through. A 20-minute walk to **Fort Freinet** to the west will reward you with fantastic views of Le Luc plain and beyond to the foothills of the Alps.

For Kids

• **Village des Tortues** The Tortoise Village at Gonfaron is a conservation centre for Hermann's tortoises, a rare species found only on the Massif and in Corsica. You can observe tortoises in their natural environment, visit the clinic for injured tortoises, the nursery for young tortoises, and the laboratory where nests and eggs are monitored. There is also a walking trail with information points in English to help you learn more about this endangered species. The best time of the year to visit is spring, when the tortoises are more active. They hatch from May to June, and hibernate from November to March (tel: 04 94 78 26 41; www.tortues.com, open daily 9–7, Mar–Nov, expensive, under 4 free).

The rooftops of La Garde-Freinet viewed from the walkway around Fort Freinet

✜ 179 D3
Tourist Office
✉ 1 place Neuve
☎ 04 94 43 67 41; www.ville-lagarde.fr
🕐 Mon–Sat 10–12:30, 3–6, Sun 10–12:30, Easter–Oct; Tue–Sat 10–12:30, 2–5, Nov–Easter

🔟 Les Arcs-sur-Argens

This attractive medieval village in the Argens valley, south of Draguignan, has a well-restored old quarter called **Le Parage**, which rises to the ruins of a 13th-century castle. From here, there are superb views of the Massif des Maures and the surrounding vineyard country, producing Côtes de Provence wines. The **Maison des Vins Côtes de Provence** (tel: 04 94 99 50 20), on the N7 south of the village, is an ideal place to taste and learn about some of the wines produced in the region. You can also buy wine here for very reasonable prices. The **Église St-Jean-Baptiste** (open daily 10–2, 2–5) has a large Provençal-style *crèche* tableau depicting Le Parage as it once was, and a 15th-century polyptych by Jean de Troyes.

Just a few kilometres outside Les Arcs-sur-Argens is the **Château Ste-Roseline**. The property dates back to the 10th century, and produces some of the most prestigious wine in the area. The château began as an abbey, and Roseline, the daughter of the Marquis of Villeneuve, was born here. She became a Carthusian nun, and was the mother superior here for many years until her death in 1329. Her body lies in a glass case in the vineyard's chapel, an important pilgrimage site with strong artistic significance. In 1978, the **Chapelle de Ste-Rosaline** was decorated by Marc Chagall with a beautiful mosaic representing the Angel's Meal. The chapel also has a stained-glass window designed by Jean Bazaine and Raoul Ubac, sculptures by Giacometti, and an alterpiece depicting St Roseline in a nativity scene with her parents. In addition to the chapel and cloister, the historic estate of Château Ste-Roseline has an excellent old vineyard, cellar door wine sales, a restaurant and well-established gardens. Musical and cultural events are held here regularly.

✜ 179 D4
Tourist Office
✉ Place Général de Gaulle
☎ 04 94 73 37 30
🕐 Mon–Fri 9–12, 2–5

Château Ste-Roseline
✉ Les Arcs-sur-Argens
☎ 04 94 99 50 30;
www.sainte-roseline.co

Where to... Stay

Prices
Expect to pay per double room, per night
€ under €80   €€ €80–€150   €€€ over €150

LES ARCS-SUR-ARGENS

Logis du Guetteur €€
The comfortable bedrooms in this beautifully restored 11th-century castle have panoramic views over the village and mountains. Meals are served in the cosy basement in winter, or on a terrace overlooking the outdoor pool in summer.
➕ 179 D4 ⊠ Place du Château
☎ 04 94 99 51 10; www.logisduguetteur. com ⊗ Closed Feb

BORMES-LES-MIMOSAS

Le Bellevue €
This simple family-run hotel has spectacular views over red roofs to the sparkling sea, and is good value in this often expensive part of the world. There's a friendly restaurant that serves fresh seafood and local Provençal dishes.
➕ 178 C2 ⊠ 12 place Gambetta
☎ 04 94 71 15 15;
www.bellevuebormes.fr.st
⊗ Closed mid-Nov to mid-Jan

COGOLIN

La Maison du Monde €€
This small, comfortable hotel with friendly service is excellent value, considering its 10km (6-mile) proximity to St-Tropez . It has 12 rooms decorated with furnishings from around the world, a shady garden and outdoor pool, and provides a welcome retreat from the crowds by the coast.
➕ 179 D3 ⊠ 63 rue Carnot
☎ 04 94 54 77 54;
www.lamaisondumonde.fr
⊗ Closed Nov–Mar except Christmas, New Year and Feb school hols

GASSIN

Le Mas de Chastelas €€–€€€
Situated just outside St-Tropez and surrounded by Côtes de Provence vineyards, this traditional shuttered farmhouse is covered in creeper and decorated with bright Provençal fabrics. The restaurant serves exceptional regional cuisine.
➕ 179 E2 ⊠ Quartier Bertaud
☎ 04 94 56 71 71
⊗ Closed Nov–Dec

GASSIN

La Palmeraie €€
Attractive, self-catering accommodation in small villas clustered round two swimming pools, just 3km (2 miles) from the beaches of St-Tropez. The excellent facilities include a restaurant, tennis courts, bar, children's playground. Cars, bicycles and TVs available to rent.
➕ 179 D3 ⊠ Quartier La Boal ☎ 04 94 55 68 00 ⊗ Closed Nov–Jan

RAMATUELLE

Camping Kon Tiki €–€€
A popular camping ground on the edge of Pampelonne beach, with mobile homes available to let. You can also bring your own caravan (trailer) or mobile home, or pitch your own tent. Grocery store, restaurant, bar, tennis court and hot showers on site.
➕ 179 E2 ⊠ Route des Plages
☎ 04 94 55 96 96;
www.campazur.com
⊗ Closed Nov–Mar

La Ferme d'Augustin €€–€€€
This three-star hotel, close to the beach, has comfortable rooms in a

charmingly rustic setting. Terraces look out over the garden and outdoor pool (which is heated and has hydro-massaging jets). Inside there are beamed ceilings and a cosy fireplace in the lounge.

📍 179 E2 🗺 Route de Tahiti 📞 04 94 55 97 00; www.fermeaugustin.com 🕐 Closed mid-Oct to mid-Mar

La Vigne de Ramatuelle €€€

Chic yet characterful vineyard villa near St-Tropez's famous beaches and nightspots.

📍 179 E2 🗺 Route des Plages 📞 04 94 79 12 50; www.hotel-vignederamatuelle.com 🕐 Closed mid-Oct to Mar

Villa Marie €€€

On the hill overlooking Pampelonne, this chic boutique hotel and spa is a place of pure indulgence. Each spacious room is stylishly decorated. Meals can be taken in the restaurant or out on the terrace. Enjoy the pool and open-air bar on a balmy evening.

📍 179 E2 🗺 Ramatuelle 📞 04 94 97 40 22; www.villamarie.fr 🕐 Closed early Oct–Apr

ST-TROPEZ

Hôtel Le Baron Lodge €–€€

This hotel at the foot of the citadel has 14 peaceful double rooms and a homely, comfortable atmosphere. The airy rooms look onto the harbour or towards the citadel. It's an easy walk downhill to the port. A lovely place to stay, without being excessively luxurious. Limited reserved parking for guests.

📍 179 E3 🗺 23 rue de l'Aïoli 📞 04 94 97 06 57; www.hotel-le-baron.com 🕐 Closed mid-Nov to mid-Dec

Hôtel Byblos €€€

Byblos is the jet set's hotel of choice. Doormen keep out the riff-raff, reserving the sophisticated interior for the privileged guests. Inside, small villas, flower gardens and neat patios are clustered around a pool, fitness centre and boutiques. In summer, Byblos is the venue for the chic nightclub, Les Caves du Roy, and Alain Ducasse's restaurant, Spoon (▶ 156).

📍 179 E3 🗺 Avenue Paul Signac 📞 04 94 56 68 00; www.byblos.com 🕐 Closed Nov to mid-Apr

Château de la Messardière €€€

This luxurious hotel, set on a private hillside with views over the sea and the Gulf of St-Tropez, is truly palatial: a 19th-century castle, just a stone's throw from the beach. A large swimming pool, fitness and beauty centre, tennis courts and a well-renowned restaurant are also on site.

📍 179 E3 🗺 Route de Tahiti 📞 04 94 56 76 00; www.messardiere.com 🕐 Closed early Oct–late Mar

Hôtel Les Lauriers €

A two-star hotel set a little away from the action, on a street behind the place des Lices. The rooms are pleasant and cool, and there's a shady garden to escape the heat.

📍 179 E3 🗺 Rue du Temple 📞 04 94 97 04 88 🕐 Closed Nov–Mar

Hôtel Lou Cagnard €–€€

This comfortable budget hotel is an excellent option, with rooms that are airy, clean and simple. Enjoy breakfast in the lovely, leafy garden on a sunny morning. Private parking available.

📍 179 E3 🗺 18 avenue Paul Roussel 📞 04 94 97 04 24; www.hotel-lou-cagnard.com 🕐 Closed Nov–Dec

Hôtel la Maison Blanche €€€

This beautiful old town house is stylishly decorated in a minimalist fashion, with white dominating the colour palette. Situated on the place des Lices, the port is only a short walk away.

📍 179 E3 🗺 15 place des Lices 📞 04 94 97 52 66; www.hotellamaisonblanche.com

Where to...
Eat and Drink

Prices

Expect to pay for a three-course meal for one, excluding drinks and service

€ under €25   €€ €25–€60   €€€ over €60

BORMES-LES-MIMOSAS

L'Escondudo €€

Wholesome regional dishes, flavoured with herbs from the surrounding hills, served on a sunny bougainvillaea-filled terrace.

🕀 178 C2 ⊠ 2 ruelle du Moulin 🕾 04 94 71 15 53 🕑 Thu–Mon dinner only; Thu, Fri, Mon low season

Lou Portaou €€

Market-fresh Provençal cuisine in a pretty, hidden corner of the village.

🕀 178 C2 ⊠ 1 rue Cubert des Poètes 🕾 04 94 64 86 37 🕑 Closed Mon pm, and Tue mid–Sep to mid–Jun

COLLOBRIÈRES

La Petite Fontaine €

Try some regional delicacies of the Massif des Maures, washed down with a glass of local wine.

🕀 178 C3 ⊠ 1 place de la République 🕾 04 94 48 00 12 🕑 Closed Sun pm–Mon

LA GARDE-FREINET

Longo Maï €€

This cosy, intimate restaurant at the heart of the Massif des Maures provides the perfect venue to taste *cassoulet Provençal* (a hotpot of white beans, pork and white wine), served by the log fire in winter.

🕀 179 D3 ⊠ D558, Massif des Maures 🕾 04 94 55 59 60 🕑 Closed Sun pm–Mon

LES ARCS-SUR-ARGENS

Le Bacchus Gourmand €€

After learning about and sampling Côtes de Provence wines at the Maison du Vin Côtes de Provence (▶ 152), head upstairs for some wonderful Provençal cuisine, accompanied by quality local wine.

🕀 179 D4 ⊠ N7 🕾 04 94 47 48 47 🕑 Closed Sun, Oct–Mar

GRIMAUD

Les Santons €€

This popular restaurant is one of the region's best, so book well ahead in summer and on weekends. The freshest local ingredients are used to make classic French and Mediterranean dishes. Impeccable service and elegant surroundings.

🕀 179 D3 ⊠ N558 🕾 04 94 43 21 02 🕑 Mon, Thu–Sun 12–2:30, 7–10; Tue–Wed 7–10

ST-TROPEZ

La Bouillabaisse €€

A speciality fish restaurant in an old fisherman's cottage on the beach.

🕀 179 E3 ⊠ Plage de la Bouillabaisse 🕾 04 94 97 54 00 🕑 Mid-Oct to mid-May; closed dinner Sun–Thu

Le Café €€

Formerly known as Le Café des Arts, this cosy bar/stylish restaurant has a long history as a centre for intellectual and artistic debate, and was also the reception venue for Rolling Stone Mick Jagger's wedding to Bianca Perez Morena de Macias in 1971. An archetypal French bar with brown leather couches, wooden fittings and prominently displayed pétanque trophies. Have a meal or a coffee on the terrace while watching a game of pétanque.

street overlooking the Chapelle de la Misericorde. Excellent value.

➕ 179 E3 ☒ 5 place des Lices ☎ 04 94 97 44 69; www.lecafe.fr ⏰ Food daily 12–2.30, 7.30–11; café 8 am–midnight

Chez Fuchs €€

This friendly, unpretentious, family-run bar-*tabac* serves a wide range of cigars and hearty bistro meals. Traditional dishes and a lively atmosphere make tiny Chez Fuchs hugely popular. Book ahead.

➕ 179 E3 ☒ 7 rue des Commerçants ☎ 04 94 97 01 25 ⏰ Closed Sun–Mon

La Citadelle €€

This tiny, atmospheric restaurant overflows onto the street. Don't miss the scrumptious tarte tatin.

➕ 179 E3 ☒ 1 rue Aire du Chemin ☎ 04 94 54 81 19 ⏰ Closed Nov–Mar

L'Eau à la Bouche €–€€

Simple, homey cuisine on a sunny pavement terrace in a cobbled back-

Sénéquier €€

You can't miss the distinctive red awnings on the waterfront, for this is one of the best-known spots in town and a must for breakfast. There's no denying the coffees are on the pricey side, but this is really the place to be on a sunny morning in St-Tropez.

➕ 179 E3 ☒ Quai Jean-Jaurès ☎ 04 94 97 00 90 ⏰ Daily, summer 8 am–2 am; winter 8–8

Spoon Byblos €€€

Enshrined within the exclusive Hôtel Byblos (➤ 154), Spoon Byblos aims to encompass world cuisine and offers an inventive menu which can be read horizontally, with the food divided into numbered columns: dish (1), sauce (2) and accompaniment (3). You can mix and match elements from each column to create your own culinary masterpiece. The food at Spoon Byblos is influenced by the different cultures and produce of the

Mediterranean, combining the flavours of the Riviera, Italy, Catalonia, Andalucia, Tunisia and Morocco.

➕ 179 E3 ☒ Avenue du Maréchal Foch ☎ 04 94 56 68 20; www.byblos.com/spoonbyblos ⏰ Daily 8 pm to 11 pm or midnight, mid-Apr to mid-Oct

La Table du Marché €–€€

An elegant informal bistro-cum-deli, with star chef Christophe Leroy at the helm, serving Provençal dishes created from fresh market produce. The set menu offers good value for dinner, or call in for afternoon tea and choose from the tempting array of pastries and cakes displayed at the counter. You can also stock up on quality olive oil, wine and other regional specialities while you're here.

➕ 179 E3 ☒ 38 rue Georges Clemenceau ☎ 04 94 97 91 91; www.christophe-leroy.com ⏰ Daily 8 am–midnight

Maison Leï Mouscardins €€€

Sitting among the yachts and cruisers on St-Tropez's famous port, you can expect nothing but the freshest seafood to be on the menu at this renowned quayside restaurant. A seafood platter, accompanied by a chilled bottle of white wine, makes a perfect lunch.

➕ 179 E3 ☒ Tour de Portalet ☎ 04 94 97 29 00 ⏰ Closed Sat noon, Sun eve, Mon, and Nov–Feb

Pizzeria du Vieux Port €–€€

The pizzas and set menu here are reasonably priced for a restaurant right on the waterfront at St-Tropez, and the view is superb.

➕ 179 E3 ☒ Quai Frédéric Mistral ☎ 04 94 97 20 49 ⏰ Summer daily 12 pm–1 am, winter 12 pm–11 pm

Where to...
Shop

FOOD AND DRINK

A trip to St-Tropez is not complete without sampling the creations from **La Tarte Tropézienne** (36 rue Clemenceau, tel: 04 94 97 71 42, www.tarte-tropezienne.com). The shop takes its name from the tart – a rich cake sandwich filled with custard and topped with sugar – that was popular with Brigitte Bardot during the filming of *Et Dieu Créa la Femme (And God Created Woman)* in 1956. Confectioner Alexandre Micka created the tart while he was catering for the actors of the film, and the invention was named by Bardot herself.

Nestled between vineyards in Gassin, **La Maison des Confitures** (chemin Bourrian, tel: 04 94 43 41 58), has more than 500 varieties of

jam, including some typically regional ones (thyme, lavender, fig and nut) and savoury ones (such as onion).

At the **Petit Village** in Gassin (Carrefour de la Foux, tel: 04 94 56 32 04), you can buy the wines of the *Maîtres Vignerons*, which are considered among the best Côtes de Provence wines. You can also stock up on local wines in Les Arcs-sur-Argens at the **Maison du Vins Côtes de Provence** (➤ 152).

MARKETS

St Tropez's **Marché aux Poissons** (place aux Herbes, open daily 7 am–1 pm) is a small fish market which provides a different view of life in the town. Try Mediterranean fish such as red mullet, scorpion fish and rainbow wrasse. Credit cards are not accepted.

The **Marché Provençal** (place des Lices, St-Tropez, open Tue, Sat 8–1) has typical Provençal food, as well as an antiques corner and

some local crafts. Credit cards are not accepted.

Marché Collobriérois (place de la Libération, Collobrières, Thu, Sun 8–1) is a lively farmers' market with a good range of chestnut products, from *marrons glacés* and chestnut jam to chestnut-wood wickerwork. Cork products and other regional specialities such as olives and honey are also sold. Credit cards are not accepted.

PROVENÇAL GOODS

Tropézienne fashion history was made with the invention of the Tropézienne sandal in 1927, a Roman-gladiator-style sandal favoured by the likes of Picasso. At **Rondini's** (16 rue Georges Clemenceau, tel: 04 94 97 19 55 www.nova.fr/rondini), the family who originally brought this sandal to the town continue to do so today. The sandals come in a variety of styles for around €100 and are a popular souvenir of St-Tropez.

You can get **L'Occitane** products just about anywhere, but the little boutique in St-Tropez is a lovely place to buy a scented souvenir of Provence (rue Georges Clemenceau, www.loccitane.com).

Pépinières Cavatore (chemin de Bénat, tel: 04 94 00 40 23; www.pepinierescavatore.com) in Bormes-les-Mimosas is a nursery specialising in mimosa – visit in February to see the trees in full bloom. It's worth a visit, even if you aren't planning on buying anything. Credit cards are not accepted.

At **Pipes Courrieu** (58–60 avenue Georges Clemenceau, Cogolin, tel: 04 94 54 63 82; www.courrieupipes.fr, open Mon–Sat 9–12, 2–6), pipes have been made by the same family since 1802, using the methods which have been passed from father to son. They are made out of briar from Maures' mountains and marked with a silver cockerel, the emblem of Cogolin village.

Where to...
Be Entertained

NIGHTLIFE

There is no shortage of exclusive clubs in St-Tropez. One of the best known is **Les Caves du Roy** in Hotel Byblos (avenue Paul Signac/avenue Foch, tel: 04 94 56 68 00, open Jul–Aug daily 11 pm–5 am; Apr–Jun, Sep–Oct Fri–Sat 11 pm–5 am). This well-established haunt of the rich and famous can prove difficult to get into, so try to arrive early and look beautiful. Admission is free, but drink prices are extortionate.

La Bodega de Papagayo (résidences du Nouveau Port, tel: 04 94 79 29 50) is a restaurant-nightclub near the Old Port. It has a terrace with great views, and is a good place for a bit of celebrity spotting.

Clubby music pumping into the small hours makes it popular with the young crowd. Bands perform almost every night during the high season.

The VIP Room (résidences du Nouveau Port, tel: 04 94 97 14 70, open May–Sep daily 9 pm–5 am; mid-Oct to Apr 9 pm–3 am) is all class, and to get inside you must be a VIP, or at least look as if you might be. The crowd here loves to dance, and the music will keep everyone up on their feet all night.

On the first floor of classy Hôtel Sube, **Bar Anglais** (Hôtel Sube, 15 quai Suffren, tel: 04 94 97 30 04, open daily 7:30 am–1 am or 3 am May–Oct) has a good range of beers on tap, and some great cocktails, best enjoyed on the tiny balcony,

which has views over the port. If you're not into clubbing, **Octave Café** (place de la Garonne, St-Tropez, tel: 04 94 97 22 56) is a stylish café, with comfy chairs, low tables, and lounge and live music. You'll find jazz musicians playing in a small back-bar area.

FESTIVALS

The area is packed with festivals and events. Check with local tourist offices for further information and exact dates.

In **February**, Bormes-les-Mimosas' famous festival, the Corso Fleuri, celebrates the coming of spring and thus the yellow, vanilla-scented flower after which the village is named.

April brings the Fête de la Transhumance to Collobrières, a celebration of the traditional moving of flocks of sheep.

In **mid-May**, St-Tropez's tribute to its headless patron, St Torpes (or Tropez), takes place at the *Bravade*.

St-Tropez's second festival, Bravade des Espagnols, takes place on **15 June**.

Across France, **14 July** is Bastille Day, commemorating the start of the French Revolution with the storming of the Bastille prison.

August is a great month for local celebrations everywhere. Among them are Collobrières' Grande Fête des Fontaines, celebrated in style, with rosé wine spurting from the town's fountain. The Festival de Ramatuelle, featuring theatre and music, takes place in August (▶ 142).

Throughout **September**, Bormes-Les-Mimosas is a hotbed of competition as the World Pétanque Championships take place. At the end of the month, St-Tropez hosts the Nioulargue yacht race.

Collobrières celebrates the Fête de la Chataigne in **October**, in conjunction with the chestnut harvest. There's lively street entertainment and more chestnut products than you could ever consume.

Walks and Tours

1 Cap Martin Coast

Walk

DISTANCE 6km (4 miles) **TIME** 1.5 hours (longer if you continue to Monte-Carlo)
START/END POINT Cap Martin/ Cabbé or Monte-Carlo. Note, the journey back to the start point involves a train ride, so check timetables ahead ✚ 181 E3

East of Monaco and close to the Italian border, Cap Martin is a rich suburb of Menton, with mansions set among sweet-smelling mimosa and olive trees. This long, linear walk (you return by train) along the Cap Martin coast takes in some of the most attractive scenery on the Côte d'Azur. The sapphire sea sparkles on your left; sweet honeysuckle, mimosa and rhododendrons bloom on your right; and coastal towns lie ahead towards the principality of Monaco.

1–2

If you are driving to Cap Martin, there is a **parking area** at the seaward end of avenue Winston Churchill on the Cap. From here, walk farther towards the end of the Cap, past **Le Roc Martin** restaurant (on the left) and come to a wide path at the edge of the sea. The path is called **promenade Le Courbusier**, after the influential 1920s architect.

Le Corbusier was connected with this area through his association with designer Eileen Gray, whose house is near by. The start of the path is marked by a sign for **Ville de Roquebrune-Cap Martin.**

2–3

Follow the promenade Le Courbusier as it hugs the coastline, skirting the edges of private gardens and smart hotels.

Cap Martin Watchtower

The headland at Cap Martin is perfectly positioned to provide good views of the area, and has long been used as a lookout point. The ruins of a fortified medieval watchtower can be found at the centre of the headland today. Also here are the remains of an 11th-century priory, where it is said an arrangement was made between the monks who lived here and the local people, whereby if the tower's bell rang, the people would come to the aid of the monks. One night, the prior rang the bell to test the people's response, and they came running to help, only to find nothing the matter. A few nights later, when the priory was raided by pirates, the townspeople left the ringing bell unanswered and the monks of the priory were all killed.

The path heads west along the edge of Cap Martin, providing spectacular views of Monaco and the sea. **Eileen Gray's house**, designated a historic monument in 1998, is hidden from view, below the path that continues up the western side of the Cap.

3–4

There are several places along the path where steps lead up to the Cap, but a good option is to continue on to **Cabbé**, where

A sea angler casting his line from Cap Martin

there is a rail connection back to **Carnolès**. From Carnolès station you can return to the **parking area** by heading towards the sea, and then following the coastal path back to where you started.

4–5

To extend the walk beyond Cabbé, the path continues into **Monte-Carlo**, offering a grand entrance into the principality. Between Cabbé and Monte-Carlo the path sometimes strays onto the road. There are train connections from Monaco back to Carnolès station.

Tips
- Consult a train timetable before you set out, and time your walk so that you can meet a train at Cabbé to take you back to Carnolès.
- Bring a raincoat if it is a windy day or the sea is rough, as the promenade can be splashed by waves.
- It is best to take this walk in the afternoon, when the hottest part of the day has passed and the sun is at a good angle for the views.

Rhododendrons bloom along the path in early summer

Taking a break
Cap Martin has expensive, high-quality restaurants. Less expensive places can be found at the other end of the walk in Cabbé.

2 St-Tropez
Walk

Stroll around St-Tropez's glamorous high-class shops and marina, detour at an art gallery, continue on towards the old heart of the town and climb La Citadelle, where you can take in a wonderful vista across the whole town and bay.

DISTANCE 2km (1.2 miles) **TIME** 2 hours, plus time for visits
START/END POINT Place des Lices (park at parking des Lices) **⊞** 179 E3

1–2
Start at **place des Lices**, a large open area where serious games of pétanque take place under the shade of plane trees, and markets are held on Tuesdays and Saturdays.

2–3
Take the **rue Georges Clemenceau** (with Café Clemenceau on the corner) away from the place des Lices towards the port. Stop off at **La Tarte Tropézienne** (➤ 157) to experience the eponymous sponge cake filled with custard cream that was invented here in the 1950s and has enjoyed enormous popularity ever since. Upmarket boutiques proliferate along this pedestrianised street, and all the

way down to the harbour. Cross the main street and turn left at **quai Gabriel Péri**. The Musée de l'Annonciade (➤ 141, closed Tuesday) sits on the corner ahead, where the quay bears right. The permanent collection

here includes many pointillist and fauvist works dating from the end of the 19th century, when St-Tropez was at the centre of the artistic avant-garde.

3–4
Walk back along the quay, so that the water is on your left. You should get a wonderful view of the luxury boats in the harbour from here. Take a couple of minutes to look at the founding father of St-Tropez, Pierre-André de Suffren, an 18th-century admiral whose **statue** will be on your right. Farther along the quay, pick up a town map from the **tourist office** on the right. The famous red-terraced **Café Sénéquier** (➤ 156) is here too. Stop by for a coffee, looking out over the harbour, the yachts and passers-by.

A game of pétanque in the place des Lices, St-Tropez

Taking a break

Tarte Tropézienne (➤ 157)
Sénéquier (➤ 156)
Chez Fuchs (➤ 156)
Le Café (➤ 155)

4–5

Follow the waterfront until you come to **Môle Jean-Reveille**, the jetty enclosing the port. Climb up some steps to the paved jetty to enjoy a sweeping view of the town on one side and the Bay of St-Tropez on the other. From the *môle*, head down to the **Tour du Portalet** and enter a little street at the base of the tower, rue Portalet, with **Leï Mouscardins** (➤ 156) on the corner. Turn left into rue St-Ésprit and then the first-left into rue du Puits. Turn left into **place de l'Hôtel de Ville** and take the third right into rue St-Jean to reach the **Église de St-Tropez** (➤ 140). Turn right down rue du Clocher, and right again at rue Commandant Guichard, where you'll find the church's entrance. The church's bright pink bell tower houses the bust of St Torpes (or Tropez), the town's patron saint, who is celebrated in an annual

procession at the Bravade de St-Torpes in May (➤ 140).

5–6

Return to the **place de l'Hôtel de Ville** and turn right to walk through the Porte du Revelen (an arch at the end of the street). On the other side of the arch is the small **Port des Pêcheurs**, the fishermen's port that originally made up St-Tropez. Turning around, walk up the rue des Ramparts, left across the small place des Ramparts, and take rue des Quatre-vents until you come to some steps at the end of the street. Turn right down rue de l'Aïoli, take a left between two anchors (across from Baron Lodge), and climb up the steps leading towards **La Citadelle** (➤ 140–141). Dating back to the 16th century, the citadel houses the **Musée Naval** (➤ 141).

6–7

From the citadel, retrace your path down the steps and cross the road to enter the pedestrian-only rue de la Citadelle. Continue down this street until a minor crossroad, where you should turn right into rue des Commerçants. On the right is **Chez Fuchs** (➤ 156), where, past the thousands of cigars, a spiral staircase leads up towards a popular Provençal bistro.

7–8

Outside Chez Fuchs, take the first left down a small alley, rue de Marché, which leads towards **place aux Herbes**, a tiny but lovely square where a daily market is held. An arch on the left leads into the **fish market**, where freshly caught fish is sold by local fishmongers.

8–9

Continue on through the fish market to come out at the **tourist office**. Cross the road into the boutique-lined rue François Sibilli, past place de la Garonne, and continue on along rue François Sibilli to return to the place des Lices, where you should reward yourself with a coffee at **Le Café** (➤ 155).

3 Vence to Grasse
Drive

DISTANCE 44km (27.5 miles) **TIME** Allow a half-day with visits
START POINT Vence ✚ 180 B3 **END POINT** Grasse ✚ 180 A3

1–2
Leave Vence on the **D2210** signposted Grasse and Tourrettes-sur-Loup. After 3km (2 miles), just off the road, is **Château Notre-Dame-des-Fleurs**. This magnificent 19th-century castle became a contemporary art foundation in 1993 and contains a permanent collection of works by Matisse, Dufy and Chagall.

2–3
Continue along the **D2210** to **Tourrettes-sur-Loup**. Tourrettes is a lovely medieval village on a rocky ridge. The village is popular with artists and artisans, but perhaps best known for its production of violets (▶ 11, 21).

3–4
Eight kilometres (5 miles) farther on, you will arrive at **Pont-du-Loup**. From here it is worth taking a short detour to **Le Bar-sur-Loup**.

The national flag flying from the highest point of Tourrettes-sur-Loup

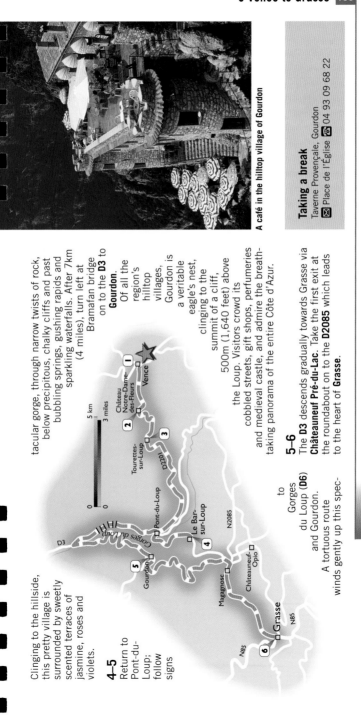

A café in the hilltop village of Gourdon

Taking a break
Taverne Provençale, Gourdon
Place de l'Église ☎ 04 93 09 68 22

tacular gorge, through narrow twists of rock, below precipitous, chalky cliffs and past bubbling springs, gushing rapids and sparkling waterfalls. After 7km (4 miles), turn left at Bramafan bridge on to the **D3** to **Gourdon**.

Of all the region's hilltop villages, Gourdon is a veritable eagle's nest, clinging to the summit of a cliff, 500m (1,640 feet) above the Loup. Visitors crowd its cobbled streets, gift shops, perfumeries and medieval castle, and admire the breathtaking panorama of the entire Côte d'Azur.

5–6

The **D3** descends gradually towards Grasse via **Châteauneuf Pré-du-Lac**. Take the first exit at the roundabout on to the **D2085** which leads to the heart of **Grasse**.

Clinging to the hillside, this pretty village is surrounded by sweetly scented terraces of jasmine, roses and violets.

4–5

Return to Pont-du-Loup; follow signs

to Gorges du Loup (**D6**) and Gourdon. A tortuous route winds gently up this spec-

Map labels: Vence ①, Château Notre-Dame-des-Fleurs ②, Tourettes-sur-Loup ③, D2210, Pont-du-Loup, Gorges du Loup, D3, Le Bar-sur-Loup ④, N2085, Gourdon ⑤, Châteauneuf-Opio, Magagnosc, Grasse ⑥, N85

5 km / 3 miles

4 Exploring Inland from the Côte d'Azur

Drive

This circular route into the countryside which lies behind the principality of Monaco contrasts some of the prettiest – and busiest – villages and towns of the Côte d'Azur with the peace and natural beauty of the Parc National du Mercantour.

DISTANCE 150km (93 miles) **TIME** Allow a full day for this drive, and be aware that the roads inland from the coast are often winding and slow **START/END POINT** Menton ✚ 181 E4

Flags flying from the tollgate on the 11th-century bridge over the **Bevera River at the heart of Sospel**

1–2

Start from **Menton** (▶ 72–73), a pretty and curiously Italian town on the French side of the border. There's a **museum** by the waterfront to the poet, playwright and film director Jean Cocteau (1889–1963), which is worth a quick look if you have time. Pick up the road in the town centre signed **Autoroute (Nice, Italia) and Sospel**. Follow signs for Sospel on the winding **D2566**, passing under the A8 and through Castillon-Neuf. Go over the railway crossing and turn left, following signs

down to Sospel. Go over **Col de Braus** (1,002m/3,287 feet) and descend through hairpin bends almost into L'Escarène. Just after a railway bridge turn right, signposted to Lucéram and Peïra-Cava. Continue on this road to reach the attractively jumbled medieval hilltop village of **Lucéram**.

for Moulinet and Col de Turini. The bridge at Sospel, with its central tower, was rebuilt in the 20th century after the 11th-century original was blown up during World War II.

2–3

Bear left at a bend on to the **D2204**. The road climbs to Col St-Jean, with great views back

3–4

Go through Lucéram, and at the next junction, on a steep hill, bear left, following signs for Turini. There are many more hairpin bends to negotiate before you reach the superb viewpoint of **Peïra-Cava**. To the east, the view is of the magnificent Parc National du Mercantour.

4–5

Continue north from Peïra-Cava to the next viewpoint, **Col de Turini**. The mountain pass stands at 1,607m (5,272 feet), and this is a good place for a break and refreshment at the hotel **Les Trois Vallées**.

5–6

Turn left on to the **D70**, following signs for La Bollène-Vésubie and Nice. Descend with care, and after about 10km (6 miles), just after the Chapelle-St-Honorat tunnel, look out for a small **chapel** on the left, on a bend. There are fabulous views from the parking area here.

6–7

Continue on this road through La Bollène-Vésubie and at a T-junction (intersection) turn left on to the **D2565**, signed for Nice and St-Martin-Vésubie (Vésubie is the name of the river which runs through here). This brings you to the valley floor. Follow signs for Lantosque and

Nice, going straight on at first, then left along the main road. After 1km (0.6 miles) divert right to go through **Lantosque** village, then rejoin the main road. Continue southwards through **St-Jean-de-la-Rivière**. About 1km (0.6 miles) beyond St-Jean fork left on to the **D19**, signed Nice par Levens. This road becomes narrower as it ascends the valley. Go through a tunnel just before Duranus and look for a viewpoint on the right. The **Saut des Français** looks out from sheer cliffs. Stay on the road into **Levens**, an appealing old town with two 18th-century chapels standing on two sides of the square, and a grand gateway – the remnant of a castle that has long since disappeared.

Taking a break

Les Trois Vallées hotel-restaurant stands at the high point of this tour, at the Col de Turini ☎ 04 93 04 23 23. There are also several bars and restaurants in Sospel.

7–8

Leave Levens on the **D19**, following signs for Nice, and passing Tourette-Levens. Soon after St-André the road passes under the A8. Turn left at traffic lights here, signed to Sospel. Cross a river and go straight over another set of traffic lights, passing under the A8 again. Take the next right turn, signed Route de Turin, cross the river and a level (grade) crossing, then turn left at traffic lights, signed La Trinité and Drap. At the roundabout (traffic circle) take the road signed for La Turbie and Laghet, and follow the **D2204a** up a winding valley to **Laghet**. There a hairpin bend takes the road sharply right.

Pass under the A8 once more, and turn left at the next junction, an autoroute slip road,

following signs to Menton. Turn left at the next junction, signed for La Turbie and Monaco, and stay on this road to the ancient Roman village of **La Turbie** (▶ 66). Its outstanding monument is the Trophée des

Alpes, a triumphal arch built by Augustus Caesar around 6 BC. After La Turbie bear left past a hotel, signed Roquebrune and Menton, and turn right at traffic lights at the bottom of the hill, signed Nice and Beausoleil. At the next lights turn left, signed to Cap Martin. As it leaves the heart of the village the road veers sharp left – go straight ahead here, signed for Mayerling and Cap Martin, to reach the sea. Follow the coast road back to **Menton**.

The picturesque village of La Bollène-Vésubie

GETTING ADVANCE INFORMATION

Websites

Département Tourist Information:
● Alpes-Maritimes: www.guideriviera.com
● Var: www.tourismevar.com

Tourist Offices
● www.cannes.fr
● www.monaco-tourisme.com
● www.nicetourism.com
● www.saint-tropez.st
● www.franceguide.com

● Online resources with information in English: www.provencebeyond.com www.provenceweb.fr www.angloinfo.com
● Route planner: www.theAA.com

BEFORE YOU GO

WHAT YOU NEED

● Required
○ Suggested
▲ Not required
△ Not applicable

Some countries require a passport to remain valid for at least six months beyond the date of entry – contact their consulate or embassy or your travel agent for details.

	UK	Germany	USA	Canada	Australia	Ireland	Netherlands	Spain
Passport (or National Identity Card where applicable)	●	●	●	●	●	●	●	△
Visa (regulations can change – check before your journey)	▲	▲	▲	▲	▲	▲	▲	▲
Onward or Return Ticket	▲	▲	▲	▲	▲	▲	▲	▲
Health Inoculations (tetanus and polio)	▲	▲	▲	▲	▲	▲	▲	▲
Health Documentation (➤ 174, Health)	●	●	●	●	●	●	●	●
Travel Insurance	○	○	○	○	○	○	○	○
Driver's Licence (national)	●	●	●	●	●	●	●	●
Car Insurance Certificate	○	○	n/a	n/a	n/a	○	○	○
Car Registration Document	●	●	n/a	n/a	n/a	●	●	●

WHEN TO GO

Côte d'Azur

High season   Low season

JAN	FEB	MAR	APR	MAY	JUN	JUL	AUG	SEP	OCT	NOV	DEC
12°C	14°C	14°C	18°C	21°C	27°C	28°C	28°C	25°C	22°C	17°C	14°C

☀ Sun   ☁ Cloud   🌧 Wet   🌦 Sun/Showers   🌧 Very wet

Temperatures are the **average daily maximum** for each month, although they can rise to 35°C (95°F) in July and August. Spring starts in March when the mimosa and almonds come into bloom on the coast, and it is usually warm enough to sit outside on the terrace in April. Summers are hot and dry, and the coastal areas are very crowded. The autumn months (September and October) can be very pleasant, although there may be occasional thunderstorms. Colder weather arrives in November, with snow settling on high ground in December.

In the UK	In the US	In Australia	In Canada
French Tourist Office	French Tourist Office	French Tourist Office	French Tourist Office
178 Piccadilly	444 Madison	Level 20	1981 avenue
London	Avenue	25 Bligh Street	McGill College
W1V OAL	16th Floor	Sydney NSW 2000	Suite 490
☎ 0906 824	New York NY10022	☎ 02 9231 5244	Montreal H3A 2W9
4123	☎ 212/838 7800		☎ 514/876 9881

GETTING THERE

By Air Nice-Côte d'Azur is the main airport in the region, but there are also international flights from within Europe to Marseille-Provence and to the smaller airport just outside St-Tropez, at La Mole.

From the UK Carriers include France's international airline, Air France (tel: 0845 084 5111 in UK; 0802 802 802 in France; www.airfrance.com), British Airways (tel: 0845 773 3377; www.ba.com), easyJet (tel: 0871 750 0100; www.easyjet.com) and Ryanair (tel: 0870 156 9569; www.ryanair.com). The flight time from London to Nice is around 2 hours.

From the US and Canada Delta Air Lines operates a few direct flights between New York and Nice-Côte d'Azur, but passengers from most US and Canadian cities will usually have to change at London (Heathrow, Gatwick and Stansted) or Paris. Delta Air Lines (tel: 1800/241 4141 in US; www.delta.com), American Airlines (tel: 1800/433 7300 in US; www.aa.com) and Air Canada (tel: 1888/247 2262 in Canada; www.aircanada.com). The flying time direct from New York to Provence is around 8 hours.

By Rail SNCF, the national carrier, operates high-speed train (TGV) services from the Gare de Lyon in Paris to Nice. The journey takes about 6 hours (www.tgv.co.uk). The Eurostar passenger train service (tel: 0870 518 6186 in UK; www.eurostar.com) from London Waterloo via the Channel Tunnel to Paris Gare du Nord takes 2.5 hours.

By Sea Several ferry companies operate regular services from England and Ireland to north and northwest France. Crossing times from England vary from 35 minutes to 9 hours, and from Ireland around 14 to 18 hours.

TIME

France is on Central European Time, one hour ahead of Greenwich Mean Time (GMT +1). From late March, when clocks are put forward one hour, until late October, French summer time (GMT +2) operates.

CURRENCY AND FOREIGN EXCHANGE

Currency The euro (€) is the official currency of France and Monaco. Notes (bills) are issued in denominations of €5, €10, €20, €50, €100, €200 and €500 and coins are in denominations of 1, 2, 5, 10, 20 and 50 cents, and €1 and €2.

Exchange You can exchange travellers' cheques at some banks and at bureaux de change at airports, main railway stations or in some department stores, and exchange booths. All transactions are subject to a commission charge, so you may prefer to rely on cash and credit cards. Travellers' cheques issued by American Express and VISA may also be changed at many post offices.

Credit cards are widely accepted in shops, restaurants and hotels. VISA (Carte Bleue), MasterCard (Eurocard) and Diners Club cards with four-digit PINs can be used in most ATM cash dispensers. Some smaller shops and hotels may not accept credit cards – always check before you book in.

GMT	Nice	USA New York	Germany	Spain	Australia
12 noon	1 pm	← 7 am	→ 1 pm	→ 1 pm	→ Sydney 10 pm

WHEN YOU ARE THERE

CLOTHING SIZES

UK	Rest of Europe	USA	
36	46	36	
38	48	38	
40	50	40	
42	52	42	Suits
44	54	44	
46	56	46	
7	41	8	
7.5	42	8.5	
8.5	43	9.5	
9.5	44	10.5	Shoes
10.5	45	11.5	
11	46	12	
14.5	37	14.5	
15	38	15	
15.5	39/40	15.5	
16	41	16	Shirts
16.5	42	16.5	
17	43	17	
8	34	6	
10	36	8	
12	38	10	
14	40	12	Dresses
16	42	14	
18	44	16	
4.5	38	6	
5	38	6.5	
5.5	39	7	
6	39	7.5	Shoes
6.5	40	8	
7	41	8.5	

NATIONAL HOLIDAYS

1 Jan	New Year's Day
27 Jan	St Devote's Day (Monaco only)
Mar/Apr	Easter Sunday and Monday
1 May	Labour Day
8 May	VE Day (France only)
May/Jun	Whit Sunday and Monday
Jun	Corpus Christi (Monaco only)
14 Jul	Bastille Day (France only)
15 Aug	Assumption
1 Nov	All Saints' Day
11 Nov	Remembrance Day (France only)
19 Nov	Monaco National Holiday (Monaco only)
25 Dec	Christmas Day

OPENING HOURS

○ Shops
● Offices
● Banks
● Post Offices
● Museums/Monuments
● Pharmacies

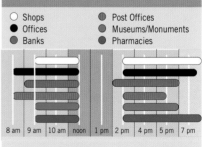

8 am | 9 am | 10 am | noon | 1 pm | 2 pm | 4 pm | 5 pm | 7 pm

☐ Day   ☐ Midday   ☐ Evening

Shops In summer the afternoon opening time of shops is from 4 to 8 or 9 pm. Most shops close on Sunday and many on Monday. Small food shops open from 7 am and may open on Sunday morning. Large department stores do not close for lunch, and hypermarkets open 10 am to 9 or 10 pm but may shut on Monday morning.

Banks Banks are closed on Sunday as well as Saturday or Monday.

Museums Museums and monuments have extended summer hours. Many close one day a week; either Monday (municipal ones) or Tuesday (national ones).

EMERGENCY NUMBERS

POLICE 17

FIRE 18

AMBULANCE 15

PERSONAL SAFETY

The Police Municipale (blue uniforms) carry out police duties in cities and towns. The Gendarmes (blue trousers, black jackets, white belts), the national police force, cover the countryside and smaller places. The CRS deal with emergencies and also look after safety on beaches. Monaco has its own police.

To avoid danger or theft:
• Do not use unmanned roadside rest areas at night.
• Cars, especially foreign cars, should be secured.
• Beware of pickpockets.

Police assistance:
 17 from any call box

TELEPHONES

 number when phoning from outside the principality). Most public phones use a phone card (*télécarte*), sold in units of 50 or 120 at France Telecom shops, post offices, tobacconists, newsagents and at railway stations. Cheap call rates generally apply Mon–Fri 7 pm–8 am, Sat–Sun all day.

All telephone numbers in France comprise ten digits (eight in Monaco). There are no area codes except for Monaco (377 precedes

International Dialling Codes
Dial 00 followed by

UK:	44
USA / Canada:	1
Irish Republic:	353
Australia:	61
New Zealand:	64

POST

 The PTT (*Poste et Télécommunications*) deals with mail and telephone services. Outside main centres, post offices open shorter hours and may close 12–2. Letter boxes are yellow. Post offices usually have an ATM.

ELECTRICITY

The power supply throughout France is 220 volts AC, 50 Hz. Sockets accept two-round-pin continental-style plugs. Visitors from the UK will need a plug adaptor and US visitors will need a voltage transformer.

TIPS/GRATUITIES

Tipping is normal for all services. As a general guide:

Taxis	Change from note (bill)
Tour guides	€3–5
Porters	€3 per bag
Chambermaids	€2 per day
Cafés/bars	Leave change
Hairdressers	Change from note (bill)
Restaurant workers	Service always included. Leave a note if service has been exemplary

CONSULATES

UK
☎ 04 91 15 72 10
☎ 04 93 62 13 56

US
☎ 04 91 54 92 00
☎ 04 93 88 89 55

Germany
☎ 04 91 16 75 20
☎ 04 93 83 55 25

Ireland
☎ 04 93 61 50 63

Canada
☎ 04 93 92 93 22

HEALTH

 Insurance Citizens of EU countries receive reduced-cost emergency health care with relevant documentation (European Health Insurance Card), but private medical insurance is still advised, and essential for all other visitors.

Dental Services As for general medical treatment (see above, Insurance), nationals of EU countries can obtain dental treatment at reduced cost. Around 70 per cent of standard dentists' fees are refunded, but private medical insurance is still advised for all.

Weather July and August are likely to be sunny and very hot. When sightseeing, cover up, apply a good sunscreen, wear sunglasses and a hat, and drink plenty of fluids.

Drugs Pharmacies – recognised by their green cross sign – have highly qualified staff able to offer medical advice, provide first-aid and prescribe a wide range of drugs, although some are available by prescription (*ordonnance*) only.

Safe Water Tap water is safe to drink, and restaurants will often bring a carafe of water to the table, although you may prefer to buy bottled water. Never drink from a tap marked *eau non potable* (not drinking water).

CONCESSIONS

Students/Youths Holders of an International Student Identity Card (ISIC) are entitled to discounted admission to museums and sights, air and ferry tickets and meals in some student cafeterias. Holders of the International Youth Travel Card (or GO 25 Card) qualify for similar discounts as ISIC holders.

Senior Citizens If you are over 60 you can get discounts (up to 50 per cent) in museums, on public transport and in places of entertainment. You will need a Carte Vermeil, which can be purchased from the *Abonnement* office of any main railway station. You may get a discount if you show your passport.

TRAVELLING WITH A DISABILITY

France has made great headway in providing access and facilities for visitors with disabilities. However, some tourist offices, museums and restaurants that are in historic, protected buildings are still not fully accessible. A telephone call before going to a restaurant is a good idea to arrange for an easily accessible table. The Association des Paralysés de France (17 boulevard Auguste Blanqui, 75013, Paris, tel: 01 40 78 69 00; www.apf.asso.fr) provides information on wheelchair access.

CHILDREN

Children are welcomed in most hotels and restaurants. Baby-changing facilities are excellent in newer museums and attractions, but limited elsewhere.

TOILETS

Modern unisex, self-cleaning, coin-operated toilets are found on the streets of most major cities. In smaller towns and villages, free public toilets can normally be found by the market square or near tourist offices. Cleanliness varies, and some older or more remote establishments may have a squat toilet. Café toilets are for the use of customers only.

SURVIVAL PHRASES

Yes/no **Oui/non**
Hello **Bonjour/bonsoir**
Goodbye **Au revoir**
How are you? **Comment allez-vous?**
Please **S'il vous plaît**
Thank you **Merci**
Excuse me **Excusez-moi**
I'm sorry **Pardon**
You're welcome **De rien/avec plaisir**
Do you have...? **Avez-vous...?**
How much is this? **C'est combien?**
I'd like... **Je voudrais...**

DIRECTIONS

Is there a phone box around here?
  **Y a-t-il une cabine téléphonique
  dans le coin?**
Where is...? **Où se trouve...?**
...the nearest Métro **le Métro le plus
  proche**
...the telephone **le téléphone**
...the bank **la banque**
...the toilet **les toilettes**
Turn left/right **tournez à gauche/droite**
Go straight on **allez tout droit**
The first/second (on the right)
  le premier/le deuxième (à droite)
At the crossroads **au carrefour**

IF YOU NEED HELP

Could you help me, please?
  Pouvez-vous m'aider?
Do you speak English?
  Parlez-vous anglais?
I don't understand
  Je ne comprends pas
Could you call a doctor quickly,
  please? **Voulez-vous vite appeler un
  médecin, s'il vous plaît?**

RESTAURANT

I'd like to book a table **Puis-je
  réserver une table?**
A table for two please **Une table pour
  deux personnes, s'il vous plaît**
Do you have a fixed price menu?
  Vous avez un menu prix fixe?
Could we see the menu please?
  Nous pouvons avoir la carte?
Could I have the bill please?
  L'addition, s'il vous plaît
A bottle/glass of... **Une bouteille/un
  verre de...**

MENU READER

apéritifs appetisers
boissons alcoolisées
  alcoholic beverages
boissons chaudes hot beverages
boissons froides cold beverages
carte des vins wine list
coquillages shellfish
fromage cheese
gibier game
hors d'oeuvres starters
légumes vegetables
plats chauds hot dishes
plats froids cold dishes
plat du jour dish of the day
pâtisserie pastry
plat principal main course
potages soups
service compris service included
service non compris
  service not included
spécialités régionales
  regional specialities
viandes meat courses
volaille poultry

NUMBERS

0 **zéro**	12 **douze**	30 **trente**	110 **cent dix**
1 **un**	13 **treize**	31 **trente et un**	120 **cent vingt**
2 **deux**	14 **quatorze**	32 **trente-deux**	200 **deux cents**
3 **trois**	15 **quinze**		300 **trois cents**
4 **quatre**	16 **seize**	40 **quarante**	400 **quatre cents**
5 **cinq**	17 **dix-sept**	50 **cinquante**	500 **cinq cents**
6 **six**	18 **dix-huit**	60 **soixante**	600 **six cents**
7 **sept**	19 **dix-neuf**	70 **soixante-dix**	700 **sept cents**
8 **huit**	20 **vingt**	80 **quatre-vingts**	800 **huit cents**
9 **neuf**		90 **quatre-vingt-dix**	900 **neuf cents**
10 **dix**	21 **vingt et un**	100 **cent**	
11 **onze**	22 **vingt-deux**	101 **cent un**	1,000 **mille**

agneau lamb
ail garlic
ananas pineapple
anguille eel
banane banana
beurre butter
bifteck steak
bière (bière pression) beer (draught beer)
boeuf beef
boudin noir/blanc black/white pudding
brochet pike
cabillaud cod
calmar squid
canard duck
champignons mushrooms
chou cabbage
choucroute sauerkraut
chou-fleur cauliflower
choux de Bruxelles Brussels sprouts
citron lemon
civet de lièvre jugged hare
concombre cucumber
confiture jam
coquilles Saint-Jacques scallops
cornichon gherkin
côte/côtelette chop
côtelettes dans l'échine spare ribs
couvert cutlery
crevettes grises shrimps
crevettes roses prawns
croque monsieur toasted ham and cheese sandwich
cru raw
crustacés seafood
cuisses de grenouilles frogs' legs
cuit (à l'eau) boiled
eau mineral

gazeuse/non gazeuse sparkling/still mineral water
ecrevisse crayfish
entrecôte sirloin steak
entrées first course
épices spices
épinards spinach
épis de maïs corn (on the cob)
escargots snails
farine flour
fenouil fennel
fèves broad beans
figues figs
filet de boeuf fillet
filet mignon fillet steak
filet de porc tenderloin
fines herbes herbs
foie gras goose liver
fraises strawberries
framboises raspberries
frit fried
friture deep-fried
fruit de la passion passion fruit
fruits de la saison seasonal fruits
gaufres waffles
gigot d'agneau leg of lamb
glace ice-cream
glaçons ice cubes
grillé grilled
groseilles redcurrants
hareng herring
haricots blancs haricot beans
haricots verts french beans
homard lobster
huîtres oysters
jambon blanc/cru/fumé ham (cooked/Parma style/smoked)
jus de citron lemon juice
jus de fruits fruit juice

jus d'orange orange juice
lait demi-écrémé/entier milk semi-skimmed/full-cream
langouste crayfish
langoustine scampi
langue tongue
lapin rabbit
lentilles lentils
lotte monkfish
loup de mer sea bass
macaron macaroon
maïs sweetcorn
marron chestnut
menu du jour/à la carte menu of the day/à la carte
morilles morels
moules mussels
mousse au chocolat chocolate mousse
moutarde mustard
myrtilles bilberries
noisette hazelnut
noix walnut
noix de veau fillet of veal
oeuf à la coque/dur/au plat egg soft/hard-boiled/fried
oignon onion
origan oregano
pain au chocolat croissant with chocolate centre
part portion
pêche peach
petite friture fried fish (whitebait or similar)
petits (biscuits) salés savoury biscuits
petit pain roll
petits pois green peas

pintade guinea fowl
poire pear
pois chiches chick peas
poisson fish
poivre pepper
poivron green/red pepper
pomme apple
pommes de terre potatoes
pommes frites chips
poulet (blanc) chicken (breast)
prune plum
pruneaux prunes
queue de boeuf oxtail
ragoût stew
ris de veau sweetbread
riz rice
rôti de boeuf (rosbif) roast beef
rouget red mullet
saignant rare
salade verte lettuce
salé/sucré salted/sweet
saumon salmon
saucisses sausages
sel salt
soupe à l'oignon onion soup
sucre sugar
thon tuna
thym thyme
tripes tripe
truffes truffles
truite trout
truite saumonée salmon trout
vapeur (à la) steamed
venaison venison
viande hachée minced meat/mince
vin blanc white wine
vin rosé rosé wine
vin rouge red wine
vinaigre vinegar
xérès sherry

Atlas

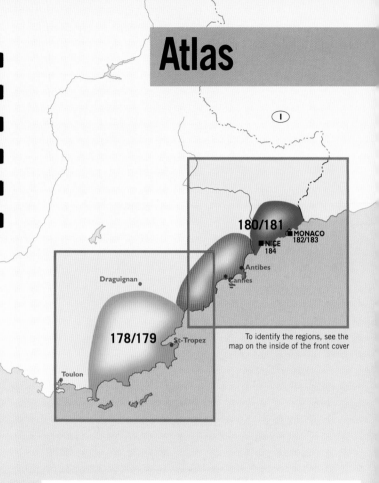

①

180/181

■ MONACO
182/183

■ NICE
184

● Antibes

● Cannes

Draguignan ▫

178/179

▫ St-Tropez

Toulon

To identify the regions, see the
map on the inside of the front cover

Regional Maps

━━━━ Major route
━━━━ Motorway/main road
─·─·─ International boundary
─··─··─ Regional boundary
▢ City
▫ Town/village

✈ Airport
▢ Featured place of interest

178–181

City Plans

═══ Main road/minor road
━━━ Railway
▣ Place of interest
● Metro

▮ Important building
▮ Park

182/183

184

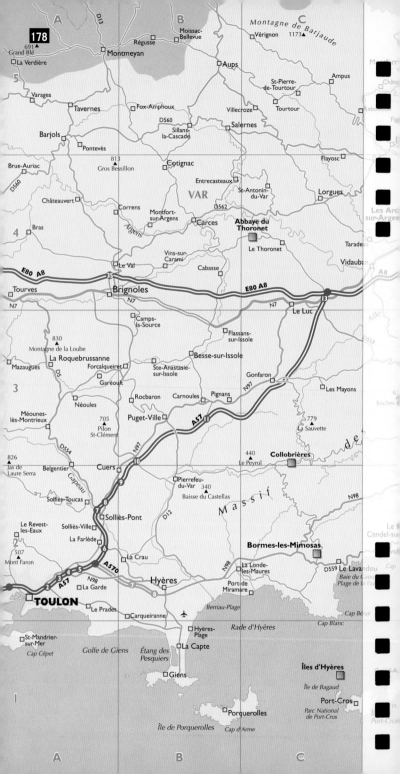

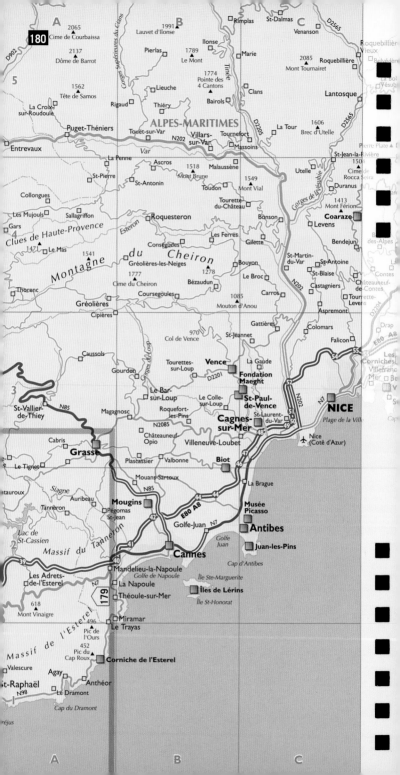

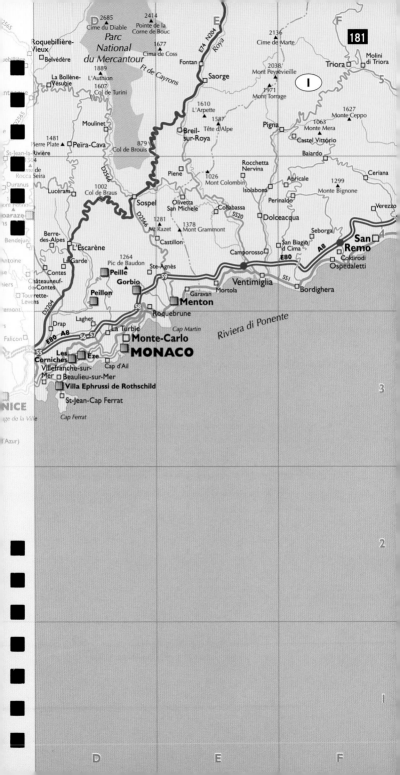

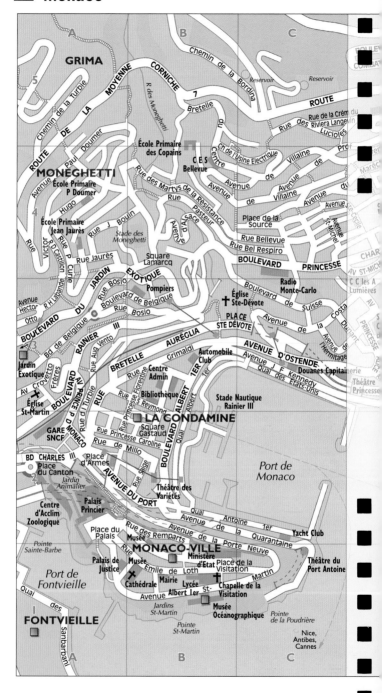

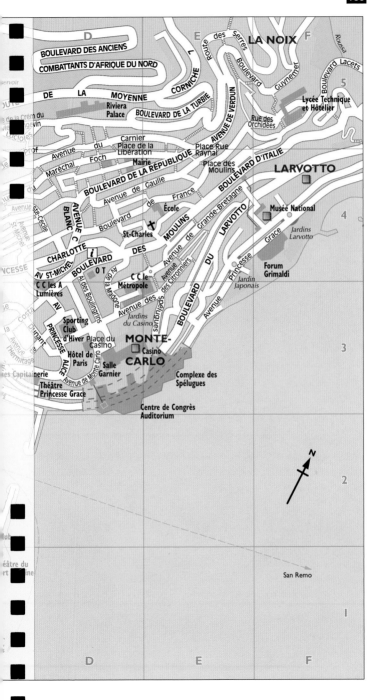

BOULEVARD DES ANCIENS
COMBATTANTS D'AFRIQUE DU NORD

LA NOIX

D

E

F

5

DE   LA   MOYENNE
Riviera
Palace

CORNICHE
BOULEVARD DE LA TURBIE

Route des Serres
Boulevard
Guynemer
Boulevard Lacets
Roussa

AVENUE DE VERDUN

Lycée Technique
et Hôtelier

Rue des
Orchidées

Carnier
du
Place de la
Libération

Avenue
Maréchal   Foch

Place Rue
Raynal

BOULEVARD D'ITALIE

LARVOTTO

BOULEVARD DE LA RÉPUBLIQUE

Mairie

Place des
Moulins

Avenue de Gaulle

de   France

Musée National

École

Boulevard

MOULINS

LARVOTTO

Jardins
Larvotto

Grace

AVENUE BLANC C

St-Charles

Avenue   de   Grande-Bretagne

DU

Avenue

CHARLOTTE

DES

Avenue   des   Citronniers

BOULEVARD

Princesse

Forum
Grimaldi

AV ST-MICHEL

O T

C C le
Métropole

BOULEVARD

Jardin
Japonais

C C les A
Lumières

Al des Boulingrins

Av de la Madone

Avenue des Spélugues

Avenue

Princesse

AV

Avenue des

Jardins
du Casino

Sporting
Club
d'Hiver

Place du
Casino

MONTE-

PRINCESSE

Hôtel de
Paris

Casino

ALICE

Salle
Garnier

Avenue de Monte Carlo

CARLO

Complexe des
Spélugues

Capitainerie

Théâtre
Princesse Grace

Centre de Congrès
Auditorium

3

4

N

2

San Remo

1

D

E

F

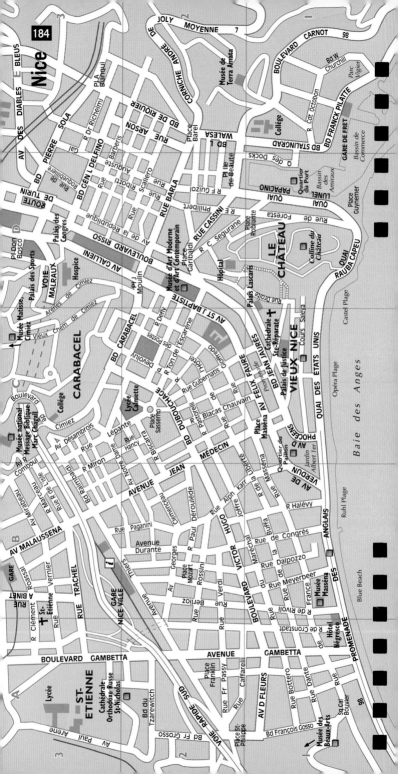

STREET INDEXES

Monaco

Albert 1er, Boulevard 182 B2
Albert 1er, Quai 182 B2
Alsace, Avenue d' 182 B4
Anciens, Boulevard des 183 D5
Antoine II, Quai 182 B2
Armes, Place d' 182 A2
Aug Vento, Rue 182 A3
Belgique, Boulevard de 182 A3
Bellevue, Rue 182 C4
Bel Respiro, Rue 182 C4
Bosio, Rue 182 A3
Boulingrins, Al des 183 D3
Bretelle Auréglia, Rue 182 A3
Bretelle du Centre 182 B5
Canton, Place du 182 A2
Carnier, Avenue du 183 D4
Casino, Place du 183 D3
C Blanc, Avenue 183 D4
Charles III, Boulevard 182 A2
Ch de l'Usine Electrique 182 B4
Chemin de la Bordina 182 B5
Chemin de la Turbie 182 A5
Citronniers, Avenue des 183 E4
Combattants d'Afrique du Nord 183 D5
Costa, Avenue de la 182 C3
Crém du Riviera Langevin, Rue de la 182 C5
Crovetto Frères, Avenue 182 A3
D Castillon, Rue 182 A4
Emile de Loth, Rue 182 B1
Etats-Unis, Quai des 182 C3
France, Boulevard de 183 D4
Gastaud, Square 182 B2
Gaulle, Avenue de 183 D4
Grande-Bretagne, Avenue de 183 E4
Grimaldi, Rue 182 B3
Guynemer, Boulevard 183 E5
Hector Otto, Avenue 182 A3
Hermitage, Avenue de l' 182 C3
H Labande, Rue 182 A3

I Turbie, Rue d 182 A2
Italie, Boulevard d' 183 E4
Jardin Exotique, Boulevard du 182 A3
Jaurès, Rue 182 A4
J Bouin, Rue 182 A4
J F Kennedy, Avenue 182 C3
Lacets, Boulevard 183 F5
Lamarcq, Square 182 B4
Larvotto, Boulevard du 183 E3
Libération, Place de la 183 D5
Lucioles, Rue des 182 C5
Madone, Avenue de la 183 D4
Maréchal Foch, Avenue du 182 C4
Martys de la Résistance, Rue des 182 B4
Millo, Rue de 182 A2
Monte Carlo, Avenue de 183 D3
Moulins, Boulevard des 183 D4
Moulins, Place des 183 E4
Moyenne Corniche, Route de la 182 C5
Orchidèes, Rue des 183 F5
Ostende, Avenue d' 182 C3
Palais, Place du 182 A2
Pasteur, Rue 182 B4
Paul Doumer, Avenue 182 A4
P Curie, Rue 182 A4
Port, Avenue du 182 A2
Porte Neuve, Avenue de la 182 B2
Prince P D Monaco, Avenue 182 A3
Princesse Alice, Avenue 183 D3
Princesse Caroline, Rue 182 A2
Princesse Charlotte, Boulevard 182 C4
Princesse Florestine, Rue 182 A2
Princesse Grace, Avenue 183 E3
Prof, Avenue de 182 C4
Quarantaine, Avenue de la 182 B2
Rainier III, Boulevard 182 A3
Raynal, Place Rue 183 E5
Remparts, Rue des 182 B2
République, Boulevard de la 183 D4
Saige, Rue 182 B2
Ste-Cecile, Avenue 182 C4
Ste Dévote, Place 182 B3
St-Martin, Avenue 182 B1

St-Michel, Avenue 182 C4
St-Michel, Avenue 183 D4
Sanbarbani, Quai des 182 A1
Serres, Route des 183 E5
Source, Place de la 182 C4
Spélugues, Avenue des 183 D3
S Reymond, Rue 182 B3
Suisse Dunant, Boulevard de 182 C3
Turbie, Boulevard de la 183 E5
Verdun, Avenue de 183 E5
Victor Hugo, Rue 182 A4
Villaine, Avenue de 182 C4
Visitation, Place de la 182 B1

Nice

A Blanqui, Place 184 E3
Alph Karr, Rue 184 B2
André de Joly Moyenne 7, Corniche 184 E2
Anglais, Promenade des 184 A1
Arson, Rue 184 E2
Auguste Gal, Rue 184 D2
Barberis, Rue 184 D3
Barel, Place 184 E2
Barla, Rue 184 D2
Beaute, Place Ile de 184 D2
Berlioz, Rue 184 B2
Binet, Rue a 184 B3
Biscarra, Rue 184 C2
Blacas Chauvain, Rue 184 C2
Bottero, Rue 184 A1
Buffa, Rue de la 184 A2
Caffarelli, Rue 184 A2
Cal Bouvier, Sq 184 A1
Carabacel, Boulevard 184 C3
Carnot 98, Boulevard 184 E1
Cassini, Rue 184 D2
Cdt Octobon, Rue 184 E1
Chem de Cimiez, Vieux 184 C3
Cimiez, Arenes de 184 C3
Cimiez, Boulevard de 184 C3
Clément Roassal, Rue 184 A3
Congrés, Rue de 184 B1
Cronstadt, Rue de 184 A1
C Segurane, Rue 184 D2
Dalpozzo, Rue 184 B1
Dante, Rue 184 A1
Defly, Rue 184 C2

Désambrois, Avenue 184 C3
Diables Bleus, Avenue des 184 E3
Docks, Quai des 184 D1
Don Bosco, Place 184 D3
Droite, Rue 184 D1
Dr Richelmi, Rue 184 E3
Dubouchage, Boulevard 184 C2
Durante, Avenue 184 B2
E Philibert, Rue 184 D2
Etats Unis, Quai des 184 C1
Félix Faure, Avenue184 C1
Fleurs, Avenue d' 184 A1
F Guizol, Rue 184 D2
Foresta, Rue de 184 D1
France, Rue de 184 A1
Franck Pilatte, Boulevard 184 E1
François Gosso, Boulevard184 A1
Franklin, Place 184 A2
Fr Grosso, Boulevard 184 A2
Gallieni, Avenue 184 D3
Gambetta, Avenue 184 A2
Gambetta, Boulevard 184 A3
Garibaldi, Place 184 D2
Gén L Delfino, Boulevard 184 D3
Georges Clemenceau, Avenue 184 B2
Gioffredo, Rue 184 C2
Gubernatis, Rue 184 C2
Guynemer, Place 184 D1
Fr Passy, Rue 184 A2
Halévy, Rue 184 B1
Hancy, Rue 184 C2
Jean Jaurés, Boulevard 184 C1
Jean Médeci, Avenue 184 B2
J Moulin, Place 184 D2
Lépante, Rue 184 C3
L'Hôtel des Postes, Rue de 184 C2
Liberté, Rue de la 184 B1
L'isle, Rue R de 184 B3
Lunel, Quai 184 D1
L Walesa, Boulevard 184 E2
Malaussena, Avenue 184 B3
Malraux, Voie 184 D3
Marceau, Rue 184 B3
Maréchal Joffre, Rue du 184 B1
Massena, Place 184 C1
Masséna, Rue 184 B1

Meyerbeer, Rue 184 B1
Mirabeau, Avenue 184 B3
Miron, Rue 184 B3
Mozart, Place 184 B2
Notre Dame, Avenue 184 B2
Paganini, Rue 184 B2
Papacino, Quai 184 D1
Pastorelli, Rue 184 C2
Paul Arene, Avenue 184 A3
Paul Déroulède, Rue 184 B2
P Devoluy, Rue184 C2
Phocéens, Avenue d' 184 C1
Pierre Sola, Boulevard 184 D3
Raimbaldi, Boulevard 184 B3
Rapide Sud, Voie 184 A2
Rauba Capeu, Quai 184 D1
R Comboul, Avenue 184 D3
République, Avenue de la 184 D2
Ribotti, Rue 184 D2
Riquier, Boulevard de 184 E2
Risso, Boulevard 184 D2
Rivoli, Rue de 184 B1
Robilante, Place 184 D1
Roquebilliere, Rue de 184 D3
Rossini, Rue 184 B2
St J Baptiste, Avenue 184 C2
St-Philippe, Place 184 A2
Saleya, Cours 184 C1
Sasserno, Place 184 C2
Scaliero, Rue 184 D2
Stalingrad, Boulevard 184 E1
Thiers, Avenue 184 B2
Ton de l'Escaréne, Rue 184 C2
Trachel, Rue 184 B3
Turin, Route de 184 D3
Tzarewitch, Boulevard du 184 A2
Victor Hugo, Boulevard 184 B1
Verdí, Rue 184 B2
Verdun, Avenue de 184 B1
Vernier, Rue 184 B3
W Churchill, Boulevard 184 E1

Picture Credits

The Automobile Association wishes to thank the following photographers,
companies and picture libraries for their assistance in the preparation of this book.

Abbreviations for the picture credits are as follows – (t) top; (b) bottom; (l) left;
(r) right; (c) centre; (AA) AA World Travel Library

Front and Back Cover: (t) AA/R Strange; (ct) AA/A Baker; (c) B Hall; (b) AA/C Sawyer;
Spine AA/R Strange

2i AA/R Strange; 2ii AA/C Sawyer; 2iii AA/C Sawyer; 2iv AA/A Baker; 2v AA/C Sawyer;
3i AA/R Strange; 3ii AA/A Baker; 3iii AA/B Smith; 3iv AA/C Sawyer; 5 AA/R Strange;
6t AA; 6c AA; 6b AA; 7t AA/C Sawyer; 7b AA; 8 AA/R Strange; 9 AA/A Baker; 10 AA/
E Meacher; 10/11 AA/R Strange; 10b AA/C Sawyer; 11 AA/A Baker; 12t AA/C Sawyer;
12c AA/A Baker; 12/13 AA/C Sawyer; 13 AA/A Baker; 14 AA/T Oliver; 15t Rex Features;
15c Rex Features; 16t IENA/UCIL/Cocinor/The Kobal Collection/Mirkine;
16c Rex Features; 17 Rex Features; 18 AA/C Sawyer; 19 AA/C Sawyer; 20/21 AA/
N Ray; 21 J M Follet/Archives Automobile Club de Monaco; 22c AA/A Baker;
22b Fete du Lemon, Menton; 23 AA/C Sawyer; 35 AA/C Sawyer; 36 AA/C Sawyer;
37t AA/C Sawyer; 37b AA/C Sawyer; 38c AA/C Sawyer; 38b AA/C Sawyer; 39t AA/
R Moore; 39b AA/C Sawyer; 40l Musee Matisse; 40/41 AA/C Sawyer; 42 AA/C Sawyer;
43 Collection Musée des Beaux-Arts de Nice; 44t AA/R Strange; 44c AA/C Sawyer;
45 AA/C Sawyer; 46/47 AA/C Sawyer; 47 AA/C Sawyer; 48 AA/C Sawyer; 49 AA/
R Strange; 50 AA/R Strange; 51 AA/R Strange; 52 AA/C Sawyer; 59 AA/A Baker;
60 AA/A Baker; 61 AA/R Strange; 62 Villa Ephrusi de Rothschild, ©Culture
Espaces/Véran; 63t AA/A Baker; 63c AA/C Sawyer; 64 AA/R Strange; 65 AA/C Sawyer;
66 AA/C Sawyer; 66/67 AA/A Baker; 68 AA/C Sawyer; 69 AA/A Baker; 70 AA/C Sawyer;
71 Villa Ephrusi de Rothschild, ©Culture Espaces; 72t AA/A Baker; 72/73 AA/
R Strange; 74 AA/A Baker; 76 AA/C Sawyer; 83 AA/C Sawyer; 85c AA/A Baker;
85b AA/A Baker; 86 AA/A Baker; 87t AA/A Baker; 87b AA/A Baker; 88/89 AA/A Baker;
89 T Middleton; 90 AA/R Strange; 91 T Middleton; 92t AA/R Strange; 92c AA/A Baker;
93 T Middleton; 94/95 AA/C Sawyer; 96 AA/A Baker; 105 AA/R Strange; 107l AA/
R Strange; 107r AA/R Strange; 108c AA/C Sawyer; 108b AA/C Sawyer; 109t AA/A Baker;
109b AA/C Sawyer; 110/111 AA/C Sawyer; 110b AA/R Strange; 111 AA/C Sawyer;
112 AA/C Sawyer; 113 AA/C Sawyer; 115 AA/R Strange; 116 AA/C Sawyer; 118 AA/
C Sawyer; 119 Joy of Life or, Antipolis, 1946 (oil on canvas), Picasso, Pablo
(1881–1973)/Musee Picasso, Antibes, France,/The Bridgeman Art Library –
©Succession Picasso/DACS 2007; 120 AA/C Sawyer; 121 AA/A Baker; 122 AA/
C Sawyer; 123 AA/R Moore; 124 AA/C Sawyer; 133 AA/A Baker; 134 AA/B Smith;
135 AA/R Strange; 136 AA/C Sawyer; 137t AA/R Strange; 137b AA/A Baker;
138 AA/R Strange; 139 AA/C Sawyer; 138/9 AA/C Sawyer; 140c AA/C Sawyer;
140b AA/C Sawyer; 141 AA/C Sawyer; 142 AA/R Strange; 143 B Hall; 144 AA/A Baker;
145 AA/R Strange; 146t AA/A Baker; 146b AA/A Baker; 147 AA/A Baker; 148 AA/
R Strange; 150 AA/T Oliver; 152 AA/T Oliver; 159 AA/B Smith; 161l AA/T Oliver;
161r AA/W Voysey; 162 AA/C Sawyer; 164 AA/R Strange; 165 AA/A Baker; 166 AA/
R Moore; 168 AA/T Oliver; 169 AA/C Sawyer; 173t AA/C Sawyer; 173cl AA/M Jourdain;
173cr AA/C Sawyer
Every effort has been made to trace the copyright holders, and we apologise in advance
for any unintentional omissions or errors. We would be pleased to apply any correc-
tions in any following edition of this publication.

Questionnaire

Your recommendations...

We always encourage readers' recommendations for restaurants, night-life or shopping
– if your recommendation is used in the next edition of the guide, we will send you a
FREE AA Spiral Guide of your choice. Please state below the establishment name,
location and your reasons for recommending it.

_____

_____

_____

_____

_____

Please send me AA Spiral _____

(see list of titles inside the back cover)

About this guide...

Which title did you buy?

_____ AA Spiral

Where did you buy it? _____

When? m m / y y

Why did you choose an AA Spiral Guide? _____

_____

_____

_____

_____

Did this guide meet your expectations?

Exceeded ☐   Met all ☐   Met most ☐   Fell below ☐

Please give your reasons _____

_____

_____

_____

_____

continued on next page...

Were there any aspects of this guide that you particularly liked?

_____
_____
_____
_____
_____

Is there anything we could have done better?

_____
_____
_____
_____

About you...

Name (Mr/Mrs/Ms) _____

Address _____

_____ Postcode _____

Daytime tel no _____ email _____

Please _only_ give us your email address and mobile phone number if you wish to hear from us about other products and services from the AA and partners by email or text or mms.

Which age group are you in?

Under 25 ☐   25–34 ☐   35–44 ☐   45–54 ☐   55–64 ☐   65+ ☐

How many trips do you make a year?

Less than one ☐   One ☐   Two ☐   Three or more ☐

Are you an AA member? Yes ☐   No ☐

About your trip...

When did you book? mm/ y y   When did you travel? mm/ y y

How long did you stay? _____

Was it for business or leisure? _____

Did you buy any other travel guides for your trip? ☐ Yes   ☐ No

If yes, which ones? _____
_____

Thank you for taking the time to complete this questionnaire. Please send it to us as soon as possible, and remember, you do not need a stamp (unless posted outside the UK).